U/PL

THE UTILITY PROGRAMMING LANGUAGE STANDARD

V1.0

Brian L. Decker

Copyright © 2021 Brian L. Decker

All rights reserved.

ISBN: 9798510149012

"People who are really serious about software should make their own hardware"
– Alan Kay

"GOTO – A programming tool that exists primarily to allow structured programmers to complain about unstructured programmers."
– Raymond Simard

Contents

ACKNOWLEDGMENT i
1. U/PL Standard 2
2. CONFORMING IMPLEMENTATION 5
   2.1 Conforming Programs 5
   2.2 Implementation Conformance 6
   2.3 Errors 7
   2.4 Exceptions 7
   2.5 Relationship to the ANSI Standard 8
3. SYNTAX AND DEFINITIONS 10
   3.1 Method of Syntax Specification 10
   3.2 Definition of Terms 13
4. PROGRAM ELEMENTS, LINES AND BLOCKS 21
   4.1 Characters 21
   4.2 Program 23
   4.3 Program Annotation 27
   4.4 Identifiers 27
5. NUMBERS 31
   5.1 Numeric Constants 31
   5.2 Numeric Variables 33
   5.3 Numeric Expressions 34
   5.4 Implementation-Supplied Numeric Functions 37
   5.5 Numeric Assignment Statement 44
   5.6 Numeric Arithmetic and Angle 45

6. STRINGS	49
6.1 String Constants	49
6.2 String Variables	50
6.3 String Expressions	52
6.4 Implementation-Supplied String Functions	54
6.5 String Assignment Statements	58
6.6 String Declarations	60
7. ARRAYS	62
7.1 General Description	62
7.2 Array Declarations	64
7.3 Numeric Arrays	68
7.4 String Arrays	72
8. CONSTANTS	76
9. VARIABLES	79
10. CONTROL STRUCTURES	83
10.1 Relational Expressions	83
10.2 Control Statements	85
10.3 Loop Structures	88
10.4 Decision Structures	92
10.5 Expressions	96
11. PROGRAM SEGMENTATION	100
11.1 User-Defined Functions	101
11.2 Subprograms	108
11.3 Linking	117
12. INPUT AND OUTPUT	119
12.1 Internal Data	119
12.2 Input	122

12.3 Output	126
12.4 Formatted Output	132
12.5 Array Input and Output	138
13. FILES	**144**
13.1 File Operations	148
13.2 File Pointer Manipulation	163
13.3 File Data Creation	168
13.4 File Data Retrieval	181
13.5 File Data Modification (Expanded U/PL only)	192
14. EXCEPTION HANDLING AND DEBUGGING	**197**
14.1 Exception Handling (Expanded U/PL only)	197
14.2 Debugging (U/PL and Expanded U/PL)	206
15. GRAPHICS	**210**
15.1 Coordinate Systems	210
15.2 Attributes and Screen Control	216
15.3 Graphic Output	219
APPENDIX 1	**223**
ORGANIZATION OF THE U/PL STANDARD	223
APPENDIX 2	**225**
COMBINED LIST OF CONSTRUCT RULES	225
APPENDIX 3	**246**
COMMON KEYWORDS, COMMANDS AND FUNCTIONS	246
APPENDIX 4	**272**
EXCEPTION CODES	272
INDEX	**278**

ACKNOWLEDGMENT

Many thanks to my dearest wife Hadley, whose patient support and inspiration made this work possible.

1. U/PL Standard

The availability of inexpensive and easy to program microcontrollers and a resurgence in "techno-archeology" has spurred a great deal of interest in the "dead languages" of the past. Cobol, Forth, Fortran, APL, PL/I, Algol, Pascal and BASIC have experienced a renaissance and are once again being put to use – both by amateurs and professionals. New languages are being developed that expand on or mirror these earlier languages – but unlike those earlier languages which were intended for general purpose use, these Utility Programming Languages are designed and implemented to perform specific functions on electro-mechanical and/or state-machine systems. The U/PL Standard is designed to promote the interchangeability of these Utility Languages and their programs among a variety of microcontrollers and low power microprocessors. In addition to supporting the procedural and functional systems that are built around them, Utility Programming also seeks to retain limited backwards-compatibility with the ECMA and ANSI standards which were supported from the late 1970's to early 1990's. Utility Language Implementations and their programs which conform to this Standard will be classified as written in "U/PL".

This Standard establishes:

- the syntax of a program written in U/PL.
- The formats of data and the precision and range of numeric representations which are acceptable as input to a system being controlled by a program written in U/PL.
- The formats of data and the minimum precision and range of numeric representations and the minimum length and set of characters in strings which can be generated as output by a system being controlled by a program written in U/PL.
- The semantic rules for interpreting the meaning of a program written in U/PL.
- The errors and exceptional circumstances which will be detected and the manner in which such errors and exceptional circumstance will be handled.

Utility Programming Languages may be designed and implemented for interactive use – requiring input by a User – or as fully automated systems operating with or without sensor, time or status based inputs. This Standard does not restrict conformance to one or the other, and in many cases a combination of both will be implemented. Because U/PL is an imperative, procedural, state-based programming language it is ideal for use in non-interactive systems (autonomous and/or PLC type devices) which require a robust control system that is can auto-boot and self initiate to a known state without user control.

This Standard is not meant to preclude the use of any particular implementation technique, for example interpreters, incremental or one-pass compilers or emulators (regardless of platform).

The organization of the Standard is outlined in Appendix 1. The method of syntax specification used is explained in Appendix 2. Common keywords, commands and functions are outlined in Appendix 3.

1.1 Related Standards
ECMA-6: 7-Bit Input/Output Coded Character Set, 4th Edition

ECMA-35: Code Extension Techniques

ECMA-53 : Representation of Source Programs for Program Interchange: APL, COBOL, FORTRAN, Minimal BASIC and PL/1

ECMA-55 : Minimal BASIC

ECMA-116: Extended BASIC

ANSI X3.113-198X: American National Standard for BASIC

ANSI X3.30-1985: Information Systems – Representation for Calendar Date and Ordinal Date for Information Interchange

ANSI X3.42-1975: The representation of Numerical Values in Character Strings for Information Interchange

ANSI X3.60-1978: Minimal BASIC

ANSI x3.124-1985: Information Systems – Computer Graphics – Graphic Kernal System

ASCII ISO/IEC 646

ISO 2014: Writing of Calendar dates in all-numeric form

ISO 2711: Representation of Ordinal Dates

ISO 3307: Representation of Time of the Day

ISO 7942: Graphical Kernel System

IEC 559: Binary Floating-Point Arithmetic for Microprocessor Systems

2. CONFORMING IMPLEMENTATION

This Standard specifies two levels of the language: U/PL and Expanded U/PL. In addition, this Standard defines an optional Graphics module which is not required in either form of implementation to meet conformance.

U/PL includes all the parts defined in Section 4 to 13, with the exception of those portions of Section 13 that describes Expanded files and Section 14.1, Exception Handling. All the keywords, listed in 3.2.13 are reserved words.

Expanded U/PL includes all the parts defined in Section 4 to 14. The keywords, listed in 3.2.13 under the heading Expanded U/PL are reserved words.

The graphics module is specified in section 15. It is optional, and it can be used together either with U/PL or Expanded U/PL.

There are two aspects of the conformance to the language defined in this Standard: conformance by a program written in the U/PL language, and conformance by an implementation which processes such programs.

Broadly speaking, the conformance requirements are structured so that any program conforming to this standard will produce the same results when executed by any implementation conforming to the standard (though some implementation-defined features are noted in Appendix 3).

2.1 Conforming Programs

A program conforms to this Standard only when both of the following conditions are met:

- the program and each statement or other syntactic element contained therein is syntactically valid according to the syntactic rules specified by this Standard as belonging to that level of implementation
- the program as a whole violates none of the global constraints imposed by this level of the Standard on the application of the syntactic rules.

2.2 Implementation Conformance

An implementation conforms to the appropriate level of this Standard only when all of the following conditions are met:

- it accepts and processes all programs conforming to that level of this Standard
- it reports reasons for rejecting any program which does not conform to this Standard (either by error messages or specific references to the non-conforming section of the Standard in software documentation)
- it interprets errors and exceptional circumstances according to the specifications of this Standard appropriate to the level of its implementation
- it interprets the semantics of each statement of a conforming program according to the specifications in this Standard appropriate to the level of its implementation
- it interprets the semantics of a conforming program as a whole according to the specifications in this Standard, appropriate to the level of its implementation
- it accepts as input, manipulates, and can generate as output numbers of at least the precision and range specified in this Standard appropriate to the level of its implementation
- it accepts as input, manipulates, and can generate as output strings of at least the length and composed of at least those characters specified in this Standard appropriate to the level of its implementation
- it is accompanied by documentation available to the user that describes the actions taken in regard to features referred to as "undefined" or "implementation-defined" in this Standard appropriate to the level of its implementation
- it is accompanied by documentation available to the user that describes and identifies all enhancements to the language defined in this Standard appropriate to the level of its implementation.

This Standard makes no requirement concerning the interpretation of the semantics of any statement or program as a whole that does not conform to this Standard.

2.3 Errors

This Standard does not include specific requirements for reporting syntactic errors in the text of a program, and implementations conforming to this Standard may accept programs written in an Expanded language without having to report all constructs not conforming to this Standard.

Whenever a statement or other program element does not conform to the syntactic rules provided by this Standard, and that statement or other program element does not have a clear, well documented implementation-defined meaning an error must be reported. Errors should be reported in a clear and well documented way and whenever feasible the implementation should indicate the erroneous statement and the position of the error within the statement. This is particularly important when working in an interpreted environment as errors may be easily identified and corrected.

2.4 Exceptions

An exception is a circumstance during execution of a program when an implementation recognizes that the semantic rules of this Standard cannot be followed or that some resource constraint is about to be exceeded. All exceptions described in this Standard will be detected, reported and processed when they occur, unless some mechanism provided in 14.1 (Expanded U/PL only) or an enhancement to this Standard has been invoked by the user to handle exceptions.

In the absence of programmer-specified recovery procedures, exceptions will be handled by the recovery procedures specified in this Standard. If no recovery procedure is specified in this Standard, or if restrictions imposed by the hardware or the operating environment make it impossible to follow the procedure specified in this Standard, then the way in which the exception is handled depends on the context:

- If the exception occurred in the invocation of a function or subprogram, then the exception is "propagated back" to the invoking statement in the invoking program unit.
- If this propagation procedure reaches the main-program, or if the exception occurred in the main- program, then the exception will be handled by terminating the program.

The way in which the exception handling mechanism reports an exception is implementation-defined, except that the contents of the report will identify at least the exception code and the line number of the line in which the original exception occurred .

Except in the case of files, when several exceptions are caused by the execution of a single statement of a program, this Standard does not specify an order in which these exceptions will be detected or reported. If an implementation determines that a particular statement in a conforming program will always cause an exception when executed, the implementation may issue a warning to the user. Nonetheless, the implementation must accept and execute the program, according to the normal semantic rules specified herein.

2.5 Relationship to the ANSI Standard

This U/PL Standard defines a subset of the ANSI BASIC Standard, ANSI X3.113-198X.

The ANSI standard defines a set of modules, only one of which (the Core module) is mandatory. On the other hand, only the graphics module is optional in the U/PL standard.

Programs written in U/PL will run on implementations conforming to the ANSI standard if the implementation implements at least the Core module. Provided that the implementation-defined elements are defined in a compatible way in the two implementations, the programs will act in the same way and give the same results.

Programs written in Expanded U/PL will run on implementations conforming to the ANSI Standard if the implementation implements at least the Core module and the Expanded Files module. Provided that the implementation-defined elements are defined in a compatible way in the two implementations, the program will act in the same way and give the same results. The reverse will not always be true. In view of the modular nature of the ANSI standard, programs conforming to the ANSI standards will run on an ECMA BASIC or U/PL implementation only if they use the set of facilities defined in the U/PL Standard.

A further difference exists in reserved words. All keywords defined in U/PL are reserved and cannot be used as identifiers. Only a limited number of keywords is reserved in the ANSI Standard. Thus, programs written in ECMA MINIMAL BASIC or U/PL will run on an ANSI implementation, with the limitations defined above. A program written in ANSI BASIC, and which uses only the facilities defined in ECMA MINIMAL BASIC or the U/PL standard, is not granted to run on an ECMA MINIMAL BASIC implementation, unless the limitations on identifiers have been observed.

The graphics module is a subset of the ANSI one. Thus, programs conforming to the Standard graphics module will run on an ANSI implementation, but programs conforming to the ANSI module will not run on a ECMA MINIMAL BASIC or U/PL implementation unless they use only the facilities defined in section 15 of this standard.

3. SYNTAX AND DEFINITIONS

3.1 Method of Syntax Specification

The syntax, through a series of rewriting rules known as "constructs", define syntactic objects of various types, such as a *program* or *expression*, and describes which strings of symbols are objects of these types.

In the syntax, upper-case-letters, digits, and (possibly hyphenated) lower-case words are used as "metanames", i.e., as names of syntactic objects. Most of these metanames are defined by constructs in terms of other metanames. In order that this process terminates, certain metanames are designated as "terminal" metanames, and constructs for them are not included in the syntax. It should be noted in particular that all upper-case-letters are terminal metanames which denote both themselves and their lower-case equivalents (except in the constructs defining upper-case-letters and lower-case-letters, in which the letters denote only themselves). The digits are terminal metanames which denote themselves. In addition, the construct "[implementation-defined]" is not a unique syntactic object, but each occurrence of it is defined by each implementation in an appropriate fashion for the object in question. In some cases, a recommendation as to the representation of the object is given in the corresponding remarks section.

We illustrate further details of the syntax by considering the following examples. The construct:

    fraction = period integer

indicates that a fraction is a period followed by an integer. Since "period" is a terminal metaname (i.e., it does not occur on the left-hand side of any construct), the semantics in 4.1 identify the particular character denoted by a period.

What is integer? The construct:

    integer = digit digit*

indicates that an integer is a digit followed by an arbitrary number of other digits. An asterisk is a syntactic operator indicating that the object it follows may be repeated any number of time, including zero times.

What is a digit? The construct:

digit = 0/1/2/ 3/4/5/ 6/7/8/9

indicates that a digit is either a 0, a 1, ..., or a 9. The slant is a syntactic operator meaning "or" and is used to indicate that a metaname can be rewritten in one of several ways. Since the digits are terminal metanames, our decipherment of the syntax for a fraction comes to an end. The semantics in 4.1 identify the digits in terms of the characters they represent.

A question-mark is a syntactic operator like the asterisk, indicating that the object it follows may be omitted. For example, the construct:

exrad = E sign? integer

indicates that an exrad consists of the letter E or e followed by an optional sign followed by an integer.

Parentheses may be used to group sequences of metanames together. For example:

variable-list = variable (comma variable)*

defines a variable-list to consist of a variable followed by an arbitrary number of other variables separated by commas. If we wish parentheses actually to appear in syntactic objects, rather than just wish to use them to describe syntactic objects, then we indicate their presence by the metanames "left-parenthesis" and "right-parenthesis".

When several syntactic operators occur in the same construct, the following order of precedence is employed. The operators "?" and "*" apply only to the word or parenthesized expression they immediately follow. The operator "/" applies to the sequence of words and expressions, separated by spaces, which occur since the beginning of the entire expression, the last "/", or the last unmatched left parenthesis. Thus, for example, significand = integer period? / integer? fraction is equivalent to significand = (integer (period)?) / ((integer)? fraction)

Spaces in the syntax are used to separate terms in a construct from each other. Special conventions are observed regarding spaces in U/PL programs.

Some syntactic objects are defined by more than one construct. For example, the construct:

simple-variable > simple-numeric-variable

may also be configured as:

simple-variable > simple-string-variable.

Those two constructs are equivalent to the single construct below

(provided no other definition of simple-variable exists)

simple-variable = simple-numeric-variable / simple-string-variable.

In all cases, a greater-than-sign is used in place of an equals-sign to indicate a multiple definition, such definitions are equivalent to a single definition containing the various right-hand sides separated by slants.

In order to maintain equivalency among the ECMA, ANSI and U/PL standards, constructs not used in this Standard but referenced in others are identified by the construct: [removed].

As an illustration of the method of syntax specification, following is a description of the syntax of this method. The terminal metanames occurring below are defined within the U/PL standard as:

1. construct = metanames spaces (equals-sign / greater-than-sign) spaces syntax-expression

2. metaname = lower-case-letter metacharacters*

3. metacharacter = lower-case-letter / hyphen

4. spaces = space* end-of-line? space* space

5. syntax-expression = syntax-term (spaces ? slant spaces? syntax-term)*

6. syntax-term = syntax-factor (spaces syntax-factor)*

7. syntax-factor = syntax-primary repetition?

8. syntax-primary metaname / digit digit* / upper-case-letter upper-case-letter* / left-parenthesis space* syntax-expression space* right-parenthesis

9. repetition

3.2 Definition of Terms

For the purposes of this Standard, the following terms have the meanings indicated below. In cases where the meanings correlate with definitions in other standards, these meanings will supersede those uses.

3.2.1 Autorun

The processing of programs in an environment where no provision is made for user interaction. Programs conforming to the U/PL Standard may be interactive or non-interactive, and such interaction may be produced by user I/O or peripheral inputs (i.e., an analog signal crossing a pre-defined threshold). An Autorun program may be stored in EEPROM or may reside in removable media such as an SD card or USB drive. Such a program will begin execution from a predefined starting state upon system power on or system reset and continue operation until halted by system power down or an interrupt command.

3.2.2 Command

Commands are direct mode instructions that are executed immediately upon pressing enter. Examples of common Commands are LIST, DISPLAY and RUN.

3.2.3 Display zone

A contiguous set of character positions in a display output line which may contain an evaluated DISPLAY statement element.

3.2.4 End-of-line

The character(s) or indicator which identifies the termination of a line. Lines of three kinds may be identified in U/PL: program lines, display lines and input reply lines. End-of-line may vary between the three cases and may also vary depending upon context. Thus, for example, an end of input line may vary on a given system depending on the terminal or input device being used in interactive or Autorun mode.

Typical examples of end-of-line are carriage-return, carriage-return-line-feed, and an end of record (such as end of file or EOL).

3.2.5 Error
A flaw in the syntax of a program which causes the program to be incorrect, even if such program can be run by the system. A professionally designed U/PL editor or IDE will evaluate the program for errors while it is being written and notify the programmer with an appropriate error message prior to execution.

3.2.6 Exception
A circumstance arising in the course of executing a program when an implementation recognizes that the semantic rules of this Standard cannot be followed or that some resource constraint is about to be exceeded. Certain exceptions (nonfatal exceptions) may be handled by automatic recovery procedures specified in this Standard. These and other exceptions may also be handled by recovery procedures specified in the program. If no recovery procedure is given in this Standard (fatal exceptions) or if restrictions imposed by the hardware or operating environment make it impossible to follow the given procedure, and if no recovery procedure is specified in the program, then the way in which the exception is handled depends on the context. If the exception occurred in an invocation of a function, picture, or subprogram, then the exception is 'propagated back' to the invoking statement of the invoking program unit If this propagation procedure reaches the main program, or if the exception occurred in the main program, then the exception will be handled by terminating the program. Program termination does not require that data or program state prior to the Exception need to be maintained to meet the requirements of this Standard.

3.2.7 External
With respect to procedures, refers to a procedure lexically not contained within a larger program-unit.

3.2.8 Function
Functions are standard processes which are executed by a U/PL interpreter or compiler that are represented by a Keyword. Functions serve as built in "subprograms" so that the programmer is not required to provide detailed instructions to the system in order to perform every task – though care should be taken when designing or implementing a U/PL program to verify that the required Functions are present in the version being used. INPUT is an example of a function that executes multiple system tasks – it stops program execution while in RUN state, displays a prompt, receives input, determines if the input is of the correct form, executes the assignment or evaluation of the input and either places the system back in RUN state or halts the program and displays an appropriate error message.

3.2.9 Identifier
An individual character or character string used to name a variable, an array, an array-value, an exception- handler, a function, subprogram, or a program. The character or character string may not be an Operator or reserved Keyword.

3.2.10 Imperative
The U/PL programming paradigm is Imperative –the system running a program changes from state to state as directed by explicit Commands and/or Statements.

3.2.11 Interactive mode
The processing of programs in an environment which permits the user to respond directly to the actions of individual programs and to control the commencement and termination of those programs.

3.2.12 Internal
With respect to record-type, refers to data representations such that both the type and exact value of the written data are preserved and retrievable by subsequent read operations. With respect to procedures, refers to a procedure lexically contained within a larger program: unit and sharing data with that unit.

3.2.13 Keyword

A character string, usually with the spelling of a commonly used or mnemonic word, which provides a distinctive identification of a statement or a component of a statement of a programming language. Keywords are considered reserved and may not be used as an identifier.

The primary reserved keywords in U/PL are:

ABS, ACCESS, AND, ANGLE, APPEND, AREA, ARITHMETIC, ARRAY, ASC, ASK, AT, AUTO, BASE, BEGIN, BREAK, CALL, CASE, CAUSE, CELLS, CHOICE, CLEAR, CLIP, CLOSE, COLLATE, COLOR, CONNECT, CONTINUE, DATA, DATUM, DEBUG, DECIMAL, DECLARE, DEF, DEGREES, DELAY, DELETE, DEVICE, DIM, DISCONNECT, DISPLAY, DO, DRAW, ELAPSED, ELSE, ELSEIF, END, ERASABLE, ERASE, EVENT, EXCEPTION, EXIT, EXLINE, EXTERNAL, EXTRACT, EXTYPE, FILETYPE, FIRST, FIXED, FOR, FROM, FUNCTION, GET, GO, GOSUB, GOTO, GRAPH, HANDLER, HEIGHT, IF, IMAGE, IN, INPUT, INTERNAL, IS, JUSTIFY, KEY, KEYED, LAST, LENGTH, LET, , LIMIT, LINE, LINES, LINK, LIST, LOCATE, LOOP, MARGIN, MAT, MESSAGE, MISSING, MIX, MULTIPOINT, MLFT, MFWD, MRIGHT, MRWD, NAME, NATIVE, NEXT, NOT, NUMERIC, OF, OFF, ON, OPEN, OPTION, OR, ORGANIZATION, OUT, OUTIN, OUTPUT, PARACT, PARSTOP, PICTURE, PIXEL, PLOT, POINT, POINTER, POINTS, PORT, PROCESS, PROGRAM, PROMPT, PUT, RADIANS, RSEED, RANGE, READ, RECEIVE, RECORD, RECSIZE, RECTYPE, RELATIVE, REM, RENUMBER, REST, RESTORE, RETRY, RETURN, REWRITE, SAME, SEIZE, SELECT, SEND, SEQUENTIAL, SET, SETTER, SERVOCTR, SERVOLFT, SERVORGT, SERVOPOS, SHARED, SIGNAL, SIZE, SKIP, STANDARD, START, STATUS, STEP, STOP, STREAM, STRING, STRUCTURE, STYLE, SUB, TAB, TEMPLATE, TEXT, THEN, THERE, TIME, TIMEOUT, TO, TRACE, TRUNCATE, UNTIL, URGENCY, USE, USING, VALUE, VARIABLE, VIEWPORT, WHEN, WHILE, WINDOW, WITH, WRITE, ZONEWIDTH.

Depending on the implementation of U/PL that you are using or developing there are likely many additional Keywords that may not be used as an Identifier. Care should be taken when developing documentation and Error messages to clearly communicate to the user when a reserved keyword is improperly used.

3.2.14 Line

A single transmission of characters which may contain an assignment, command, data, function or operator and terminates with an end-of-line. A single line immediate-mode program does not require a Line Number. A multi-line program requires that every line begins with a unique positive-integer Line Number which serves as the Identifier for the Statement(s) it contains. Program execution begins with the numerically lowest Line Number and continues in numeric order until the END statement is reached with the following exceptions:

- A GOTO statement shifts the program execution to a location defined by a Line Number within the statement. Program execution will skip the Line Numbers which are numerically greater than the Line containing the GOTO statement and numerically lesser than the Line Number defined by the GOTO statement and continue from that Line.

A GOSUB statement shifts the program execution to a location defined by a Line Number within the statement. Program execution will skip the Line Numbers which are numerically greater than the Line containing the GOSUB statement and numerically lesser than the Line Number defined by the GOSUB statement and continue until a RETURN statement is reached. The RETURN statement will shift program execution to the Line one numeric increment above that which the GOSUB was executed from.

- A READ statement shifts the program execution to the DATA statement identified by the Line Number indexed by the READ pointer. The READ pointer is to be reset to the numerically lowest DATA Line Number by the RESTORE statement.
- A LINK-statement is executed, or
- A STOP-statement or end-statement is executed.

The end-statement will serve both to mark the physical end of the main-program and to terminate execution of the program when encountered.

3.2.15 Native

With respect to record-type, refers to a record with a specified structure for the fields within the record, to be compatible with records generated by other languages on the same system. With respect to numeric or string data, refers to data for which certain semantic rules are left implementation-defined (e.g., collating sequence, precision) to be directly implementable on the host hardware.

3.2.16 Nesting
A set of statements is nested within another set of statements when:

- the nested set is physically contiguous, and
- the nesting set (divided by the nested set) is non-null.

3.2.17 Operator
Operators define what how numeric or string data are compared or manipulated from one system state to another when a program is run. Some operators like the plus sign (+) or minus sign (-) are used to commit calculations. Others, such as the greater than sign (>) or less than sign (<) are used for data comparison. Operators may be used to generate an output that is independent of assignment or they may be used to generate new data which replaces a previous assignment or creates a new variable or constant.

3.2.18 Overflow
With respect to numeric operations, the term applied to the condition which exists when a prior operation has attempted to generate a result which exceeds MAXNUM, or which exceeds the maximum value that can be represented by the declared format of a fixed-point variable or array. With respect to string operations, the term applied to the condition which exists when a prior operation has attempted to generate a result which has more characters than can be contained in a string of maximal length, as determined by the language processor. With respect to string assignment, the term applied to the condition which exists when a prior operation has attempted to assign a value that is longer than the declared or default maximum of a string-variable or string-defined-function.

3.2.19 Procedural
The Procedural code paradigm is a subset of the use of an Imperative architecture. This paradigm uses a linear top-down approach and treats data and procedures as two different entities. Based on the concept of a

procedure call, Procedural Programming divides the program into procedures, which are also known as routines or functions which directly instruct a device on how to finish a task in logical steps.

Simply put, Procedural Programming involves writing down a list of instructions to tell the system what it should do step-by-step to finish the task at hand.

3.2.20 Program Unit
A self-contained part of a U/PL program consisting either of the main-program, which is the sequence of lines up to and including the line containing an END statement, or of an external-sub-def or external-function-def.

3.2.21 Rounding
The process by which the representation of a value with lower precision is generated from a representation of higher precision taking into account the value of that portion of the original number which is to be omitted. In an integer only U/PL implementation, the rounding process converts its argument by rounding to the nearest integer. In a U/PL implementation that is capable of floating-point arithmetic, any number that is exactly halfway between two integers (that is, of the form *integer*+0.5), then it is rounded to the one that is even (divisible by 2).

3.2.22 Significant digits
The contiguous sequence of digits between the high-order nonzero digit and the low-order non-zero digit, without regard for the location of the radix point. Commonly, in a normalized floating point internal representation, only the significant digits of a representation are maintained in the significance.

NOTE: The Standard requires that the ability of a conforming implementation to accept numeric representations be measured in terms of significant digits rather than the actual number of digits (that is including leading or trailing zeroes) in the representation.

3.2.23 State
The digital system running a U/PL program operates in a large but finite "state space" – it has a limited set of discrete configurations within which the system shifts in accordance with the clock signal, commands and/or

input (user, external or internal). The current State of the system consists of its mode, variable assignments, active commands and/or operators.

3.2.24 Statement
Statements are instructions that are preceded by a line number and are not executed until the system is placed into a RUN state. U/PL does allow for instructions to be utilized as both Commands and Statements – for example DISPLAY may be used as a Command in direct mode or as a Statement to be executed while in RUN mode.

3.2.25 Truncation
The process by which the representation of a value with lower precision is generated from a representation of higher precision by merely deleting the unwanted low order digits of the original representation. The Truncate process converts its argument by truncating toward zero; that is, the result is the integer of the same sign as the argument, and which has the greatest integral magnitude not greater than that of the argument.

3.2.26 Underflow
With respect to numeric operations, the terms applied to the condition which exists when a prior operation has attempted to generate a result, other than zero, which is less in magnitude than machine infinitesimal.

3.2.27 U/PL
A term applied as a name to the most current member of a class of languages which utilize similar syntaxes and semantic meanings which originated with the original BASIC language developed by John G. Kemeny and Thomas E. Kurtz at Dartmouth College in 1964. The term "BASIC" is an acronym for Beginner's All-purpose Symbolic Instruction Code – this has been superseded by the use of "U/PL" which is the proper acronym for Utility Programming Language. U/PL is an imperative, procedural, state-based programming language which generates programs which are transportable across current microcontroller architectures in standard form and microprocessors in Expanded form – though characteristics of either may be present in conforming installations.

4. PROGRAM ELEMENTS, LINES AND BLOCKS

A U/PL program is a sequence of lines containing statements. Each line is itself a sequence of characters.

4.1 Characters

4.1.1 General Description
The character set for U/PL is contained in ISO/IEC 646 (US-ASCII)

4.1.2 Syntax

1. character = quotation-mark / non-quote-character

2. quoted-string-character = double-quote / non-quote-character

3. non-quote-character = ampersand / apostrophe / asterisk / circumflex-accent / colon / comma / dollar-sign / equals-sign / exclamation-mark / greater-than-sign / left-parenthesis / less-than-sign / number-sign / percent-sign / question-mark / right-parenthesis / semicolon / slant / underline / unquoted-string-character

4. double-quote = quotation-mark quotation-mark

5. unquoted-string-character = space / plain-string-character

6. plain-string-character = digit / letter / period / plus-sign / minus-sign

7. digit = 0/1/2/3/4/5/6/7/8/9

8. letter = upper-case-letter / lower-case-letter

9. upper-case-letter = A/B/C/D/E/F/G/H/I/J/K/L/M/N/O/P/Q/R/S/T/U/V/W/X/Y/Z

10. lower-case-letter = a/b/c/d/e/f/g/h/i/j/k/l/m/n/o/p/q/r/s/t/u/v/w/x/y/z

11. other character = [implementation-defined]

The syntax as described generates programs which contain no spaces other than those occurring in remark-strings, in certain quoted-strings, unquoted-strings, and literal-strings, or where the presence of a space is explicitly indicated by the metaname space.

Special conventions will be observed regarding spaces. With the following exceptions, spaces may occur anywhere in a U/PL program without affecting the execution of that program and may be used to improve the appearance and readability of the program. Spaces will not appear:

- immediately preceding the line-number of a line
- within line-numbers
- within keywords
- within identifiers
- within numeric-constants
- within multicharacter relation symbols

In addition, spaces which appear in quoted-strings, unquoted-strings, and format- strings will be significant (though spaces which precede or follow an unquoted- string are not part of that string).

All keywords in a program, when used as such, will be preceded and followed by some character other than a letter, digit, underline or dollar-sign. A keyword may also be followed by an end-of-line.

4.1.3 Examples
None.

4.1.4 Semantics
The letters will be the set of capital (upper-case) and small (lower-case) letters contained in the ASCII character set in positions 4/1 to 5/10 and 6/1 to 7/10, respectively.

The digits will be the set of Arabic digits contained in the character set in position 3/0 to 3/9.

The remaining characters will correspond to the remaining graphic characters in position 2/0 to 2/15, 3/10 to 3/15, 5/14, and 5/15 of the ASCII character set.

The characters defined by the ASCII standard will apply when the standard collating sequence is in effect, either by default or by explicit use of a COLLATE option. The coding for the native collating sequence will be implementation-defined.

All characters other than letters denote themselves. Letters denote themselves within quoted-strings, unquoted-strings and line-input-replies. Corresponding upper¬ case-letters and lower-case-letters will be equivalent when used in identifiers and keywords. Quoted-string-characters also denote themselves, except for the double quote, which denotes one occurrence of the quotation-mark in the value of the string.

4.1.5 Exceptions
None.

4.1.6 Remarks
Other-characters may be defined by an implementation to be part of the character set for U/PL. These characters may be used in strings and may be accepted as characters in data supplied in response to a request for input or generated as the value of the CHR$ function. The effects of these other-characters are implementation- defined.

Programs written using other-characters (except for end-of-line characters) are not themselves standard-conforming programs.

4.2 Program
A U/PL program is a sequence of lines. Each line contains a unique line-number which facilitates program editing and serves as a label for the statement contained in that line.

A U/PL program is divided logically into a number of program-units. The first of these is the main-program, which is terminated by an end-line. Following the main- program may be zero or more external-sub-def or external-function-def.

Certain logical groupings of lines within a U/PL program are called blocks.

4.2.1 Syntax
Some of the syntax elements below are available only in Expanded U/PL implementations.

The Utility Programming Language Standard

1. program > program-name-line? main-program procedure-part*
2. program-name-line= line-number PROGRAM program-name function parm-list?
3. program-name = routine-identifier
4. main-program = unit-block* end-line
5. unit-block = internal-proc-def / block
6. internal-proc-def tail > internal-function-def / internal-sub-def / detached-handler
7. block > statement-line / loop / if-block / select-block /image-line / protection-block
8. statement-line = line-number statement tail
9. line-number = digit digit*
10. statement > declarative-statement / imperative-statement / conditional-statement
11. declarative-statement > data-statement / declare-statement / dimension-statement / null-statement / option-statement / remark-statement
12. imperative-statement > array-assignment / array-input-statement / array-line-input-statement / array-display-statement / array-read-statement / array-write-statement / ask-statement / break-statement / call-statement / cause-statement / close-statement / debug-statement / erase-statement / exit-do-statement / exit-for-statement / exit-function-statement / exit-handler-statement / exit-sub-statement / gosub-statement / goto-statement / handler - return-statement / input-statement / line-input-statement / link-statement / numeric-function-set-statement / open-statement / display-statement / randomize-statement / read-statement / restore-statement / return-statement / set-statement / stop-statement / string-function-set-statement / trace-statement / write-statement
13. stop statement = STOP
14. conditional-statement = if-statement / on-gosub-statement / on-goto-statement
15. tail = tail-comment? end-of-line
16. end-of-line = [implementation-defined]
17. end-line = line-number end-statement tail

18. end-statement = END
19. procedure-part = remark-line* procedure
20. procedure > external-function-def / external-sub-def
21. remark-line = line-number (null-statement / remark-statement) end-of-line
22. line > case-line / case-else-line / do-line / else-line / elseif-then-line / end-function-line / end-handler-line / end-if-line / end-line / end-select-line / end-sub-line / end-when-1ine / external-function-line / external-sub-line / for-line / handler-line / internal-def-line / internal-function-line / internal-sub-line / if-then-line / image-line / loop-line / next-line / program-name-line / remark-line / select-line / statement-line / use-line / when-line / when-use-name-line
23. program-unit > main-program / procedure
24. line-continuation = ampersand space* tail ampersand

A program will be composed of a sequence of lines. Exactly one of these lines will be an end-line; the lines up to and including this end-line constitutes the main- program. Line-number zero is not allowed; leading zeroes will have no effect. Lines will occur in ascending line-number order. All references to line-numbers within a program-unit will be to line-numbers of lines within that program-unit. The number of digits in a line-number will not exceed 5. The value of a line-number will not exceed 50000.

The manner in which the end of a line is detected is determined by the implementation, e.g., the end-of-line may be a carriage-return character, a carriage- return character followed by a line-feed character, an end of line function or the end of a physical record.

A physical line in a program will contain at most 256 characters before each end-of- line indicator.

At any place where a space may be used, except in quoted-strings, unquoted-strings, literal-strings, and remark-strings, a line-continuation may be substituted for a space with no effect other than that of the space it replaces.

Parameters in the program-name-line will not be explicitly dimensioned or declared in the main-program.

4.2.2 Examples

```
100 PROGRAM Graphic      & ! This program draws a graph
& (*,                    & ! x is x-coordinate
& y)                     ! y is y-coordinate
999 END
```

4.2.3 Semantics

The program-name-line is the operand of the `LINK`-statement. The relationship between the program-name and the program-designator in a program executing a `LINK`-statement is implementation-defined. Parameters in the program- name- line are evaluated as described in 9.1. Their scope is the main-program. For a program executed in isolation, the program-name has no effect. The effect of a parameter-list in a program-name-line for a program executed in isolation is implementation-defined.

Lines in a program will be executed in sequential order, starting with the first line, until

- some other action is dictated by execution of a line, or
- an exception occurs (unless, in Expanded U/PL, it is a nonfatal exception which is not handled by a user defined exception-handler), or
- a `LINK`-statement is executed, or
- a stop-statement or end-statement is executed.

The end-statement will serve both to mark the physical end of the main-program and to terminate execution of the program when encountered.

Execution of a stop-statement will also cause termination of execution of the program.

4.2.4 Exceptions
None.

4.2.5 Remarks
References to non-existent line-numbers in a program-unit are syntax errors. Implementations may therefore treat them as exceptions if they are documented as such.

4.3 Program Annotation

4.3.1 General Description
U/PL programs may be annotated by comments at the end of program lines or by separate remark-statements.

4.3.2 Syntax
       1. remark-statement = REM remark-string

       2. remark-string = character*

       3. null-statement = tail-comment

       4. tail-comment = exclamation-mark remark-string

Line-continuation will not occur in remark-strings.

4.3.3 Examples
```
REM FINAL CHECK
COMPUTE AVERAGE
```

4.3.4 Semantics
If the execution of a program reaches a line containing a remark-statement or null- statement, then it will proceed to the next line with no other effect.

A tail-comment has no effect upon the execution of the line in which it occurs. The remark-string in the tail-comment serves solely as a comment about the line.

4.3.5 Exceptions
None.

4.3.6 Remarks
None.

4.4 Identifiers

4.4.1 General Description
Identifiers are used to name variables, arrays, array-values, functions, programs, subprograms, and exception-handlers.

4.4.2 Syntax

1. identifier > numeric-identifier / string-identifier / routine-identifier
2. numeric-identifier = letter identifier-characters*
3. identifier-character = letter / digit / underline
4. string-identifier = letter identifier-character*dollar-sign
5. routine-identifier = letter identifier-character*

An identifier will contain at most 128 characters, including the dollar-sign in the case of a string identifier.

A given numeric-identifier may name a simple-numeric-variable, a one-dimensional, two-dimensional, or three-dimensional numeric-array, a numeric-function, or a numeric- array- value, but not more than one of these in a program-unit. Likewise, a given string-identifier may name a simple-string-variable, a one-dimensional, two- dimensional or three-dimensional string-array, a string-function, or a string-array- value, but not more than one of these in a program-unit.

A given identifier may name an internal-subprogram, an internal-function-def or a detached-handler but not more than one of these in a program-unit. A given routine-identifier will not name more than one of an external-function-def, an external-sub-def or a main-program in a program.

A numeric-identifier which names an external-function-def may not be used as a routine-identifier. The names of the no-argument supplied functions or array-values `CON`, `DATE`, `EXLINE`, `EXTYPE`, `IDN`, `MAXNUM`, `PI`, `RND`, `TIME`, `TRANSFORM` and `ZER` will not be used as numeric- identifiers to name any other entity. The names of the no-argument supplied functions or array-values `DATE$`, `NUL$`, and `TIME$` will not be used as string- identifiers to name any other entity. Keywords listed may not be used as identifiers.

4.4.3 Examples
X
sum
A$
last__names$
INVERT

4.4.4 Semantics
Each program-unit is a distinct entity in that identifiers used to name variables, arrays, detached-handlers, internal-function-definitions, or internal-procedures defined within program-units will be local to each invocation of the program-unit in which they occur, i.e., they will name different objects in different program-units and in different invocations of the same program-unit. Identifiers used to name supplied-functions or program-units, however, will be global to the entire program, i.e., they will name the same object wherever they occur.

If the name of implementation-supplied function or the keyword TAB is implicitly or explicitly defined or declared as the identifier of a user-defined function, array, or variable, then the defined declared interpretation of the identifier will override the interpretation specified by the Standard within the scope of the definition or declaration. Therefore, within that scope, the implementation-supplied function or the tab-call will be unavailable.

Within any program-unit, identifiers which differ only in the cases of the letters they contain will denote the same objects (e.g., Xl identifies the same object as xl). Identifiers which differ in any other respect will denote different objects.

4.4.5 Exceptions
None.

4.4.6 Remarks
No implementation-defined enhancement to this Standard may extend the list of words unavailable for use as simple-variables. Since all arrays must be declared, and since all defined-functions must be declared or defined in the program- unit in which they are referenced, implementations may supply built-in functions other than those specified in this Standard provided that

any declaration for such identifiers within a program overrides the implementation-supplied interpretation. Note, however, that in some cases the use of a parameterless function supplied by an implementation as an enhancement would be syntactically indistinguishable from a variable having the same name. Therefore, implementations which provide such functions must also provide a syntactic means for identifying them as functions. Examples of such syntax are a requirement to declare such functions explicitly in any program-unit where they are used or requiring the use of empty parentheses (e.g., n NEWFUNCTION()") with reference to such functions.

An operating system may impose additional restrictions on the length and form or identifiers for procedures which are compiled independently of the main-program.

A supplied-function may be overridden by defining a user-defined function or simple-variable with the same name.

In U/PL, an identifier may have the same spelling as a keyword (other than DISPLAY, ELSE, REM or NOT).

5. NUMBERS

Numbers constitute one of two primitive data types in U/PL (the other is strings). With numbers are associated constants, variables, and implementation-supplied functions, from which expressions can be formed.

5.1 Numeric Constants

5.1.1 General Description

Numeric-constants denote scalar numeric values. A numeric-constant is a decimal representation, in positional-notation, of a number. There are four general syntactic forms of numeric-constants:

- implicit point unscaled representation d...d
- explicit point unscaled representation ds..drd...d
- explicit point scaled representation sd...drd...dEsd..,d
- implicit point scaled representation sd...dEsd...d

where d is a digit, r is a period, s is an optional sign, and E is the explicit character E or e. A numeric-constant not preceded by a sign is assumed to be positive.

5.1.2 Syntax

1. constant > numeric-constant

2. numeric-constant = sign? numeric-rep

3. sign = plus-sign / minus-sign

4. numeric-rep = significand exrad?

5. significand = integer period? / integer? fraction

6. integer = digit digit*

7. fraction = period integer

8. exrad = E sign? integer

5.1.3 Examples
```
-21
1E10
5e-1
.4E+1
500.
1.2
.255
```

5.1.4 Semantics
The value of a numeric-constant is the number represented by that constant. n E" and M e M stand for "times ten to the power"; if no sign follows the symbols E and e, then a plus-sign is understood.

A program can contain numeric-constants which have an arbitrary number of digits. An imp Indentation must retain either the exact value of a numeric-cons tant, or that value rounded to an implementation-defined precision. The implementation-defined precision for numeric constants will not be less than ten or six significant decimal digits, depending on upon whether the arithmetic option in force DECIMAL or NATIVE is respectively. Numeric-constants can also have an arbitrary number of digits in the exrad, though nonzero constants whose magnitude is outside an implementation-defined range may be treated as exceptions. Nonzero constants whose magnitudes are less than machine infinitesimal will be replaced by zero, while constants whose magnitudes are larger than MAXNUM will be reported as causing an overflow.

5.1.5 Exceptions
- The evaluation of a numeric-constant causes an overflow (1001, fatal).

5.1.6 Remarks
It is recommended that implementations report constants whose magnitudes are less than machine infinitesimal as underflows (1501,

nonfatal replace by zero and continue). In an Expanded U/PL implementation, this permits interception by exception handlers.

Although this Standard contains no provision for named constants, their effect can be achieved through no-argument defined-functions.

5.2 Numeric Variables

5.2.1 General Description

Numeric-variables may be either simple-numeric-variables or references to elements of numeric-arrays.

5.2.2 Syntax

    1. variable > numeric-variable

    2. numeric-variable = simple-numeric-variable / numeric-array-element

    3. simple-numeric-variable = numeric-identifier

    4. numeric-array-element = numeric-array subscript-part

    5. numeric-array = numeric-identifier

    6. subscript-part = left-parenthesis subscript (comma subscript)*

    right-parenthesis

    7. subscript = index

    8. index = numeric-expression

    9. simple-variable > simple-numeric-variable

    10. array-name > numeric-array

The number of subscripts in a subscript-part will be one, two, or three.

5.2.3 Examples

```
X sum

V(4)

table(i, j+1)
```

5.2.4 Semantics

At any instant in the execution of a program, a numeric-variable is associated with a single numeric value. The value associated with a numeric-variable may be changed by the execution of statements in the program. Simple-numeric-variables are declared implicitly through their appearance in a program-unit. The scope of a numeric-variable will be the program-unit in which it appears, unless it is a parameter of an internal-function-definition.

An index is a numeric-expression whose value will be rounded to the nearest integer; the rounded value of X is defined to be INT(X+.5). A numeric-array-element is called a subscripted numeric-variable and refers to the element in the array selected by the value(s) of the subscript(s). The acceptable range of values must be explicitly declared in a dimension-statement or a declare-statement. Subscripts will have values within the appropriate range.

At the initiation of execution, the values associated with all numeric-variables will be implementation-defined.

5.2.5 Exceptions

- A subscript is not in the range of the declared bounds (2001, fatal).

5.2.6 Remarks

Since initialization of variables is not specified, and hence may vary from implementation to implementation, programs that are intended to be transportable should explicitly assign a value to each variable before any expression involving that variable is evaluated.

There are many commonly used alternatives for associating implementation-defined initial values with variables; it is recommended that all variables be recognizably undefined in the sense that an exception will result from any attempt to access the value of any variable before that variable is explicitly assigned a value (3101, nonfatal: supply an implementation-defined value and continue).

5.3 Numeric Expressions

5.3.1 General Description

Numeric-expressions may be constructed from numeric-variables, numeric-reps, and numeric-function-refs using the operations of addition, subtraction, multiplication, division, and exponentiation (i.e., raising to a power).

5.3.2 Syntax

1. expression > numeric-expression

2. numeric-expression = sign? term (sign terra)*

3. term = factor (multiplier factor)*

4. factor = primary (circumflex-accent primary)*

5. primary = numeric-rep numeric-variable / numeric-function-ref / left-parenthesis numeric-expression right-parenthesis

6. numeric-function-ref > numeric-function function-arg-list?

7. numeric-function = numeric-defined-function / numeric-supplied function

8. function-arg-list = left-parenthesis function-argument (comma function-argument)*right-parenthesis

9. function-argument = expression / actual-array

10. actual-array = array-name

11. multiplier = asterisk / slant

The number and types of arguments in a numeric-function-ref will agree with the number and types of corresponding parameters in the definition of the numeric- function. An actual-array will have the same number of dimensions as the corresponding parameter. Whenever numeric arguments are passed to an external-function-definition, the `ARITHMETIC` options in effect for the external-function-definition and the invoking program-unit must agree. Each numeric-function referenced in an expression within a program-unit will either be implementation-supplied or will be defined in an internal-function-def or declared in a declare-statement occurring in a lower-numbered line, within the same program-unit, than the first reference to that numeric-function.

5.3.3 Examples

```
3*X - Y 2
cost*quantity + overhead
2~(-X)
SQR(X'2+Y'2)
value(X, Y, a$) 26
```

5.3.4 Semantics

The formation and evaluation of numeric-expressions follows the normal algebraic rules. The symbols circumflex-accent O, asterisk (*), slant (/), plus-sign (+)> and minus-sign (-) represent the operations of exponentiation, multiplication, division, addition, and subtraction or negation, respectively. Unless parenthesis dictate otherwise, exponentiations will be performed first, then multiplications and divisions, and finally additions, subtractions, and negations. In the absence of parenthesis, operations of the same precedence will be evaluated from left to right. Thus A-B-C will be interpreted as (A-B)-C; A~B~C, as (A B) C; A/B/C, as (A/B)/C; -A+B as (-A)+B; and -A~B as -(A B).

If an underflow occurs in the evaluation of a numeric-expression, then the value generated by the operation which resulted in the underflow will be replaced by zero.

For those mathematical operators which are associative, commutative, or both, full use of these properties may be made in order to revise the order of evaluation of the numeric-expression except where constrained by the use of parenthesis.

0~0 is defined to be 1.

A numeric-function-ref is a notation for the invocation of a predefined algorithm, into which the argument values, if any, will be substituted for the parameters used in the function-definition. The result of evaluating a numeric-function, achieved by the execution of the defining algorithm, will be a scalar numeric value which replaces the numeric-function-ref in the numeric- expression.

5.3.5 Exceptions
- Evaluation of a numeric-expression results in division by zero (3001, fatal).
- Evaluation of a numeric-expression results in an overflow (1002, fatal).
- Evaluation of the operation of exponentiation results in a negative number being raised to a non-integral power (3002, fatal).
- Evaluation of the operation of exponentiation results in zero being raised to a negative power (3003, fatal).

5.3.6 Remarks
The accuracy with which the evaluation of a numeric expression takes place may vary from implementation to implementation, though care should be taken when developing a unique implementation that the accuracy allows for successful utilization.

It is recommended that implementations report underflow as an exception (1502, nonfatal: replace by zero and continue). In an Expanded U/PL implementation, this permits interception by exception handlers.

Implementations may evaluate primaries and operations within a numeric-expression in any order which is consistent with the semantics as defined by this Standard. Of course, an operation must be evaluated after its operands. For example, in the expression M A+B+C+D*E n , the primaries and additions may be evaluated in any order. However, the multiplication must be performed before the addition implied by the third plus-sign, since the product M D*E n is one of the operands of that addition.

5.4 Implementation-Supplied Numeric Functions

5.4.1 General Description
Predefined algorithms are supplied by the implementation for the evaluation of commonly used numeric functions. Additional functions related to other features of this Standard are defined in 6.4, 7.1 and 7.2.

5.4.2 Syntax
        1. numeric-supplied-function > ABS / ACOS / ANGLE / ASIN / ATN / CEIL / COS / COSH / COT / CSC / DATE / DEG / EPS / EXP / FP / MAXNUM / INT / IP / LOG / LOGIO /

```
LOG2 / MAX / MIN / MOD / PI / RAD / REMAINDER / RND /
ROUND / SEC / SGN / SIN / SINH / SQR / TAN / TANH /
TIME / TRUNCATE
```

2. randomize-statement = RSEED

5.4.3 Examples

```
RSEED
```

5.4.4 Semantics

The values of the numeric-supplied functions, as well as the number of arguments required for each function, will be as described below. In all cases, X and Y stand for numeric-expressions, and N stands for an index, i.e., the rounded integer value of a numeric-expression. Each function accepts numeric arguments within the range of the negative number with the largest magnitude to the largest positive number, except where noted. For functions which return a value in angle measure (`ACOS`, `ANGLE`, `ASIN` and `ATN`), the value will be in radians unless `OPTION ANGLE DEGREES` is in effect, when the value will be in degrees. In the semantics below, "pi" (lower-case) stands for the true value of that constant.

Functions:

`ABS(X)`

The absolute value of X.

`ACOS(X)`

The arccosine of X in radians or degrees, where 0 < ACOS(X) < pi; X will be in the range -1 < X < 1.

`ANGLE(X, Y)`

The angle in radians or degrees between the positive x-axis and the vector joining the origin to the point with coordinates (X, Y), where -pi < ANGLE(X, Y) < pi. X and Y must not both be 0. Note that counterclockwise is positive, e.g., ANGLE(1,1) = 45 degrees.

ASIN(X)

The arcsine of X in radians or degrees, where -pi/2 < ASIN(X) < pi/2; X will be in the range -1 < X < 1.

ATN(X)

The arctangent of X in radians or degrees, i.e., the angle whose tangent is X, where -(pi/2) < ATN(X) < (pi/2).

CEIL(X)

The smallest integer not less than X.

COS(X)

The cosine of X, where X is in radians or degrees.

COSH(X)

The hyperbolic cosine of X.

COT(X)

The cotangent of X, where X is in radians or degrees.

CSC(X)

The cosecant of X, where X is in radians or degrees.

DATE

The current date in decimal form YYDDD, where YY are the last two digits of the year and DDD is the ordinal number of the current day of the year, e.g., the value of DATE on May 9, 1977 was 77129. If there is no calendar available, then the value of DATE will be -1.

DEG(X)

The number of degrees in X radians.

EPS(X)

The maximum of (X-X', X"-X, sigma) where X' and X" are the predecessor and successor of X and sigma is the smallest positive value representable. If X has no predecessor then X'=X and if X has no successor then X n =X". Note EPS(O) is the smallest positive number representable by the implementation and is therefore implementation-defined. Note also that PS may produce different results for different arithmetic options.

`EXP(X)`

The exponential of X, i.e., the value of the base of natural logarithms (e = 2.71828...) raised to the power X; if `EXP(X)` is less than machine infinitesimal, then its value will be replaced by zero.

`FP(X)`

The fractional part of X, i.e., X - IP(X).

`INT(X)`

The largest integer not greater than X, e.g., `INT(1.3)=1` and `INT(-1.3) = -2`.

`IP(X)`

The integer part of X, i.e., SGN(X)*INT(ABS(X)).

`LOG(X)`

The natural logarithm of X; X will be greater than zero.

`LOGIO(X)`

The common logarithm of X; X will be greater than zero.

`LOG2(X)`

The base 2 logarithm of X; X will be greater than zero.

`MAX(X, Y)`

The larger (algebraically) of X and Y.

`MAXNUM`

The largest finite positive number representable and manipulable by the implementation; implementation-defined. `MAXNUM` may represent different numbers for different arithmetic options.

`MIN(X, Y)`

The smaller (algebraically) of X and Y.

`MOD(X, Y)`

X modulo Y, i.e., X-Y*`INT`(X/Y). Y will not equal zero.

`PI`

The constant 3.14159... which is the ratio of the circumference of a circle to its diameter.

`RAD(X)`

The number of radians in X degrees.

`REMAINDER(X, Y)`

The remainder function, i.e., X-Y*IP(X/Y). Y will not equal zero.

`RND`

The next pseudo-random number in an implementation-defined sequence of pseudo-random numbers uniformly distributed in the range 0 < `RND` < 1.

If no randomize-statement is executed, then the `RND` function will generate the same sequence of pseudo-random numbers each time a program is run. Execution of a randomize-statement will override this implementation-supplied sequence of pseudorandom numbers, generating a new (and unpredictable) starting point for the list of pseudo-random numbers used subsequently by the `RND` function. The sequence of pseudo random numbers will be global to the entire program, not local to individual program-units.

`ROUND(X, N)`

The value of X rounded to N decimal digits to the right of the decimal point (or -N digits to the left if N < 0); i.e., `INT`(X*10~N+.5)/10~N.

`SEC(X)`

The secant of X, where X is in radians or degrees.

`SGN(X)`

The sign of X: -1 if X < 0, 0 if X = 0, and +1 if X > 0.

SIN(X)

The sine of X, where X is in radians or degrees.

SINH(X)

The hyperbolic sine of X.

SQR(X)

The non-negative square root of X; X will be non-negative.

TAN(X)

The tangent of X, where X is in radians or degrees.

TANH(X)

The hyperbolic tangent of X.

TIME

The time elapsed since the previous midnight, expressed in seconds, e.g., the value of TIME at 11:15 AM is 40500. If there is no clock available, then the value of TIME will be -1. The value of TIME at midnight will be zero (not 86400).

TRUNCATE(X, N)

The value of X truncated to N decimal digits to the right of the decimal point (or -N digits to the left if N < 0); i.e., IP(X*10 N)/10 N.

If OPTION ANGLE DEGREES is in effect, the term "in radians or degrees" in the above list of function values will mean degrees. If OPTION ANGLE RADIANS is in effect, the term "in radians or degrees" will mean radians. The accuracy requirements for the periodic trigonometric functions SIN, COS, TAN, SEC, CSC, COT are limited to providing full accuracy of m+1 decimal digits only for arguments n the range of -2*pi to 2*pi. Loss of accuracy outside this range is limited to the result of loss of precision in performing those range reductions on arguments necessary to compute values of these functions, i.e., "SIN (x)" may be evaluated as if it were written "SIN (MOD (x, 2*pi))" and similarly for the other functions.

5.4.5 Exceptions

- The value of the argument of the LOG, LOG10, or LOG2 function is zero or negative (3004, fatal).
- The value of the argument of the SQR function is negative (3005, fatal).
- The magnitude of the value of a numeric-supplied-function is larger than MAXNUM or is mathematical infinity (1003, fatal).
- The value of the second argument of the MOD or REMAINDER function is zero (3006, fatal).
- The value of the argument of the ACOS or ASIN function is less than -1 or greater than 1 (3007, fatal).
- An attempt is made to evaluate ANGLE(0,0) (3008, fatal).

5.4.6 Remarks

In the case of implementations which do not have access to a randomizing device such as a real-time clock, the randomize-statement may be implemented by means of an interaction with the user.

This Standard requires that overflows be reported only for the final values of numeric-supplied-functions; exceptions which occur in the evaluation of these functions need not be reported, though implementations will take appropriate actions in the event of such exceptions to ensure the accuracy of the final values. When overflows are reported for the final values of numeric-supplied-functions, it is recommended that the name of the function generating the overflow be reported also.

It is recommended that, if the magnitude of the value of a numeric-supplied-function is nonzero, but less than machine infinitesimal, implementations report this as an underflow, set the value to zero (1503, nonfatal: return zero and continue). In Extended U/PL implementations, this permits interception by exception handlers.

The time-zone used for DATE and TIME is implementation-defined.

It may not be possible, for reasons of overflow, to express the year in full format in DATE. When this full format is needed, the function DATES should be used.

5.5 Numeric Assignment Statement

5.5.1 General Description
A set-statement provides for the simultaneous assignment of the computed value of a numeric-expression to a list of numeric-variables.

5.5.2 Syntax
1. set-statement > numeric-set-statement

2. numeric-set-statement = SET numeric-variable-list equals-sign numeric-expression

3. numeric-variable-list = numeric-variable (comma numeric-variable)*

5.5.3 Examples
```
SET P = 3.14159
SET A(X,3) = SIN(X)*Y + 1
SET A, Y(1), Z = 1+1
SET T(I,J), I, J = I + J
```

5.5.4 Semantics
The subscripts, if any, of variables in the numeric-variable-list will be evaluated in sequence from left to right. Next the numeric-expression on the right of the equals-sign will be evaluated. Finally, the value of that numeric-expression, if necessary rounded to the nearest value which can be retained by the variable, will be assigned to the numeric-variables in the numeric-variable-list in order from left to right.

5.5.5 Exceptions
None.

5.5.6 Remarks
Note that:

```
SET A = 1 SET A, B(A) = 2
```

is not equivalent to:

SET A = 1

SET A = 2

SET B(A) = 2

5.6 Numeric Arithmetic and Angle

5.6.1 General Description

Unless specified otherwise, the values of all numeric-variables will behave logically as floating-point decimal numbers with an implementation-defined precision of at least ten decimal digits. By use of an option-statement, a program may choose to take advantage of a more efficient, but possibly less accurate, representation for numeric values.

Unless specified otherwise the trigonometric functions require arguments or generate values in radian measure. By use of an option-statement, a program may change the angle measure of all such functions to degrees.

5.6.2 Syntax

1. option-statement = OPTION option-list

2. option-list = option (comma option)*

3. option > ARITHMETIC (DECIMAL / NATIVE / FIXED) / ANGLE (DEGREES / RADIANS)

4. declare-statement = DECLARE type-declaration

5. type-declaration > numeric-type

6. numeric-type > NUMERIC numeric-declaration (comma numeric-declaration)*

7. numeric-declaration > simple-numeric-variable

An option-statement with an ARITHMETIC option, if present at all, will occur in a lower-numbered line than any numeric-expression, or a dimension-statement or a declare-statement referencing a numeric-array or fixed-declaration in the same program-unit.

The option `ARITHMETIC FIXED` is relevant only to Extended U/PL.

A program-unit will contain at most one `ARITHMETIC` option.

An `ANGLE` option, if present at all, will occur in a lower-numbered line than any reference to any numeric-supplied-function in the same program-unit.

A program-unit will contain at most one `ANGLE` option.

A declare-statement, if present at all, must occur in a lower-numbered line than any reference to the variables declared therein.

5.6.3 Examples
```
OPTION ARITHMETIC DECIMAL, ANGLE DEGREES
```

5.6.4 Semantics
The `ARITHMETIC` option controls the logical behavior of numeric entities within the program-unit containing the option.

If `OPTION ARITHMETIC DECIMAL` is specified, or if no `ARITHMETIC` option is specified, then the values of the numeric-variables will behave logically as decimal floating-point numbers, with an implementation-defined precision, say m, of at least ten significant decimal digits and with an implementation-defined range of at least IE-38 to 1E+38.

The results of decimal computations can be described in terms of floating-point decimal intermediate results with at least m+1 decimal digits of precision (but may be implemented in some other equivalent fashion). The value of a numeric-variable will be assumed to be exact. Numeric-constants will be evaluated accurately to at least m decimal digits of precision. Numeric operations and functions will also be evaluated accurately to at least m+1 decimal digits of precision with respect to the computed value of their operands and arguments (which may themselves be intermediate results). In all cases, the intermediate result of an evaluation will be represented as a floating-point decimal number with at least ra+1 decimal digits of precision, thus, when the true result can be expressed as a decimal number with m+1 significant digits, the computed result will be exact. In no case will the error for evaluation of an individual constant, operation, or function be greater than 5 in the (m+2)nd significant digit. Implementations are free to use any method of numeric evaluation which always yields results whose absolute error (with respect to the true result) is no greater than the absolute error of the results generated by the preceding specification.

If OPTION ARITHMETIC NATIVE is specified, then the values of numeric variables and constants will be represented and manipulated in an implementation-defined fashion, with an implementation-defined precision of at least six decimal digits and with an implementation-defined range of at least 2E-38 to 1E+38. Decimal values need not be represented exactly, as long as the error is within the limits of this precision.

The ANGLE option controls the evaluation of the trigonometric functions within the program-unit containing the option. If OPTION ANGLE RADIANS is specified, or if no ANGLE option is specified, then the numeric-supplied-functions COS, COT, CSC, SEC, SIN, and TAN use arguments in radian measure, and the numeric-supplied-functions ACOS, ANGLE, ASIN and ATN generate results in radian measure.

If OPTION ANGLE DEGREES is specified, then the numeric-supplied-functions COS, COT, CSC, SEC, SIN, and TAN use arguments in degree measure, and the numeric-supplied- functions ACOS, ANGLE, ASIN, and ATN generate results in degree measure.

If the execution of a program reaches a line containing an option-statement, then it will proceed to the next line with no further effect.

A simple-numeric-variable that appears in a numeric-type will establish that variable as a simple-numeric-variable.

If execution reaches a line containing a declare-statement, it will proceed to the next line with no further effect.

5.6.5 Exceptions
None.

5.6.6 Remarks
The representations chosen for numeric values when OPTION ARITHMETIC NATIVE is specified may be the same as that for OPTION ARITHMETIC DECIMAL.

No minimum accuracy is specified for the evaluation of numeric expressions and functions when `OPTION ARITHMETIC NATIVE` has been chosen. However, it is recommended that implementations maintain at least six decimal digits of precision.

The value 2E-38 is specified for the maximum value of the lower bound of positive numbers to allow an implementation employing the IEC 559 floating point binary arithmetic to be standard conforming.

6. STRINGS

Character strings constitute one of two primitive data types in U/PL (the other is numbers). Strings consist of arbitrary sequences of characters. Their lengths are variable, not fixed, although a maximum length for a string may be specified. With strings are associated constants, variables, and implementation-supplied functions, from which expressions can be formed.

6.1 String Constants

6.1.1 General Description
A string-constant is a character string of fixed length enclosed within quotation- marks. A quotation-mark itself may be included in a string-constant by representing it by two adjacent quotation-marks.

6.1.2 Syntax

    1. constant > string-constant

    2. string-constant = quoted-string

    3. quoted-string = quotation-mark quoted-string-character* quotation-mark

The length of a string-constant, i.e., the number of quoted-string-characters contained between the quotation-marks, will be limited only by the implementation- defined maximum number of characters preceding each of end-of-line indicator (i.e., at least 132).

6.1.3 Examples
"XYZ"
"1E10"
"He said, ""Don't""."

6.1.4 Semantics
The value of a string-constant will be the sequence of all quoted-string-characters between the initial and final quotation-marks. The double-quote, when appearing inside a quoted-string ,will denote a single quotation-mark. Spaces in string- constants, including trailing spaces, will be significant. A string consisting only of two quotation-marks will represent the null string.

Upper-case-letters and lower- case-letters will be distinct within string-constants.

6.1.5 Exceptions
None.

6.1.6 Remarks
The maximum length of a string-constant is constrained by the maximum length of a physical line. The maximum length of the constant would therefore be 3 less than that for the line, allowing for a continuation character ("&"), and the leading and trailing quotation-mark, e.g.:

```
100 SET A$ = &
&"abc...unseen characters here...xyz"
```

As the maximum physical line length must be at least 132, the maximum string-constant length must be at least 129.

6.2 String Variables

6.2.1 General Description
String-variables may be either simple-string-variables or references to elements of one-dimensional, two-dimensional, or three-dimensional string-arrays. Explicit declarations of simple-string-variables are not required. A dollar-sign serves to distinguish a string-variable from a numeric-variable.

6.2.2 Syntax

    1. variable > string-variable

    2. string-variable = (simple-string-variable / string-array-element) substring-qualifier?

    3. simple-string-variable = string-identifier

    4. string-array-element = string-array subscript-part

    5. string-array = string-identifier

    6. substring-qualifier = left-parenthesis index colon index right-parenthesis

    7. simple-variable > simple-string-variable

8. array-name > string-array

6.2.3 Examples
```
K$
name$(X:Y)
ITEM$(1,n)(z:z+5)
A$(4)
table$(I,J)
```

6.2.4 Semantics
At any instant in the execution of a program, a string-variable is associated with a single string-value. The value associated with a string-variable may be changed by the execution of statements in the program.

The length of the character string associated with a string-variable can vary during the execution of a program from a length of zero characters (signifying the null or empty string) to the maximum allowed for that string-variable.

Simple-string-variables may be declared explicitly or may be declared implicitly through their appearance in a program-unit. The scope of a string-variable will be the program-unit in which it appears, unless it is a parameter of an internal-proc-def, in which case its scope is that definition.

A string-array element is called a subscripted string-variable and refers to the element in the one-dimensional, two-dimensional or three-dimensional array selected by the value(s) of the subscript(s). Subscripts will have values within the appropriate range.

The substring-qualifier provides a means for specifying a portion of the value associated with a string-variable. A$(M:N) will specify that substring of the value associated with A$ from its Mth through Nth characters (M and N are indices).

Characters in a string will be numbered from the left starting with one. There are no exceptions associated with substring-qualifiers; if either M or N is not in the range from 1 to LEN(A$), the M will be considered to be MAX(M,1) and N will be considered to be MIN(N,LEN(A$)). If M > N, even after this adjustment, then A$(M:N) will be the null string occurring before the Mth character of A$ if M < LEN(A$) or the null string immediately following A$ if M > LEN(A$). For example, if A$ = "1.23k", then A$(l:l) = "l", A$(l:3) = "123", A$(0:3) = "123", A$(2:5) = "234", A$(3:2) is the null string preceding the third character of A$, and A$(5:7) is the null string following A$. At the initiation of program execution, the values associated with all string-variables will be implementation-defined.

6.2.5 Exceptions
- A subscript is not in the range of the declared bounds (2001, fatal).

6.2.6 Remarks
Since initialization of variables is not specified, and hence may vary from implementation to implementation, programs that are intended to be transportable should explicitly assign a value to each variable before any expression involving that variable is evacuated.

There are many commonly used alternatives for associating implementation-defined initial values with variables; it is recommended that all variables be recognizably undefined in the sense that an exception will result from any attempt to access the value of any variable before that variable is explicitly assigned a value (3102, non- fatal: supply an implementation-defined value and continue).

6.3 String Expressions

6.3.1 General Description
String-expressions are composed of string-variables, string-constants, string-function-references, or a concatenation of these.

6.3.2 Syntax
   1. expression > string-expression

   2. string-expression = string-primary (concatenation string-primary)*

   3. string-primary = string-constant / string-variable / string-function-ref / left-parenthesis string-expression right-parenthesis

   4. string-function-ref = string-function function-arg-list?

5. string-function = string-defined-function / string-supplied-function

6. concatenation = ampersand

The number and types of arguments in a string-function-ref will agree with the number and types of the corresponding parameters specified in the definition of the string-function. An actual-array will have the same number of dimensions as the corresponding parameter. Each string-function referenced in an expression within a program-unit will either be implementation-supplied or will be defined in an internal-function-def or declared in a declare-statement occurring in a lower-numbered line, within the same program-unit, than the first reference to that string-function.

6.3.3 Examples
A2$ & B$(4:22) & "223"

X$(1,3)(I:J)

6.3.4 Semantics
The value of a string-expression will be the concatenation of the values of the string-primaries in the expression (e.g., if A$ = "COME " and B$ = "IN", then A$ & B$ = "COME IN" and B$ & A$ = "INCOME ").

Within a string-expression, string-primaries will be evaluated from left to right. For each string-primary, first the subscripts, if any, will be evaluated, then the substring-qualifiers, and then the value of the primary itself.

A string-function-ref is a notation for the invocation of a predefined algorithm, into which the argument values, if any, will be substituted for the parameters used in the function-def. The result of evaluating a string-function, achieved by the execution of the defining algorithm, will be a scalar string value which replaces the string-function-ref in the string-expression.

6.3.5 Exception
- Evaluation of a string-expression causes a string overflow (1051, fatal).

6.3.6 Remarks
The ampersand is used both for concatenation and line-continuation. Thus:

```
100 DISPLAY "ABC" &&
& "XYZ"
```

will display the sequence of characters ABCXYZ.

6.4 Implementation-Supplied String Functions
6.4.1 General Description
Predefined algorithms are supplied by the implementation for the evaluation of commonly used string-valued functions and numeric-valued functions whose arguments are strings.

6.4.2 Syntax
    1. string-supplied-function > (CHR / DATE / LCASE / LTRIM / REPEAT / RTRIM / STR / TIME / UCASE / USING) dollar-sign

    2. numeric-supplied-function > LEN / ORD / POS / VAL

    3. numeric-function-ref > MAXLEN left-parenthesis (simple-string-variable / string-array) right-parenthesis

6.4.3 Examples
None.

6.4.4 Semantics
The values of the implementation-supplied functions, as well as the number and types of arguments required for each function, are described below. In all cases, M represents an index, i.e., the rounded integer value of some numeric-expression; X stands for a numeric-expression; V$ represents a simple-string-variable or string-array; and A$ and B$ stand for string-expressions.

String Functions:

CHR$(M)

The one-character string consisting of the character occupying ordinal position M+l in the collating sequence for the declared character set, i.e., the first character is returned for an argument of zero. M will be at least zero and less than the number of characters in the declared character set. For example, for the standard character set, CHR$(53) = "5", and CHR$(65) = "A". The values of CHR$ for the native character set are implementation-defined. DATE$ The date in the string representation "YYYYMMDD" according to ISO 2014. For example, the value of DATE$ on May 9, 2021 was "20210509 M . If there is no calendar available, then the value of DATE$ will be "OOOOOOOO".

LCASE$(A$)

The string of characters resulting from the value associated with A$ by replacing each upper-case-letter in the string by its lower-case version.

LEN(A$)

The number of characters in the value associated with A$. Note that LEN(m,,m) = 1, since the value of the string constant consists of precisely one quotation-mark.

LTRIM$(A$)

The string of characters resulting from the value associated with A$ by deleting all leading space characters.

MAXLEN(V$)

The maximum length associated with the simple-string-variable or string-array. If there is no effective limit on string length, the value returned will be MAXNUM.

ORD(A$)

The ordinal position of the character named by the string associated with A$ in the collating sequence of the declared character set, where the first member of the character set is in ordinal position zero. The acceptable values of A$ are single characters in the character set and two-character or three-character mnemonics for characters in the character set. Values of A$ with two or more characters will be treated with upper-case-letters and lower-case- letters equivalent. The acceptable values for the standard character set are shown in Table 1. The acceptable values for the native character set are implementation-defined. For example, for the standard character set,

ORD("BS") = 8, ORD("A") = 65, ORD("a") = 97, ORD("5") = 53, ORD("SOH M) = 1, ORD("Soh M) =1, and ORD(M ABC") causes an exception.

POS(A$,B$)

The character position, within the value associated with A$, of the first character of the first occurrence of the value associated with B$. If there is no such occurrence, then POS(A$,B$) will be zero. POS(A$, MM) will be one, for all values of A$.

POS(A$,B$,M)

The character position, within the value associated with A, of the first character of the first occurrence of the value associated with B$, starting at the Mth character of A$. If the value associated with B$ does not occur within the designated portion of the value associated with A$, or if M is greater than LEN(A$), the value returned is zero. Otherwise, the value returned is equivalent to:

```
SET tempi = MAX(1, MIN(M, LEN(A$) + 1))
SET temp2$ = A$(tempi: LEN(A$))
SET temp3 = POS(temp2$, B$)
IF temp3 = 0 THEN
SET POS =0
ELSE
SET POS = temp3 + tempi - 1
END IF
```

For example, if A$ has the value "GRANSTANDING", then POS(A$,"AN",1) = 3, POS(A$,"AN",4) = 8, and POS(A$,"AN",9) = 0. POS(A$,"",M) will be MAX(M,1), as long as M <= LEN(A$).

REPEATS(A$,M)

The string consisting of M copies of A$; M > 0.

RTRIM$(A$)

The string of characters resulting from the value associated with A$ by deleting all trailing space characters.

STR$(X)

The string generated by the display-statement as the numeric-representation of the value associated with X. No leading or trailing spaces will be included in this numeric-representation. For example, STR$(123.5) = "123.5" and STR$(-3.14) = "-3.14".

TIMES

The time of day in 24-hour notation according to ISO 3307. For example, the value of TIMES at 11:15 AM is "11:15:00". If there is no clock available, then the value of TIMES will be "99:99:99". The value of TIMES at midnight is "00:00:00".

UCASE$(A$)

The string of characters resulting from the value associated with A$ by replacing each lower-case-letter in the string by its upper-case version.

USING$(A$,X)

The string consisting of the formatted representation of X, using A$ as a format-item, according to the semantics as defined by this Standard. The exceptions allowed for formatted output also apply to the USINGS function.

VAL(A$)

The value of the numeric-constant associated with A$, if the string associated with A$ is a numeric-constant. Leading and trailing spaces in the string are ignored. If the evaluation of the numeric-constant would result in a value which causes an underflow, then the value returned will be zero. For example, VAL(" 123.5 ") = 123.5, VAL("2.E-99") could be zero, and

VAL("MCMXVII")

Causes an exception.

6.4.5 Exceptions

- The value of the argument of VAL is not a valid numeric-constant (4001, fatal).
- The value of the argument of VAL is a valid numeric-constant, but evaluating this constant results in an overflow (1004, fatal).
- The value of the argument of CHR$ is not in the appropriate range (4002, fatal).
- The value of the argument of ORD is neither a valid single character nor a valid mnemonic (4003, fatal).
- The value of the second argument of REPEATS is not > 0 (4010, fatal).

6.4.6 Remarks

It is recommended that if the magnitude of the value of the VAL function is less than machine infinitesimal, implementations report this as an exception (1504, nonfatal: replace with zero and continue). In Expanded U/PL implementations, this permits interception by exception handlers.

The time zone used for DATES and TIMES is implementation-defined.

The effect of the functions UCASE$, and LCASE$ is fully defined only for the ECMA character set. For other-characters, such as accented letters, the effect is implementation-defined, and may be specified in other national version of this Standard to accommodate the needs of local alphabets.

6.5 String Assignment Statements

6.5.1 General Description
A SET-statement provides for the simultaneous assignment of the computed value of a string-expression to a list of string-variables.

6.5.2 Syntax

1. set-statement > string-set-statement

2. string-set-statement = SET string-variable-list equals-sign string-expression

3. string-variable-list = string-variable (comma string-variable)*

6.5.3 Examples

```
SET A$ = "ABC"
SET A$(I) = B$(3:4)
SET A$, B$ = "NEGATIVE DISCRIMINANT"
SET C$(7:10) = "wxyz"
SET A$ = "ABCD" &&
& "XYZ"
```

6.5.4 Semantics

The subscripts and substring-qualifiers, if any, of variables in the string-variable- list will be evaluated in sequence from left to right. Next the string-expression on the right of the equals-sign will be evaluated. Finally, the value of that string-expression will be assigned to the string-variables in the string-variable- list in order from left to right.

When a value is assigned to a string-variable with a substring-qualifier, it will replace the substring of the value of the string-variable specified by the substring- qualifier. The length of the value of the string-variable may change as a result of this replacement. For example, if A$ = "1234", then assigning "32" to A$(2:3) results in "1324", assigning "" to A$(2:3) results in "14", assigning A$(l:2) to A$(2:3) results in "1124", and assigning "5" to A$(2:l) results in "15234".

6.5.5 Exceptions

- The assignment of a value to a string-variable causes a string overflow (1106, fatal).

6.5.6 Remarks

The order of assignment of values to string-variables in the string-variable-list is important in statements such as

```
SET A$(1:2), A$(2:3) = "X"
```

where different order of assignment may produce different results.

6.6 String Declarations

6.6.1 General Description
An option-statement may be used to define an ordering on the set of all string characters.

A declare-statement may be used to set a maximum length for specified string-variables in a program-unit.

6.6.2 Syntax
    1. option > COLLATE (NATIVE / STANDARD)

    2. type-declaration > string-type

    3. string-type = STRING length-max? string-declaration (comma string-declaration)*

    4. length-max = asterisk integer

    5. string-declaration > simple-string-declaration

    6. simple-string-declaration = simple-string-variable length-max?

An option-statement with a COLLATE option, if present at all, will occur in a lower- numbered line than any string-expression, or a dimension-statement or declare- statement referencing a string-array or string-variable within the same program-unit. A program-unit will contain at most one COLLATE option.

No simple-string-variable will be declared more than once in a program-unit. A simple-string-variable which is a formal-parameter, or a parameter will not occur in a declare-statement.

6.6.3 Examples
COLLATE NATIVE
STRING*8 last_name$*20, first_name$, middle_name$

6.6.4 Semantics
The COLLATE option identifies the collating sequence to be used within a program-unit for comparing strings and for computing values of the CHR$ and ORD functions. OPTION COLLATE NATIVE specifies that the native

collating sequence of the host system will be used. OPTION COLLATE STANDARD specifies that the collating sequence will correspond to the order of the characters in Table 1. If no COLLATE option appears in a program-unit then the standard collating sequence will be used within that program-unit.

Simple-string-variables whose string-identifiers appear in string-types may have a maximum length less than or equal to the implementation-defined default value. The maximum is determined, in descending order of precedence, from:

- the length-max in the string-declaration for that variable
- the length-max in the string-type of the declare-statement containing that variable, or
- the implementation-defined default

The length-max guarantees that string values up to that length may be stored in the variable and that an attempt to store a longer value will cause a string overflow exception. The implementation-defined maximum string length default will be at least 13 characters.

A length-max of 0 in a string-type will establish the associated string-variable as having a maximum length of zero, i.e., the null string.

6.6.5 Exceptions
None.

6.6.6 Remarks
The native collating sequence may be the standard collating sequence.

The COLLATE option may be extended, on national versions of this Standard, to accommodate specific needs of local alphabets.

7. ARRAYS

7.1 General Description

The dimension-statement is used to reserve space for arrays. Unless declared otherwise, all array subscripts will have a lower bound of zero and an upper bound of ten. Thus, the default space allocation reserves space for 11 elements in one-dimensional arrays and 121 elements in two-dimensional arrays. By use of a dimension-statement, the subscript(s) of an array may be declared to have an upper bound other than ten. By use of an option-statement, the subscripts of all arrays may be declared to have a lower bound of one.

The general syntactic form of the dimension-statement is:

DIM declaration, ..., declaration

where each declaration has the form:

letter (integer) or letter (integer , integer)

The general syntactic form of the option-statement is:

OPTION BASE n

where n is either 0 or 1.

7.1.2 Syntax

    1. dimension-statement = DIM array declaration(comma array-declaration)*

    2. array-declaration = numeric-array-name left-parenthesis bounds right-parenthesis

    3. bounds= integer (comma integer)?

    4. option-statement = OPTION BASE (0/1)

7.1.3 Examples

DIM A (6), B(10,10)

7.1.4 Semantics

Each array-declaration occurring in a dimension-statement declares the array named to be either one or two dimensional according to whether one or two bounds are listed for the array. In addition, the bounds specify the maximum values that subscript expressions for the array can have.

The declaration for an array, if present at all, will occur in a lower numbered line than any reference to an element of that

array. Arrays that are not declared in any dimension-statement are declared implicitly to be one or two dimensional according to their use in the program, and to have subscripts with a maximum value of ten.

The option-statement declares the minimum value for all array subscripts; if no option-statement occurs in a program, this minimum is zero. An option-statement, if present at all, must occur in a lower numbered line than any dimension-statement or any reference to an element of an array. If an option-statement specifies that the lower bound for array subscripts is one, then no dimension-statement in the program may specify an upper bound of zero. A program may contain at most one option-statement.

If the execution of a program reaches a line containing a dimension-statement or an option-statement, then it will proceed to the next line with no other effect.

An array can be explicitly dimensioned only once.

Arrays are indexed collections of numbers or strings. Array elements can be manipulated by scalar numeric and string operations. In addition, entire arrays may be manipulated by matrix statements.

7.1.5 Exceptions

None.

7.1.6 Remarks
None.

7.2 Array Declarations

7.2.1 General Description

An option in the option-statement may be used to define the lower bound for all array subscripts within a program-unit which are not explicitly stated. By use of an option-statement the subscripts of all such arrays may be declared to have a lower bound of zero or one; if no such declaration occurs, the lower bound will be one.

Arrays may have one, two, or three dimensions. The number of dimensions and subscript bounds for each dimension are declared in the declare-statement or dimension- statement. All array-names, except those appearing in a function-parm-list or a procedure-parm-list, must be declared in one and only one such statement. If not explicitly declared, the lower subscript bound for a given dimension is one or zero, depending on the BASE option. Upper bounds must always be explicitly declared.

A one-dimensional array with subscripts 1 to 10 or 1980 to 1989 or -9 to 0 contains 10 elements. A two-dimensional array with subscript bounds 1 to 10 for each dimension contains 100 elements. Similarly, a three-dimensional array with subscript-bounds 1 to 10 for each dimension contains 1000 elements.

A declare-statement can be used to dimension numeric-arrays as well as to declare maximum lengths for string-variables and string-arrays, and to dimension string- arrays. A dimension-statement can be used to dimension arrays, but not to declare the maximum length of strings in string-arrays.

7.2.2 Syntax

1 . dimension-statement = DIM dimension-list

2 . dimension-list = array-declaration (comma array-declaration)*

3. array-declaration = numeric-array-declaration / string-array-declaration

4. numeric-array-declaration = numeric-array bounds

5. bounds = left-parenthesis bounds-range (comma bounds-range)* right-parenthesis

6 . bounds-range = signed-integer TO signed-integer / signed-integer

7. signed-integer = sign? integer

8 . string-array-declaration = string-array bounds

9. option > BASE (0 / 1)

10 . string-declaration > string-array-declaration length-max?

11 . numeric-declaration > numeric-array-declaration

12 . numeric-function-ref > MAXSIZE maxsize-argument / SIZE bound-argument / LBOUND bound-argument / UBOUND bound-argument

13. maxsize-argument = left-parenthesis actual-array right-parenthesis

14. bound-argument= left-parenthesis actual-array (comma index)? right-parenthesis

The number of bounds-ranges in "bounds" will be one, two or three. An array which is named as a formal-array of a defined-function, a subprogram or a program will not be declared in a declare-statement or dimension-statement (since the formal-array in the function-parm-list or procedure-parm-list serves as its declaration). Any other array will be declared in a lower numbered line than any reference to that array or one of its elements. Any reference to an array and its elements must agree in dimensionality with the declaration of that array in a declare- statement, a dimension-statement, or as a function-parameter or procedure-parameter.

No numeric-array or string-array will be dimensioned or declared more than once in a program-unit.

If the optional lower bound (the first signed-integer) is included in the bounds- range, it will be less than or equal to the upper bound (the second signed-integer).

If the lower bound is not specified, then the upper bound must not be less than the default lower bound, which may be zero or one, depending on the BASE option.

An option-statement with a BASE option, if present at all, will occur in a lower- numbered line than any declare-statement or dimension-statement or any MAT statement that uses a numeric-array-value in the same program-unit. A program-unit will contain at most one BASE option.

If a bound-argument does not specify an index, the actual-array must be declared as one-dimensional.

7.2.3 Examples

```
DIM A(6), B(10,10), B$(100), D(1 TO 5, 1980 TO 2020)
DIM A$(4,4), C(-5 TO 10)
A$(3 TO 21) * 8
SIZE(A,1)
SIZE(B$,2)
SIZE(X)
LBOUND(A)
UBØUND(C$,2)
```

7.2.4 Semantics

Each array-declaration declares the named array to be either one-dimensional, two- dimensional, or three-dimensional, according to whether one, two, or three bounds- ranges are specified in the bounds for the array. In addition, the bounds specify the maximum and optionally minimum values that subscripts for the array will have. If a minimum subscript is not explicitly declared and no BASE option occurs within the program-unit, then it will be implicitly declared to be one.

The BASE option in an option-statement is local to the program-unit in which it occurs and declares the minimum value for all array subscripts in that program-unit which are not explicitly declared.

If the execution of a program reaches a line containing a dimension-statement, then it will proceed to the next line with no further effect.

String-array-declarations appearing in a string-declaration may include a length-max, which sets the maximum length of each element of the string-array. As with simple string-variables, if there is no length-max in the string-declaration, then the length-max, if any, of the string-type takes effect. If there is no length-max in either, then the implementation-defined length-max, if any, will take effect.

The value of SIZE(A,N) where A is an actual-array and N is an index, will be the current number or permissible values for the Nth subscript of the array named by A (the value of N is rounded to the nearest integer, and the subscripts of A are indexed from left to right, starting at one). The value of SIZE(A) will be the current number of elements in the entire array A.

The value of MAXSIZE(A) will be the total number of elements of the entire array named by A permitted by the array-declaration.

The value of LBOUND(A,N), where A is an actual-array and N is an index, will be the current minimum value allowed for the Nth subscript of the array named by A. The value of UBOUND(A,N) will be the current maximum value allowed for the Nth subscript of array A. As in the SIZE function, the value of N is rounded to the nearest integer, and the subscripts of array A are indexed from left to right, starting at one. The LBOUND and UBOUND functions may be called with a single arguments provided that arguments is a vector, in which case the value of LBOUND and UBOUND are the current minimum and maximum values allowed for the subscript of the vector. (Here, and in the following sections, the word "vector" will mean a "one-dimensional array" and the word "matrix" will mean a "two-dimensional array").

7.2.5 Exceptions

- The value of the index in a SIZE reference is less than one or greater than the number of dimensions in the array (4004, fatal).
- The value of the index in an LBOUND reference is less than one or greater than the number of dimensions in the array (4008, fatal).
- The value of the index in a UBOUND reference is less than one or greater than the number of dimensions in the array (4009, fatal).

7.2.6 Remarks

The dimension statement is retained for compatibility with U/PL. All its capabilities are included within the declare-statement.

If an implementation supports more than three dimensions, SIZE, LBOUND, and UBOUND should work for those extra dimensions, and an exception should be generated only when an attempt is made to inquire about a dimension beyond those declared.

7.3 Numeric Arrays

7.3.1 General Description

Numeric-arrays in U/PL may be manipulated element by element. However, it is often more convenient to regard numeric-arrays as entities rather than as indexed collections of entities, and to manipulate the entire entity at once. U/PL provides a number of standard operations to facilitate such manipulations.

7.3.2 Syntax

1. The array-assignment > numeric-array-assignment

2. numeric-array-assignment = MAT numeric-array equals-sign / numeric-array-expression

3. numeric-array-expression = (numeric-array numeric-array-operator)? numeric-array / scalar-multiplier numeric-array / numeric-array-value / numeric-array-function-ref

4. numeric-array-operator = sign / asterisk

5. scalar-multiplier = primary asterisk

6. numeric-array-value > scalar-multiplier? (CON / IDN / ZER) redim?

7. redim = left-parenthesis redim-bounds (comma redim-bounds)* right-parenthesis

8. redim-bounds = (index TO)? index

9. numeric-array-function-ref= (TRN / INV) left-parenthesis numeric-array right-parenthesis

10. numeric-function-ref > DET (left-parenthesis numeric-array right-parenthesis) / DOT left-parenthesis numeric-array comma numeric-array right-parenthesis

The number of redim-bounds in a redim will be one, two, or three. A numeric-array being assigned a value by a numeric-array-assignment will have the same number of dimensions as the value of the numeric-array-expression.

The numeric-arrays in a numeric-function-ref involving DOT will be one-dimensional. There must be no more of them two redim-bounds following IDN.

The numeric-arrays in a sura or difference will have the same number of dimensions. The numeric-array serving as the argument of DET, INV or TRN will be two- dimensional.

The numeric-arrays serving as operands for the numeric-array-operator asterisk (matrix multiply) will be either one-dimensional or two-dimensional, and at least one of them will be two-dimensional.

7.3.3 Examples
In the following examples A, B and C are doubly-subscripted numeric-arrays, X, Y, and Z are singly-subscripted numeric-arrays, and W is a numeric-expression.

```
MAT A = B              MAT X = Y
MAT A = B + C          MAT X = Y - Z
MAT A = B*C            MAT X = A*Y     MAT X = Y*A
MAT A = W * B          MAT X = W * CON
MAT A = ZER(4,3)       MAT X = ZER
MAT A = INV(B)         MAT A = TRN(B)
DET(B)                 DOT(X, Y)
```

7.3.4 Semantics
Array Assignments and Redimensioning

Execution of a numeric-array-assignment will cause the numeric-array-expression to be evaluated and its value assigned to the array named to the left of the equals-sign. If necessary, this array will have its size changed dynamically, i.e., its number of dimensions will be unchanged, but its size in each dimension will be changed to conform to the size of the array which is the value of the numeric-array-expression.

When the size of a numeric-array is changed dynamically, the current upper bounds for its subscripts will be changed to conform to the new sizes. That is:

```
new_lower_bound = old_lower_bound
new_upper_bound = old_lower__bound + new__size - 1
```

The new sizes need not individually be less than or equal to the sizes determined in the array-declaration for that numeric-array, as long as the new total number of elements for the numeric-array does not exceed the total number of elements determined by the array-declaration for that array.

Array Expression

The evaluation of numeric-array-expressions will follow the normal rules of matrix algebra. The symbols asterisk (*), plus (+), and minus (-) will represent the operations of multiplication, addition, and subtraction respectively.

The dimensions of numeric-arrays in numeric-array-expressions will conform to the rules of matrix algebra. The numeric-arrays in a sum or difference will have the same sizes in each dimension. The numeric-arrays in a product will have sizes L x M and M x N for some L, M and N (in which case the product will have size L x N), or an M element vector and a size M x N matrix (in which case the product will be an N element vector), or a size L x M matrix and an M element vector (in which case the product will be an L element vector). All elements in a numeric-array will be used when evaluating a numeric-array-expression, i.e., each numeric-array will be treated as an entity. When a scalar-multiplier is present in a numeric-array-expression, the primary will be evaluated, and then each element of the numeric-array will be multiplied by this value.

If an underflow occurs in the evaluation of a numeric-array-expression, then the value generated by the operation which resulted in the underflow will be replaced by zero.

Array Values

Nu-array-values will be assigned to the numeric-array on the left of the equals sign. If no redim is present, the size of the numeric-array generated will be the same as the size of the numeric-array to which it is to be assigned. If a redim is present, a numeric-array of the dimensions specified will be generated, and the numeric-array to which it is assigned will be redimensioned as described above. In a redim-bounds, the values of the indices are the lower and upper bounds of the corresponding dimension in the associated array-value. If the redim-bounds consists of a single index, its value will be the upper bound, and the lower bound will be the current default lower bound in effect. If a redim is used with the IDN constant, then it will produce a square matrix, i.e., the number of rows will equal the number of columns. If a redim is not used with the IDN constant, the numeric-array being assigned to will be square.

The ZER constant will generate a numeric-array, all of whose elements are zero. The CON constant will generate a numeric-array, all of whose elements are one. The IDN constant will generate an identity matrix, i.e., a square matrix with ones on the main diagonal and zeros elsewhere. If only one redim-bounds is used with IDN, then the effect is just as if that redim-bounds had been specified twice.

If a scalar-multiplier is used with an IDN, ZER or CON constant, then the primary is evaluated and each non-zero element of the IDN, ZER or CON constant is replaced by the value of the primary.

Array Functions

The function TRN will produce the transpose of its argument. An N x M matrix is returned for an M x N argument.

The function INV will produce the inverse of its argument. The argument must be a square matrix.

The function DET will return the determinant of its argument. The argument must be a square matrix.

The value of DOT(X, Y) will result in a scalar value, which is the result of the inner product multiplication of the one-dimensional numeric-vectors X and Y.

7.3.5 Exceptions

- The sizes of numeric-arrays in a numeric-array-expression do not conform to the rules of matrix algebra (6001, fatal).
- The total number of elements required for a redimensioned array exceeds the number of elements reserved by the array's original dimensions (5001, fatal).
- The first index in a redim-bounds is greater than the second (6005, fatal).
- A redim-bounds consists of a single index which is less than the default lower bound in effect (6005, fatal).
- The redim following IDN does not specify a square matrix, or no redim is present and the receiving matrix is not square (6004,fatal).
- The argument of the DET function is not a square numeric matrix (6002, fatal). 50 - The argument of the INV function is not a square numeric matrix (6003, fatal).
- Evaluation of a numeric-array-expression results in an overflow (1005, fatal).
- Evaluation of DET or DOT results in an overflow (1009, fatal).
- Application of INV to a singular matrix, or loss of all significant digits (3009, fatal).

7.3.6 Remarks

It is recommended that implementations report underflow as an exception (1505, nonfatal: replace by zero and continue). In Expanded U/PL implementation, this permits interception by exception handlers.

7.4 String Arrays

7.4.1 General Description

As with numeric-arrays, string-arrays may be regarded as entities rather than as indexed collections of entities. U/PL provides the ability to concatenate and assign entire arrays of strings.

7.4.2 Syntax

1. array-assignment > string-array-assignment

2. string-array-assignment = MAT string-array substring-qualifier? equals-sign string-array-expression

3. String-array-expression = string-array-primary (concatenation string-array-primary)? / string-primary concatenation string-array-primary / string-array-primary concatenation string-primary / string-array-value

4. string-array-primary = string-array substring-qualifier?

5. string-array-value = (string-primary concatenation)? NUL dollar-sign redim?

A string-array being assigned a value by a string-array-assignment will have the same number of dimensions as the value of the string-array-expression. Two string-arrays being concatenated will have the same number of dimensions.

7.4.3 Examples
MAT A$ = A$ & B$
MAT A$ = NUL$(5,6)
MAT A$ = ("Number") & B$
MAT A$(4:6) = (" ") & B$

7.4.4 Semantics
Execution of a string-array-assignment will cause the string-array-expression to be evaluated and its value assigned to the array named to the left of the equals-sign. If appropriate, this array will have its size changed dynamically, i.e., its number of dimensions will be unchanged, but its size in each dimension will be changed to conform to the size of the array which is the value of the string-array-expression.

When the size of a string-array is changed dynamically, the current upper bounds for its subscripts will be changed to conform to the new sizes. That is:

new_lower_bound = old_lower_bound ; new_upper_bound = old_lower_bound + new_size - 1

The new sizes need not individually be less than or equal to the sizes determined in the string-array-declaration for that string-array, as long as the new total number 51 of elements for the string-array does not exceed the total number of elements determined by the array-declaration for that array.

When a string-array on the left of a string-array-assignment has a substring-qualifier, the assignment to each element of the string-array will replace the substring of the value of each element specified by the substring-qualifier. The substring-qualifier on the left will be evaluated before the string-array-expression.

String-array-expressions involve the operations of concatenation and substring extraction. Two string-arrays being concatenated will have the same size in each dimension; the concatenation will be performed element by element. When concatenation is by scalar, this scalar will be prefixed or suffixed, as appropriate, to every element of the string-array. When a substring-qualifier is applied to a string-array, then the specified substring will be extracted from each element in the array.

The order of evaluation and assignment will be as follows:

- evaluate the substring-qualifiers in the string-array on the left;
- evaluate the string-array-expression from left to right, by evaluating each string-primary or string-array-primary as follows: evaluate first the subscripts, if any, then the substring qualifiers, and then the value of the primary itself;
- concatenate;
- make the assignment.

The string-array-value NUL$ is an array all of whose elements are the null string. If a redim is not present, the size of the string-array generated will be the same as the size of the string-array to which it is to be assigned. If a redim is present, a string-array of the dimensions specified will be generated and the string-array to which it is assigned will be redimensioned as described above. The rules provided for redims with numeric-array-values apply to NUL$ as well.

7.4.5 Exceptions
- The arrays in a string-array-expression have different sizes (6101, fatal).
- The first index in a redim-bounds is greater than the second (6005, fatal).
- A redim-bounds consists of a single index which is less than the default lower bound in effect (6005, fatal).
- The total number of elements required for a redimensioned array exceeds the number of elements reserved by the array's original dimensions (5001, fatal).
- Evaluation of a string-array-expression results in a string overflow (1052, fatal).
- Assignment of a value to a string-array causes a string overflow (1106, fatal).

7.4.6 Remarks
None.

8. CONSTANTS

8.1.1 General Description

Constants can denote both scalar numeric values and string values.

A numeric-constant is a decimal representation in positional notation of a number. There are four general syntactic forms of (optionally signed) numeric constants:

- implicit point representation sd...d

- explicit point unscaled representation sd..drd..d

- explicit point scaled representation sd..drd..dEsd..d

- implicit point scaled representation sd..dEsd..d

where:

d is a decimal digit,

r is a full-stop

s is an optional sign, and

E is the explicit character E.

A string-constant is a character string enclosed in quotation marks.

8.1.2 Syntax

    1. numeric-constant > sign? numeric-rep

    2. sign = plus-sign / minus-sign

    3. numeric-rep = significand exrad?

    4. significand = integer full-stop? / integer? fraction

    5. integer = digit digit*

    6. fraction = full-stop digit digit*

    7. exrad = E sign? integer

8. string-constant = quoted-string

8.1.3 Examples
```
1500   -21.   .2551E10
5E-1   .4E+1
"XYZ"   "X- 3B2" "1E10"
```

8.1.4 Semantics
The value of a numeric-constant is the number represented by that constant. "E" stands for "times ten to the power"; if no sign follows the symbol "E", then a plus sign is understood. Spaces will not occur in numeric-constants.

A program may contain numeric representations which have an arbitrary number of digits, though implementations may round the values of such representations to an implementation-defined precision of not less than six significant decimal digits. Numeric constants can also have an arbitrary number of digits in the exrad, though nonzero constants whose magnitude is outside an implementation-defined range will be treated as exceptions. The implementation-defined range will be at least 1E-38 to 1E+38. Constants whose magnitudes are less than machine infinitesimal will be replaced by zero, while constants whose magnitudes are larger than machine infinity will be diagnosed as causing an overflow.

A string-constant has as its value the string of all characters between the quotation marks; spaces will not be ignored. The length of a string-constant, i.e., the number of characters contained between the quotation-marks, is limited only by the length of a line.

8.1.5 Exceptions
- The evaluation of a numeric constant causes an overflow (nonfatal, the recommended recovery procedure is to supply machine infinity with the appropriate sign and continue).

8.1.6 Remarks
Since this Standard does not require that strings with more than 18 characters be assignable to string variables, conforming programs can use string constants with more than 18 characters only as elements in a display-list.

It is recommended that implementations report constants whose magnitudes are less than machine infinitesimal as underflows and continue.

9. VARIABLES

9.1.1 General Description

Variables in U/PL are associated with either numeric or string values and, in the case of numeric variables, may be either simple variables or references to elements of one or two-dimensional arrays. If a variable is a reference to an array it is called a subscripted variable.

Simple numeric variables will be named by a letter followed by an optional digit.

Subscripted numeric variables will be named by a letter followed by one or two numeric expressions enclosed within parentheses.

String variables will be named by a letter followed by a dollar sign.

Explicit declarations of variable types are not required; a dollar-sign serves to distinguish string from numeric variables, and the presence of a subscript distinguishes a subscripted variable from a simple one.

9.1.2 Syntax

1. variable > numeric-variable / string-variable

2. numeric-variable > simple-numeric-variable / numeric-array-element

3. simple-numeric-= letter digit? variable

4. numeric-array-element = numeric-array-name subscript

5. numeric-array-name = letter

6. subscript = left-parenthesis numeric-expression (comma numeric-expression)? right-parenthesis

7. string-variable= letter dollar-sign

An identifier will contain at most 128 characters, including the dollar-sign in the case of a string identifier.

A given numeric-identifier may name a simple-numeric-variable, a one-dimensional, two-dimensional or three-dimensional numeric-array, a numeric-function, or a numeric- array- value, but not more than one of these in a program-unit. Likewise, a given string-identifier may name a simple-string-variable, a one-dimensional, two- dimensional or three-dimensional string-array, a string-function, or a string-array- value, but not more than one of these in a program-unit.

A given identifier may name an internal-subprogram, an internal-function-def or a detached-handler but not more than one of these in a program-unit. 20 A given routine-identifier will not name more than one of an external-function-def, an external-sub-def or a main-program in a program.

A numeric-identifier which names an external-function-def may not be used as a routine-identifier.

The names of the no-argument supplied functions or array-values CON, DATE, EXLINE, EXTYPE, IDN, MAXNUM, PI, RND, TIME, TRANSFORM and ZER will not be used as numeric- identifiers to name any other entity. The names of the no-argument supplied functions or array-values DATE$, NUL$, and TIME$ will not be used as string- identifiers to name any other entity. Keywords may not be used as identifiers in any implementation of U/PL or Expanded U/PL .

9.1.3 Examples
```
X A5V(3)W(X,X+Y/2)
S$C$
```

9.1.4 Semantics
At any instant in the execution of a program, a numeric variable is associated with a single numeric value and a string-variable is associated with a single string value. The value associated with a variable may be changed by the execution of statements in the program.

The length of the character string associated with a string variable can vary during the execution of a program from a length of zero characters (signifying the null or empty string) to 18 characters.

Simple-numeric-variables and string-variables are declared implicitly through their appearance in a program.

A subscripted variable refers to the element in the one or two-dimensional array selected by the value(s) of the subscript(s). The value of each subscript is rounded to the nearest integer. Unless explicitly declared in a dimension statement, subscripted variables are implicitly declared by their first appearance in a program. In this case the range of each subscript is from zero to ten inclusive, unless the presence of an option-statement indicates that the range is from one to ten inclusive. Subscript expressions will have values within the appropriate range.

The same letter will not be the name of both a simple variable and an array, nor the name of both a one-dimensional and a two- dimensional array.

There is no relationship between a numeric-variable and a string variable whose names agree except for the dollar-sign.

At the initiation of execution, the values associated with all variables will be implementation-defined.

Each program-unit is a distinct entity in that identifiers used to name variables, arrays, detached-handlers, internal-function-definitions, or internal-procedures defined within program-units will be local to each invocation of the program-unit in which they occur, i.e., they will name different objects in different program-units and in different invocations of the same program-unit. Identifiers used to name supplied-functions or program-units, however, will be global to the entire program, i.e., they will name the same object wherever they occur.

If the name of implementation-supplied function or the keyword TAB is implicitly or explicitly defined or declared as the identifier of a user-defined function, array, or variable, then the defined declared interpretation of the identifier will override the interpretation specified by the Standard within the scope of the definition or declaration. Therefore, within that scope, the implementation-supplied function or the tab-call will be unavailable.

Within any program-unit, identifiers which differ only in the cases of the letters they contain will denote the same objects (e.g., XI identifies the same object as xI). Identifiers which differ in any other respect will denote different objects.

9.1.5 Exceptions

- A subscript is not in the range of the explicit or implicit dimensioning bounds (fatal).

9.1.6 Remarks

Since initialization of variables is not specified, and hence may vary from implementation to implementation, programs that are intended to be transportable should explicitly assign a value to each variable before any expression involving that variable is evaluated.

There are many commonly used alternatives for associating implementation-defined initial values with variables; it is recommended that all variables are recognizably undefined in the sense that an exception will result from any attempt to access the value of any variable before that variable is explicitly assigned a value.

No implementation-defined enhancement to this Standard may extend the list of words unavailable for use as simple-variables. Since all arrays must be declared, and since all defined-functions must be declared or defined in the program- unit in which they are referenced, implementations may supply built-in functions other than those specified in this Standard provided that any declaration for such identifiers within a program overrides the implementation-supplied interpretation. Note, however, that in some cases the use of a parameterless function supplied by an implementation as an enhancement would be syntactically indistinguishable from a variable having the same name. Therefore, implementations which provide such functions must also provide a syntactic means for identifying them as functions. Examples of such syntax are a requirement to declare such functions explicitly in any program-unit where they are used or requiring the use of empty parentheses (e.g., n NEWFUNCTION()") with reference to such functions.

An operating system may impose additional restrictions on the length and form or identifiers for procedures which are compiled independently of the main-program.

A supplied-function may be overridden by defining a user-defined function or simple- variable with the same name.

10. CONTROL STRUCTURES

Control structures govern the order of execution of lines in a program, both by statements which make explicit reference to line-numbers and also by explicitly-constructed loops and decision mechanisms which make no reference to line-numbers.

10.1 Relational Expressions

10.1.1 General Description

Relational-expressions enable the values of expressions to be compared in order to influence the flow of control in a program.

10.1.2 Syntax

1. relational-expression = disjunction

2. disjunction = conjunction (OR conjunction)*

3. conjunction = relational-term (AND relational-term)*

4. relational-term = NOT? relational-primary

5. relational-primary = comparison / left-parenthesis relational-expression right-parenthesis

6. comparison = numeric-expression relation numeric-expression / string-expression relation string-expression

7. relation = equality-relation / greater-than-sign / less-than-sign / not-greater / not-less

8. equality-relation = equals-sign / not-equals

9. not-equals = less-than-sign greater-than-sign / greater-than-sign less-than-sign

10. not-less = greater-than-sign equals-sign / equals-sign greater-them-sign

11. not-greater = less-than-sign equals-sign / equals-sign less-than-sign

10.1.3 Examples

```
NOT X < Y OR A$ = B$ AND B$ = C$
A <= X AND X <= B
1 <= I AND I <= 10 AND A(I) = X
I < N AND (J > M OR A(I) < B(J))
```

10.1.4 Semantics

The relation "less than or equal to" is denoted by not-greater. The relation "greater than or equal to" is denoted by not-less. The relation "not equal to" is denoted by not-equals. The relations "greater than", "less than", and "equals" are denoted by the corresponding syntactic sign.

The relation of equality will hold between two numeric-expressions if and only if the two numeric-expressions have the same value.

The relation of equality will hold between two string-expressions if and only if the values of the two string-expressions have the same length and contain identical sequences of characters.

In the evaluation of relational-expressions involving string-expressions, the relation "less than" will be interpreted to mean "earlier in the collating sequence than", and the other relations will be defined in a corresponding manner. More precisely, if two unequal strings in a relational-expression have the same length, then one will be "less than" the other if, in the leftmost character position in which they differ, the character in that string precedes the character in the other according to the established collating sequence. If the two strings in a relational-expression have different lengths and one has zero length or is an initial 54 leftmost segment of the other, then the shorter string will be "less than" the other. Otherwise, the relationship between two strings of unequal length will be determined by the contents of the shorter string and the leftmost portion of the longer string which is of the same length as the shorter string.

The precedence of the operators AND, OR, and NOT will be as implied by the formal syntax. That is, NOT operates only on the relational-primary immediately following it, AND applies to the relational-terms immediately preceding and following it, and OR applies to the conjunctions immediately preceding and following it.

The order of evaluation of relational-expressions will be as follows. The relational-expression will take on the truth-value of the disjunction which constitutes it. The conjunctions immediately contained in the disjunction will be evaluated from left to right until a true conjunction is found or none are left. As soon as a true conjunction is found, the whole disjunction is evaluated as true, and any remaining conjunctions are not evaluated. If no true conjunctions are found, the disjunction is false. For each conjunction, the relational-terms immediately contained in it are evaluated from left to right until a false relational-term is found or none are left. As soon as a false relational-term is found, the whole conjunction is evaluated as false and any remaining relational-terms are not evaluated. If all the relational terms are true, then the conjunction is true. For each relational-term, the relational-primary immediately contained in it is evaluated, its truth value reversed if and only if NOT is also immediately contained in the term, and the resulting value assigned to the relational-term. A relational-primary will be evaluated according to the description above of the various relations, if it is a comparison. Otherwise, it will take on the value of the relational-expression immediately contained within it. This relational-expression will be evaluated by re-applying the rules of this paragraph to it.

10.1.5 Exceptions
None.

10.1.6 Remarks
The specification for evaluation of relational-expressions guarantees that certain parts of the expression will not be evaluated if not necessary. For instance, if an array A has subscripts from 1 to 10:

```
1 < X AND X < 10 AND A(X) = KEY
```

will never cause an exception for subscript out of range.

10.2 Control Statements

10.2.1 General Description
Control statements allow for the interruption of the normal sequence of execution of statements by causing execution to continue at a specified line, rather than at the one with the next higher line-number.

The goto-statement allows for an unconditional transfer. The on-goto-statement allows control to be transferred to a selected line. The gosub-statement and return- statement allow for subroutine calls. The on-gosub-statement and return-statement allow for selected subroutine calls.

10.2.2 Syntax

1. control-transfer = gosub-statement / goto-statement / if-statement / io-recovery / on-gosub-statement / on-goto-statement

2. goto-statement = (GOTO / GO TO) line-number

3. on-goto-statement = ON index (GOTO / GO TO) line-number (comma line-number)* (ELSE imperative-statement)?

4. go sub-statement = (GOSUB / GO SUB) line-number

5. return-statement = RETURN

6. on-gosub-statement = ON index (GOSUB / GO SUB) line-number (comma line-number)* (ELSE imperative-statement)?

10.2.3 Examples

```
GO TO 999
GOTO 999
ON L+1 GO TO 400, 400, 500
ON X GO TO 100, 200, 150, 9999 ELSE SET A = 1
GO SUB 5000
GOSUB 5160
ON A+7 GOSUB 1000, 2000, 7000, 4000
ON F1-2 GOSUB 4360, 4460, 4660 ELSE DISPLAY F$
```

10.2.4 Semantics

Execution of a goto-statement will cause execution of the program to be continued at the line with the specified line-number.

The index in an on-goto-statement will be evaluated and its value rounded to obtain an integer, whose value will be used to select a line-number from the list following the GOTO (the line-numbers in the list are indexed from left to right, starting with 1). Execution of the program will continue at the line with the selected line- number. If the on-goto-statement contains an ELSE clause, and the value of the index in the on-goto-statement is less than one or greater than the number of line-numbers in the list, then the imperative-statement following the ELSE will be executed; if the imperative-statement in the ELSE part does not transfer control to another line, then execution will be continued in sequence, i.e., with the line following that containing the on-goto-statement.

The execution of the gosub-statement or on-gosub-statement and the return-statement can be described in terms of stacks of line-numbers, one associated with each invocation of a program-unit or internal-proc-def (but may be implemented in some other fashion). (The stack is conceptual; the Standard does not require that this method be used). Prior to execution of the first gosub-statement or on-gosub-statement in the invocation of a program-unit or internal-proc-def, the stack in that entity will be empty. Each time a gosub-statement is executed, the line-number of the gosub-statement will be placed on top of this stack and execution of the program-unit or internal-proc-def will be continued at the line specified in the gosub-statement.

The index in an on-gosub-statement will be evaluated by rounding to obtain an integer, whose value will be used to select a line-number from the list following the GOSUB (the numbers in the list are indexed from left to right, starting with 1). The line-number of the on-gosub statement will be placed on top of the stack for the appropriate program-unit or internal-proc-def, and execution will continue at the line with the line-number selected by the index. If the on-gosub-statement contains an ELSE clause, and the value of the index in the on-gosub-statement is less than one or greater than the number of line-numbers in the list, then the imperative-statement following the ELSE will be executed and the stack of line-numbers will not be changed; if the imperative-statement in the ELSE part does not transfer control to another line, execution will then continue in sequence, i.e., with the line following that containing the on-gosub-statement.

Each time a return-statement is executed, the line-number on top of the stack will be removed from the stack and execution of the program-unit or internal-proc-def will continue at the line following the one with that line-number.

A return-statement, gosub-statement and on-gosub-statement within an internal-proc- def will interact only with the stack for that internal-proc-def. All other such statements interact only with the stack for the program-unit containing the statement.

It is not necessary that equal numbers of gosub-statements or on-gosub-statements and return-statements be executed before termination of a program-unit or internal-proc- def; the stack of line-numbers associated with the current invocation of a program- unit or internal-proc-def will be emptied upon termination of that program-unit or internal-proc-def.

10.2.5 Exceptions
- The value of the index in an on-goto-statement or an on-gosub-statement without an ELSE clause is less than one or greater than the number of line-numbers in the list (10001, fatal).
- An attempt is made to execute a return-statement without having executed a corresponding gosub-statement or on-gosub-statement within the same program-unit or internal-proc-def (10002, fatal).

10.2.6 Remarks
The syntactic element control-transfer is defined solely to permit describing limitations on transfers to line numbers. It is not generated by other constructs.

References to nonexistent line-numbers in a program-unit, including those in control- transfers, are syntax errors. There is no exception defined in this Standard for such references. Implementations may, however, choose to treat them as exceptions, if they are so documented, since the effect of non-standard programs is implementation-defined.

10.3 Loop Structures

10.3.1 General Description
Loops provide for the repeated execution of a sequence of statements. Do-loops provide for the construction of loops with arbitrary exit conditions. The for-statement and next-statement provide for the construction of counter-controlled loops.

10.3.2 Syntax
    1. loop = do-loop / for-loop

2. do-loop = do-line do-body

3. do-line = line-number do-statement tail

4. do-statement = DO exit-condition ?

5. exit-condition = (WHILE / UNTIL) relational-expression

6. do-body = block* loop-line

7. exit-do-statement = EXIT DO

8. loop-line = line-number loop-statement tail

9. loop-statement = LOOP exit-condition?

10. for-loop = for-line for-body

11. for-line = line-number for-statement tail

12. for-statement = FOR control-variable equals-sign initial-value TO limit (STEP increment) ?

13. control-variable = simple-numeric-variable

14. initial-value = numeric-expression

15. limit = numeric-expression

16. increment = numeric-expression

17. for-body = block* next-line

18. exit-for-statement = EXIT FOR

19. next-line = line-number next-statement tail

20. next-statement = NEXT control-variable

The control-variable in the next-statement which terminates a for-loop will be the same as the control-variable in the for-statement which begins the for-loop.

A for-loop contained in the for-body of another for-loop will not employ the same control-variable as that other for-loop. No line-numbers in a control-transfer outside a for-loop or do-loop will refer to a line in the for-body of that for-loop or in the do-body of that do-loop.

An exit-do-statement may only occur in a do-loop. An exit-for-statement may only occur in a for-loop.

10.3.3 Examples

```
10 DO WHILE I <= N AND A(I) <> 0
20 SET I = I + 1
30 LOOP
100 DO
110 SET I = I + 1
120 DISPLAY "MORE ENTRIES (ENTER 'NO' IF NONE)"
130 INPUT A$(I)
140 LOOP UNTIL A$(I) = "NO"
10 DO
20 INPUT X
30 IF 0 < X AND X <= 7 AND X = INT(X) THEN EXIT DO
40 DISPLAY "INPUT AN INTEGER BETWEEN 1 AND 7"
50 LOOP
100 FOR I = 1 TO 10
150 SET A(I) = I
200 NEXT I
FOR I = A TO B STEP -1
NEXT C7
```

10.3.4 Semantics

An exit-condition will be said to require exit from a loop if the value of the relational-expression following the keyword WHILE is false or if the value of the relational expression following the keyword UNTIL is true.

If execution of a program reaches a do-line, then the exit-condition, if any, in that do-line will be evaluated. If there is no exit-condition, or if it does not require exit from the loop, then execution will proceed to the next line. If the condition requires exit from the loop, then execution will continue at the line following the associated loop-line. If execution of a program reaches a loop-line, then the exit- condition in that loop-line, if any, will be evaluated. If there is no exit condition, or if it does not require exit from the loop, then execution will resume at the associated do-line; if the condition requires exit from the loop, then execution will continue at the line following the loop-line.

The action of the for-statement and the next-statement is defined in terms of other statements, as follows.

```
110 FOR v = initial-value TO limit STEP increment (lines)
150 NEXT v
```

will be equivalent to

```
110 SET own1 = limit
120 SET own2 = increment
130 SET v = initial-value
140 DO UNTIL (v-own1) * SGN(wn2) > 0 (lines)
150 SET v = v + own2
160 LOOP
```

Here v is any simple-numeric-variable, and own1 and own2 are variables associated with the particular for-loop and not accessible to the programmer. The variables own1 and own2 will be distinct from similar variables associated with other for- loops. In the above equivalence, a control-transfer to the for-line will be interpreted as a control-transfer to the first set-statement, and a control-transfer to the next-line will be interpreted as a control-transfer to the last set-statement.

In the absence of a STEP clause in a for-statement, the value of the increment will be +1.

Execution of an exit-do-statement will cause execution to continue the line following the loop-line of the smallest do-loop in which the exit-do-statement occurs. Execution of the exit-for-statement will cause execution to continue at the line following the next-line of the smallest for-loop in which the exit-for-statement occurs.

10.3.5 Exceptions
None.

10.3.6 Remarks

On exit from a for-loop through the next-statement, the value of the control-variable is the first value not used; on all other exits from a for-loop the control-variable retains its current value.

10.4 Decision Structures

10.4.1 General Description

An if-statement allows for conditional transfers, for the conditional execution of a single imperative-statement, or for the execution of one of two alternative imperative-statements.

An if-block allows for the conditional execution of a sequence of lines or for the execution of one of several alternative sequences of lines.

A select-block allows for the conditional execution of any one of a number of alternative sequences of lines, based on the value of an expression.

10.4.2 Syntax

1. if-clause = imperative-statement / line-number

2. if-block = if-then-line then-block elseif-block* else-block? end-if-line

3. if-then-line = line-number IF relational-expression THEN tail

4. then-block = block*

5. elseif-block = elseif-then-line block*

6. elseif-then-line = line-number ELSEIF relational-expression THEN tail

7. else-block = else-line block*

8. else-line = line-number ELSE tail

9. end-if-line = line-number END IF tail

10. select-block = select-line remark-line* case-block case-block* case-else-block? end-select-line

11. select-line = line-number select-statement tail

12. select-statement = SELECT CASE expression

13. case-block = case-line block*

14. case-line = line-number case-statement tail

15. case-statement = CASE case-list

16. case-list == case-item (comma case-item)*

17. case-item = constant / range

18. range = (constant TO / IS relation) constant

19. case-else-block = case-else-line block*

20. case-else-line = line-number CASE ELSE tail

21. end-select-line = line-number END SELECT tail

The constants appearing in case-statements in a select-block will be the same type (i.e., either numeric or string) as the expression in the select-statement. The ranges and constants specified in case-lists in a select-block will not overlap.

No line-number in a control-transfer outside an if-block, then-block, elseif-block, else-block, select-block, case-block, or case-else-block will refer to a line inside that if-block, then-block, elseif-block, else-block, select-block, case-block, or case-else-block, respectively, other than to the if-then-line of that if-block or the select-line of that select-block.

A line-number in a control-transfer inside an elseif-block, else-block, case-block, or case-else-block may not refer to the associated elseif-then-line, else-line, case-line or case-else-line.

10.4.3 Examples

```
IF X => Y2 THEN GOSUB 900 ELSE GOSUB 2000
IF X$ = "NO" OR X$ = "STOP" THEN SET A = 1
IF A = B THEN 100
IF A$ = B$ THEN 200 ELSE 300

10 IF X = INT(X) THEN
20 DISPLAY X; "IS AN INTEGER"
30 ELSE
40 DISPLAY X; "IS NOT AN INTEGER"
50 END IF
100 IF A = 0 THEN
110 DISPLAY "ONE ROOT"
120 ELSEIF DISC < 0 THEN
130 DISPLAY "COMPLEX ROOTS"
140 ELSE
150 DISPLAY "REAL ROOTS"
160 END IF
10 SELECT CASE A$(1:1)
20 CASE "A" TO "Z", "a" TO "z"
30 DISPLAY A$; "starts with a letter"
40 CASE "0" TO "9"
50 DISPLAY A$; "starts with a digit"
60 CASE ELSE
70 DISPLAY A$; "doesn't start with a letter or a digit"
80 END SELECT

10 SELECT CASE X
20 CASE IS < 0
30 DISPLAY X; "is negative 1
40 CASE IS > 0
50 DISPLAY X; "is positive 1
60 CASE ELSE
70 DISPLAY X; "is zero"
```

```
80 END SELECT
```

10.4.4 Semantics

If the value of the relational-expression in an if-statement is true and an imperative-statement follows the keyword THEN, then this imperative-statement will be executed; if a line-number follows the keywork THEN, then execution of the program will be continued at the line with that line-number. If the value of the relational- expression is false and an imperative-statement follow the keyword ELSE, then this imperative-statement will be executed; if a line-number follows the keyword ELSE, then execution of the program will be continued at the line with that line-number, if no ELSE is present, then execution will be continued in sequence, i.e., with the line following that containing the if-statement.

If-blocks will be executed as follows. If a then-block, elseif-block, or else-block does not contain a block, the effect is as if it did contain a block consisting of a remark-line. If the value of the relational-expression in the if-then-line is true, then execution will continue at the first line of the corresponding then-block. If false, then the relational-expressions of each corresponding elseif-then-line, if any, will be evaluated in order. As soon as a true relational-expression is found, execution will continue at the first line of the blocks of that elseif-block. If no true relational-expression is found in the elseif-then-lines, then, if an else-block is present, execution will continue at the first line of the block of that else- block. If there is no else-block, execution will continue at the line following the end-if-line. When execution reaches the end of a then-block, an elseif-block, or an else-block, it will continue at the line following the corresponding end-if-line.

The expression in a select-statement in a select-block will be evaluated and its value compared with the case-items in the case statements until a match is found. A match will occur when

- the value of the expression equals that of a constant appearing as a case-item, or
- the value is greater than or equal to that of the first constant appearing in a range containing the word TO, but less than or equal to the second, or

- the value satisfies the relationship indicated by the relation appearing before the constant in a range.

If and when a match is found, the rest of the case-block headed by the case-statement in which the match was found will be executed. If no case-item is matched, then the case-else-block, if it is present, will be executed. When execution reaches the end of a case-block or case-else-block, it will continue at the line following the end- select- line.

Nesting of blocks is permitted subject to the same nesting constraints as for-loops (i.e., no overlapping blocks).

10.4.5 Exception
- A select-block without a case-else-block is executed and no case-block is selected (10004, fatal).

10.4.6 Remarks
None.

10.5 Expressions

10.5.1 General Description
Expressions will be either numeric-expressions or string expressions.

Numeric-expressions may be constructed from variables, constants, and function references using the operations of addition, subtraction, multiplication, division and involution.

String-expressions are composed of either a string-variable or a string-constant.

10.5.2 Syntax
1. expression = numeric-expression / string-expression

2. numeric-expression = sign? term (sign term)*

3. term = factor (multiplier factor)*

4. factor = primary (circumflex-accent primary)*

5. multiplier = asterisk / solidus

6. primary= numeric-variable / numeric-rep / numeric-function-ref / left-parenthesis numeric-expression right-parenthesis

7. numeric-function = numeric-function-name ref argument-list?

8. numeric-function- = numeric-defined-function / name numeric-supplied-function

9. argument-list = left-parenthesis argument right-parenthesis

10. argument = string-expression

11. string-expression = string-variable / string-constant

10.5.3 Examples

```
3*X- Y^2A(1)+A(2)+A(3) 2^(-X)
-X/Y SQR(X^2+Y^2)
```

10.5.4 Semantics

The formation and evaluation of numeric-expressions follows the normal algebraic rules. The symbols circumflex-accent, asterisk, solidus, plus-sign and minus-sign represent the operations of involution, multiplication, division, addition and subtraction, respectively. Unless parentheses dictate otherwise, involutions are performed first, then multiplications and divisions, and finally additions and subtractions. In the absence of parentheses, operations of the same precedence are associated to the left.

A-B-C is interpreted as (A-B)-C, A^B^C as (A^B)^C, A/B/C as (A/B)/C and -A^B as -(A^B).

If an underflow occurs in the evaluation of a numeric expression then the value generated by the operation which resulted in the underflow will be replaced by zero.

0^0 is defined to be 1, as in ordinary mathematical usage.

When the order of evaluation of an expression is not constrained by the use of parentheses, and if the mathematical use of operators is associative, commutative, or both, then full use of these properties may be made in order to revise the order of evaluation of the expression.

In a function reference, the number of arguments supplied will be equal to the number of parameters required by the definition of the function.

A function reference is a notation for the invocation of a predefined algorithm, into which the argument value, if any, is substituted for the parameter which is used in the function definition. All functions referenced in an expression will either be implementation-supplied or be defined in a def-statement. The result of the evaluation of the function, achieved by the execution of the defining algorithm, is a scalar numeric value which replaces the function reference in the expression.

10.5.5 Exceptions
- Evaluation of an expression results in division by zero (nonfatal, the recommended recovery procedure is to supply machine infinity with the sign of the numerator and continue)
- Evaluation of an expression results in an overflow (nonfatal, the recommended recovery procedure is to supply machine infinity with the algebraically correct sign and continue).
- Evaluation of the operation of involution results in a negative number being raised to a non-integral power (fatal).
- Evaluation of the operation of involution results in a zero being raised to a negative value (nonfatal, the recommended recovery procedure is to supply positive machine infinity and continue).

10.5.6 Remarks
The accuracy with which the evaluation of an expression takes place will vary from implementation to implementation. While no minimum accuracy is specified for the evaluation of numerical expressions, it is recommended that implementations maintain at least six significant decimal digits of precision.

The method of evaluation of the operation of involution may depend upon whether or not the exponent is an integer. If it is, then the indicated number of multiplications may be performed; if it is not, then the expression may be evaluated using the `LOG` and `EXP` functions.

It is recommended that implementations report underflow as an exception and continue.

11. PROGRAM SEGMENTATION

U/PL provides three mechanisms for the segmentation of programs. The first provides for user-defined functions, whose values may be used in numeric-expressions and string- expressions. The second enables subprograms to be defined, which communicate via parameters and which can be invoked via a call-statement. The third enables separate programs to be executed sequentially without user intervention.

Functions and subprograms (which we refer to collectively as '•routines") are of two types: internal and external. External routines are independent program-units lexically following the main-program. Internal routines are contained within a program-unit (the main-program or an external routine) and are considered to be part of that program-unit. An internal routine cannot contain another internal routine.

In general, an external routine does not share anything (including, but not limited to, variables, DATA statements, internal routines, OPTIONS, and DEBUG status) with other program-units. Information is exchanged between external routines and other program-units by means of parameters and, in the case of external functions, returned values. In general, an internal routine shares everything with its surrounding program-unit, with the exception of its parameters. There are no local variables for internal routines. See Appendix 2 for more detail on scope rules.

Within a program-unit, a routine must always be defined or declared in a line lexically preceding its first invocation in that program-unit. It is not an error for a routine to be defined or declared without being invoked. An external routine may be invoked throughout the program; an internal routine may be invoked only from within its containing program- unit. No control-transfer within an internal or external routine may refer to a line-number outside that routine, nor may a control-transfer outside a routine refer to a line-number within it.

11.1 User-Defined Functions

11.1.1 General Description

In addition to the implementation-supplied functions provided for the convenience of the programmer, U/PL allows the programmer to define new functions within a program-unit or program.

11.1.2 Syntax

1. function-def = internal-function-def / external-function-def

2. internal-function-def = internal-def-line / internal-function-line block* end-function-line

3. internal-def-line = line-number def-statement tail

4. def-statement = numeric-def-statement string-def-statement

5. numeric-def-statement > DEF numeric-defined function function-parm-list? equals-sign numeric-expression

6. numeric-defined-function = numeric-identifier

7. string-def-statement = DEF string-defined-function length-max? function-parm-list? equals-sign string-expression

8. string-defined-function = string-identifier

9. function-parm-list = left-parenthesis function-parameter (comma function-parameter)* right-parenthesis

10. function-parameter > simple-variable / formal-array

11. formal-array = array-name left-parenthesis comma* right-parenthesis

12. internal-function-line > line-number FUNCTION (numeric-defined-function / (string-defined-function length-max?)) function-parm-list? tail

13. end-function-line = line-number END FUNCTION tail

14. external-function-def = external-function-line unit-block* end-function-line

15. external-function-line > line-number EXTERNAL FUNCTION (numeric-defined-function / (string-defined-function length-max?)) function-parm-list? tail

16. numeric-function-set-statement = SET numeric-defined-function equals-sign numeric-expression

17. string-function-set-statement = SET string-defined-function equals-sign string-expression

18. exit-function-statement = EXIT FUNCTION

19. type-declaration > def-type / internal-function-type / external-function-type

20. def-type = DEF function-list

21. internal-function-type = FUNCTION function-list

22. external-function-type = EXTERNAL FUNCTION function-list

23. function-list = defined-function (comma defined-function)*

24. defined-function > numeric-defined-function / string-defined-function

No line-number in a control-transfer outside an internal-function-def will refer to a line in an internal-function-def other than to an internal-function-line, nor will a line-number in a control-transfer inside an internal-function-def refer either to a line outside that internal-function-def or to the associated internal-function-line. A line-number in a control-transfer inside an external-function-def will not refer to the associated external-function-line. If a defined-function is defined by an external-function-def, it will not be defined more than once in the program. If a defined-function is defined by an internal- function-def, it will not be defined more than once in the containing program-unit.

Within a program-unit, no more than one function (internal or external) of a given name will be declared or defined. If a defined-function is defined by an external-function-def, then a declare- statement with external-function-type containing that defined-function will occur in a lower-numbered line than the first reference to that defined-function in the same program-unit.

If a defined-function is defined by an internal-function-def other than an internal- def-line, then either the internal-function-def, or a declare-statement with internal-function-type naming that defined-function, will occur in a lower-numbered line than the first reference to that defined-function in the same program-unit. If a defined-function is defined by an internal-def-line, then either the internal- def-line, or a declare-statement with def-type naming that defined-function, will occur in a lower-numbered line than the first reference to that defined-function in the same program-unit.

Self-recursive functions need not declare themselves; that is, if a function-def contains a reference to itself, that reference does not require a type-declaration containing the defined-function in a lower-numbered line. An exit-function statement will occur only within a function-def.

Within each function-def (other than an internal-def-line) will occur at least one numeric-function-set-statement or string-function-set-statement with defined-function the same as the defined-function in the internal-function-line or external-function- line of the function-def. The number and type of function-arguments in a numeric-function-ref or string- function-ref will agree with the number and type of function-parameters in the corresponding function-def. That is,

- The number of function-arguments will be the same as the number of function- parameters .

- The function-arguments in the function-arg-list will be associated with the corresponding function-parameters in the function-parm-list (i.e., the first with the first, the second with the second, etc.), and the types will correspond as follows:

Parameter	Argument
simple-numeric-variable	numeric-expression
simple-string-variable	string-expression
formal-array (numeric)	actual-array (numeric)
formal-array (string)	actual-array (string)

The number of dimensions of an actual-array will be one more than the number of commas in the corresponding formal-array. A formal-array will have no more than three dimensions (two commas). Whenever a numeric argument is passed to a corresponding numeric parameter in a different program-unit, the ARITHMETIC options in effect for the two program-units must agree. The ARITHMETIC option external-function-def of numeric type must agree with that of the invoking program-unit.

A given function-parameter will occur only once in function-parm-list. Function- parameters will not be explicitly declared or dimensioned within the internal- function-def or external-function-def. A defined-function appearing in a def-type or internal-function-type will be defined elsewhere in the same program-unit by an internal-def-line or internal-function-def (other than an internal-def-line), respectively.

A defined-function appearing in an external-function-type will be defined elsewhere in the program by an external-function-def.

11.1.3 Examples

```
DEF E = 2.7182818
DEF AVERAGE(X, Y) = (X+Y)/2
DEF FNA$(S$, T$) = S$ & T$
DEF Right$(A$, n) = A$( Len(A$)-n+1 : Len(A$) )
100 EXTERNAL FUNCTION ANSWER(A$)
120 SELECT CASE UCASE$(A$)
130 CASE "YES"
140 SET ANSWER=1
150 CASE "NO"
160 SET ANSWER=2
170 CASE ELSE
180 SET ANSWER=3
190 END SELECT
200 END FUNCTION
FUNCTION AVERAGE, REVERSES
```

11.1.4 Semantics

A function-def specifies the means of evaluating a function based on the values of the parameters appearing in the function-parm-list and possibly other variables or constants.

Function Parameters

When a defined-function is referenced (i.e., when an expression involving the function is evaluated), then the arguments in the function reference, if any, will be evaluated from left to right and their values will be assigned to the parameters in the function-parm-list for the function-def (i.e., arguments will be passed by value to the parameters of the function). The number of dimensions in a formal-array is one more than the number of commas in the formal-array. Upon invocation of a function- def, a formal-array has the same bounds as the corresponding actual-array. A simple- string-variable or string-array which is a function-parameter will have the implementation-defined default as its maximum length.

Function Evaluation

If a function is defined in a def-statement, then the expression in that statement will be evaluated and its value assigned as the value of the function. If a function is defined in an internal-function-def or external-function-def, then the lines following the internal-function-line or external-function-line will be executed in sequential order until

- some other action is dictated by execution of a line, or
- a fatal exception occurs, or
- a LINK-statement or stop-statement is executed, or
- an exit-function-statement is executed, or
- an end-function-line is reached.

The value of the defined-function will be set by execution of one or more numeric- function-set-statements or string-function-set-statements. Upon exit from the function-def, the value will be that most recently assigned to the defined-function in that invocation. If, upon exit, no such value has been assigned, then the result will be consistent with the implementation-defined policies for uninitialized variables. A length-max following a string-defined-function establishes the maximum length of the string value to be returned by that function-def. If no length-max is specified, then the maximum length will be the same as for a string-variable without a length-max.

An exit-function-statement, when executed, will terminate the execution of the function-def in which it is immediately contained. An end-function-line marks the textual end of a function-block, and also will terminate execution of the function- block. Execution of a stop-statement in a function-block will terminate execution of the entire program.

A function-def may refer, directly or indirectly, to the function being defined, i.e., recursive function invocations are permitted.

Lines in a function-def will not be executed unless the function it defines is referenced. If the execution of a program reaches an internal-def-line, it will proceed to the next line without further effect. If execution reaches an internal-function- line, it will proceed to the line following the associated end-function-line without further effect.

Scopes of Variables. Arrays. Channel Numbers, and Data

A function-parameter appearing in the function-parm-list of a function-def will be local to each invocation of that function-def, i.e., it will name a variable or array distinct from any variable or array with the same name outside the function-ref.

The treatment of variables and arrays which are not named as function-parameters in a function-def will depend upon whether the function-def is internal or external. If the function-def is external, then such variables and arrays will be local to each invocation of that program-unit, i.e., they will be distinct from objects with the same names outside that function-def or within other invocations of that function- def; in addition, they will be initialized or not initialized in a manner consistent with the implementation-defined policies for the main-program each time the function- def is invoked. If the function-def is internal, then those variables and arrays will be global to the containing program-unit and will retain their assigned values each time the function-def is invoked; if these values are changed during the course of executing the internal-function-def, the changes remain in effect when execution is returned to the surrounding program-unit.

With one exception, the scope of channel-numbers is always the program-unit. Nonzero channel-numbers within a function-def will be local to each invocation of that function-def if it is external and will be global to the containing program-unit in which it occurs if it is internal. Channel zero will be global to the entire program. Files will be assigned to nonzero channels within a program-unit by means of an open-statement before use. Files assigned to channels local to a function-def will be closed upon exit from that function-def.

The scope of internal data is always the program-unit. Thus, data within an external- function-def will be local to each invocation of that program-unit. Hence read- statements and restore-statements within such a function-def will refer only to data in data-statements within that function-def and not to data in other program-units. Upon invocation of such a function-def, the pointer for the data within that function-def will be reset to the beginning of the data. Data within an internal-function-def will be part of the data sequence for the containing program- unit and read-statements and restore-statements within such a function-def will refer to the entire sequence of data in that program-unit.

11.1.5 Exceptions
- A string-function-set-statement attempts to assign a value whose length exceeds the maximum for the string-defined-function (1106, fatal).

11.1.6 Remarks
Incompatible COLLATE options are allowed between an invoking and invoked program-unit (even if they communicate via string parameters) because COLLATE does not dictate the internal representation of strings, but only their order in a string comparisons and the values of the CHR$ and ORD functions.

It is not an error for an internal-function-def to appear before a declare-statement with def-type or internal-function-type containing the name of that internal function. It is not an error for a function to be defined by an internal-function-def or to appear in a declare-statement, but not to be referred to in that program-unit.

An internal-function-type or def-type may be omitted if the corresponding definition appears before first reference. An external-function-type is always required when an external-function is referenced in a program-unit.

It is not an error for a function to be defined by an internal-function-def or to appear in a declare-statement, but not to be referred to in that program-unit.

It is not an error for an internal-function-def to appear before a declare-statement with def-type or internal-function-type containing the name of that internal function.

An internal-function-type or def-type may be omitted if the corresponding definition appears before the first reference to that function. An external-function-type is always required when an external-function is referenced in a program-unit other than its own.

The requirement that both internal and external functions be declared or defined before they are used allows several program-units within a program each to contain an internal function with the same name as an external function. This facilitates the use of function libraries where the programmer may not know the names of all the external-function-defs in the library.

11.2 Subprograms

11.2.1 General Description

Subprograms provide a mechanism for the logical segmentation of programs, allowing parameters to be passed between program segments. Subprograms, like defined- functions, may be internal or external to a program-unit.

11.2.2 Syntax

1. subprogram-def = internal-sub-def / external-sub-def

2. internal-sub-def = internal-sub-line block* end-sub-line

3. internal-sub-line = line-number sub-statement tail

4. sub-statement = SUB subprogram-name procedure-parm-list?

5. subprogram-name = routine-identifier

6. procedure-parm-list = left-parenthesis procedure-parameter (comma procedure-parameter)* right-parenthesis

7. procedure-parameter > simple-variable / formal-array / channel-number

8. channel-number = number-sign integer

9. end-sub-line = line-number end-sub-statement tail

10. end-sub-statement = END SUB

11. exit-sub-statement = EXIT SUB

12. external-sub-def = external-sub-line unit-block* end-sub-line

13. external-sub-line= line-number EXTERNAL sub-statement tail

14. call-statement = CALL subprogram-name procedure-argument-list?

15. procedure-argument-list = left-parenthesis procedure-argument (comma procedure-argument)* right-parenthesis

16. procedure-argument = expression / actual-array / channel-expression

17. type-declaration > internal-sub-type / external-sub-type

18. internal-sub-type = SUB sub-list

19. external-sub-type = EXTERNAL SUB sub-list

20. sub-list = subprogram-name (comma subprogram-name)*

No line-number in a control-transfer outside an internal-sub-def will refer to a line in an internal-sub-def other than to an internal-sub-line, nor will a line-number in a control-transfer inside an internal-sub-def refer either to a line outside that internal-sub-def or to the associated internal-sub-line. A line-number in a control-transfer inside an external-sub-def will not refer to the associated external-sub-line.

If a subprogram-name is defined by an external-sub-def, it will not be defined more than once in the program. If a subprogram-name is defined by an internal-sub-def, it will not be defined more than once in the containing program-unit.

Within a program-unit, no more than one subprogram (internal or external) of a given name will be declared or defined. If a subprogram-name is defined by an external-sub-def, then a declare-statement with external-sub-type containing that subprogram-name will occur in a lower-numbered line than the first reference to that subprogram-name in a call-statement in the same program-unit.

If a subprogram-name is defined by an internal-sub-def, then either the internal-sub- def, or a declare-statement with internal-sub-type containing that subprogram-name, will occur in a lower-numbered line than the first reference to that subprogram-name in the same program-unit.

Self-recursive subprograms need not declare themselves; that is, if a subprogram-def contains a reference to itself in a call-statement, that reference does not require a type-declaration containing that subprogram-name in a lower-numbered line.

An exit-sub-statement will occur only within a subprogram-def.

The number and type of procedure-arguments in a call-statement will agree with the number and type of procedure-parameters in the corresponding subprogram-def. That is:

- The number of procedure-arguments will be the same as the number of procedure-parameters .
- The procedure-arguments in the procedure-arg-list will be associated with the corresponding procedure-parameters in the procedure-parm-list (i.e., the first with the first, the second with the second, etc.), and the types will correspond as follows:

Parameter	Argument
simple-numeric-variable	numeric-expression
simple-string-variable	string-expression
formal-array (numeric)	actual-array (numeric)
formal-array (string)	actual-array (string)
channel-number	channel-expression

An actual-array will have the same number of dimensions as the corresponding formal- array. The number of dimensions in a formal-array is one more than the number of commas in the formal-array. Whenever a numeric argument is passed to a corresponding numeric parameter in a different program-unit, the ARITHMETIC option in effect for the two program-units must agree. A given procedure-parameter will occur only once in a procedure-parm-list. Procedure-parameters will not be explicitly declared or dimensioned within the internal-sub-def or external-sub-def. The channel-number zero will not be used as a procedure-parameter.

A subprogram-name appearing in an internal-sub-type will be defined elsewhere in the same program-unit by sin internal-sub-def.

A subprogram-name appearing in an external-sub-type will be defined elsewhere in the program by an external-sub-def.

11.2.3 Examples

```
100 SUB exchange(a,b)
110 SET t = a
120 SET a = b
130 SET b = t
140 END SUB
SUB CALC(X, Y, Z$)
SUB SORT(A( ), B(,), A$, #3)
70 2000 EXTERNAL SUB OPEN (#1, fnaraes$, result)
CALL CALC (3*A+2, 7715, "NO")
CALL SORT (Zvect, Yraat), (L$), #N)
```

11.2.4 Semantics

When a call-statement is executed, control will be transferred to the subprogram named in to call-statement. Execution of the subprogram will begin at the line following the sub-line and will continue in sequential order until

- some other action is dictated by execution of a line, or
- a fatal exception occurs, or
- a `LINK`-statement is executed, or
- a stop-statement or exit-sub-statement is executed, or
- an end-sub-line is reached.

The end-sub-line serves both to mark the textual end of a subprogram and, when executed, to terminate execution of the subprogram. The exit-sub-statement, when executed, will terminate the execution of the innermost subprogram in which it is contained. When execution of a subprogram terminates, execution will continue at the line following the call-statement which initiated execution of the subprogram.

Execution of a stop-statement in a subprogram will terminate execution of the entire program.

A subprogram may call itself, either directly or indirectly through another procedure, i.e., recursive subprogram invocations are permitted.

Lines in a subprogram-def will not be executed unless the subprogram it defines is referenced through a call-statement. If execution reaches an internal-sub-line, it will proceed to the line following the associated end-sub-line without further effect.

Subprogram parameters

When a call-statement is executed, its procedure-arguments will be identified, from left to right, with the corresponding procedure-parameters in the sub-statement for the subprogram.

Procedure-arguments which are numeric-variables or string-variables without substring-qualifiers will be passed by reference, i.e., any reference to the corresponding procedure-parameter within the subprogram will result in a reference to the procedure-argument, and any assignment to the procedure-parameter will result in an assignment to the corresponding procedure-argument.

If a procedure-argument is an array element, its subscripts will be evaluated once at each entry to the subprogram.

A procedure-argument which is an expression, but not a numeric-variable or a string- variable without a substring-qualifier, will be evaluated once at each entry to the subprogram and the value so obtained will be assigned to a location local to the subprogram. This local value will be used in any reference to the corresponding procedure-parameter, and this local location will be used as the destination of any assignment to the procedure-parameter. Any necessary evaluation of procedure- arguments will take place from left to right.

References within a subprogram to the procedure-parameters which are formal-arrays will result in interferences to the corresponding arrays in the procedure-argument- list; assignments to or redimensioning of such arrays will result in assignments to or redimensioning of the corresponding arrays in the procedure-argument-list. Upon entry to the subprogram, a formal-array as a procedure-parameter has the same bounds as the corresponding procedure-argument.

For a procedure-parameter which is a simple-string-variable or string-array, the associated maximum length will be the implementation-defined default, in the case of passing by value; when passing by reference, the maximum length will be that of the corresponding procedure-argument.

If both an array and one of its elements are named as procedure-arguments in a call- statement and the array is redimensioned during execution of the subprogram, then any subsequent reference within the subprogram to the procedure-parameter associated with the array-element will produce implementation-defined results.

A procedure-argument which is a channel-expression will be evaluated once on entry to the subprogram and the resulting channel will be used whenever the value of the corresponding procedure-parameter is referenced in the subprogram.

The attributes of the file assigned to this channel will be passed unchanged to the subprogram, and changes to attributes and contents of the file within the subprogram must be immediately effective, regardless of which of the channel- numbers is used in the subsequent reference and will remain in effect upon exit from the subprogram.

A file need not be assigned to a channel designated by a procedure-argument when a call-statement is executed. If an open-statement within a subprogram assigns a file to that channel, then that assignment will remain in effect upon exit from the subprogram.

Scopes of variables, arrays, channel numbers, and data

A procedure-parameter appearing in the procedure-parm-list of a subprogram-def which has been passed by value will be local to each invocation of the subprogram-def, i.e., it will name a variable or array distinct from a variable or array with the same name outside the subprogram-def.

For a procedure-parameter which has been passed by reference, its name will be local to each invocation of the subprogram-def, but that name refers to the same object as the corresponding procedure-argument (see Subprogram parameters, above).

The treatment of variables and arrays which are not named as parameters in a subprogram-def will depend upon whether the subprogram-def is internal or external. If the subprogram-def is external, then such variables and arrays will be local to each invocation of that program-unit, i.e., they will be distinct from objects with the same names outside that subprogram-def or within other invocations of that subprogram-def; in addition, they will be initialized or not initialized in a manner consistent with the implementation-defined policies for the main-program each time the subprogram-def is invoked. If the subprogram-def is internal, then those variables and arrays will be global to the containing program-unit and will retain their assigned values each time the subprogram-def is invoked; if these values are hanged during the course of executing the subprogram-def, the changes remain in effect when execution is returned to the surrounding program-unit.

With one exception, the scope of channel-numbers which are not procedure-parameters is always the program-unit. Nonzero channel-numbers within a subprogram-def will be local to each invocation of that subprogram-def if it is external and will be global to the program-unit in which it occurs if it is internal. Channel zero will be global to the entire program. Files will be assigned to nonzero channels within a program-unit by means of an open-statement before use. Files assigned to channels local to a subprogram-def will be closed upon exit from that subprogram-def.

The scope of internal data is always the program-unit. Thus, data within sin external- sub-def will be local to each invocation of that program-unit. Hence read-statements and restore-statements within such a subprogram-def will refer only to data in data- statements within that subprogram-def and not to data in other program-units. Upon invocation of such a subprogram-def, the pointer for the data within that subprogram- def will be reset to the beginning of the data. Data within an internal-sub-def will be part of the data sequence for that program-unit and read-statements and restore-statements within such a subprogram-def will refer to the entire sequence of data in that program-unit.

11.2.5 Exceptions
None.

11.2.6 Remarks
Implementations may extend the language by making the use of an internal-sub-type optional, even when the internal-sub-defs occur after the call-statements referring to them.

An alias is said to exist for an object whenever two or more distinct names exist for the object within the same scope. When parameters are passed by reference, aliases may be created in certain circumstances. Parameter passing by value does not create aliases, since distinct objects are created for each parameter.

Any call-statement creates aliases whenever :

- channel-expressions which round to the same integer value are passed to different formal channel-numbers,
- the same actual-array is passed to different formal-arrays,
- the same simple variable or array element is passed to different formal simple-variables,
- an array is passed to a formal-array and an element of that array is passed to a formal simple-variable,
- a channel-expression is passed to an internal subprogram, or

- an argument which is not a channel-expression is passed by reference to an internal subprogram.

In the first four cases, the alias arises because two or more formal parameters name the same object, or parts of the same object. In the latter two cases, the alias arises because an object is ''visible' 1 to an internal subprogram, both as a parameter and as an object global to the entire program-unit.

When the state of an object referred to by an aliased procedure-parameter is changed, that change must be immediately effective in every subsequent reference to the object, regardless of which of the object's names is used in the reference. Events which potentially affect the state of the object referred to by a procedure-parameter include assignment, input/output operations, and array redimensioning.

Thus, the program :

```
100 DECLARE INTERNAL SUB S
110 SET A = 0
120 CALL S(A,A)
130 SUB S(B,C)
140 SET A = 1
150 SET B = 2
160 SET C = 3
170 IF A <> B OR B <> C OR A <> C THEN
180 DISPLAY "This shouldn't happen."
190 END IF
200 END SUB
210 END
```

would never display the error message in a conforming implementation.

Remarks about the following topics apply analogously to programs and subprograms:

- Program-units with different COLLATE options;
- Functions which are defined or declared, but not referenced;
- Functions which are defined before they are declared;
- The requirement that external, but not internal, functions always be declared (rather than defined);
- Internal functions with the same name in different program-units.

11.3 Linking

11.3.1 General Description

The LINK-statement allows separate programs to be executed serially without programmer intervention. Such a facility is useful for segmenting large programs.

11.3.2 Syntax

    1. LINK-statement = LINK program-designator (WITH function-arg-list)?

    2. program-designator = string-expression

The association of the function-arguments in the function-arg-list in the LINK-statement with the function parameters in the function-parm-list in the program-name-line will follow the same rules set down for defined-functions.

11.3.3 Examples

```
LINK "PROG2"
LINK A$ WITH (X, FILENAMES$)
```

11.3.4 Semantics

A LINK-statement will terminate execution of the current program, close all files, and initiate execution of the program designated by the program-designator. The way in which a program is associated with its program-designator is implementation- defined.

If the program being LINKED to contains a program-name-line, then the arguments of the LINK-statement are evaluated and assigned to the corresponding parameters in the program-name-line (i.e., parameters are passed by value). The bounds of a formal- array will therefore be adjusted to equal those of the corresponding actual-array, in accordance with the rules for passing array parameters to functions.

It is implementation-defined whether upper-case-letters and lower-case-letters are treated as equivalent in a program-designator.

The initial values of variables in a LINKED-to program are implementation-defined.

11.3.5 Exceptions
- The program identified by the program-designator is not available (10005, fatal).
- The number and type of arguments in a LINK-statement do not agree with the number and type of the corresponding parameters in the program-name-line of the program being LIINKED to, or a program-name-line with a function-parm-list is not present (4301, fatal).
- An actual-array does not have the same number of dimensions as the corresponding formal-array (4302, fatal).

Numeric parameters are passed between programs with a LINK-statement and the ARITHMETIC options of the program-units disagree (4303, fatal).

11.3.6 Remarks
In a typical implementation a program-designator will be the name of a file containing that program. The program LINKED to need not be a U/PL program.

If exception 4301, 4302, or 4303 occurs, it may be reported by the LINKED -from program, the LINKED -to program, or some intermediate system program.

12. INPUT AND OUTPUT

Input and output facilities are provided for the interaction of a U/PL program with collections of data. Data may be obtained by a program from statements within that program, from a standard source external to that program, or from a named source external to that program. Output data may be directed to a standard destination external to that program or to named destination external to that program.

12.1 Internal Data

12.1.1 General Description

The read-statement provides for the assignment of values to variables from a sequence of data created from one or more data-statements. The restore-statement allows data in a program to be reread.

12.1.2 Syntax

1. read-statement = READ (missing-recovery colon)? variable-list

2. variable-list = variable (comma variable)*

3. missing-recovery = IF MISSING THEN io-recovery-action

4. io-recovery-action = exit-do-statement / exit-for-statement / line-number

5. restore-statement = RESTORE line-number?

6. data-statement = DATA data-list

7. data-list = datum (comma datum)*

8. datum = constant / unquoted-string

9. unquoted-string = plain-string-character / plain-string-character unquoted-string-character* plain-string-character

An io-recovery-action containing an exit-for-statement will occur only within a for- body. An io-recovery-action containing an exit-do-statement will occur only within a do-body.

If a line-number occurs in a restore-statement, the line-number will refer to a line containing a data-statement.

12.1.3 Examples
```
READ X, , Z
READ IF MISSING THEN 1350: X(1), A$
RESTORE
RESTORE 1000
DATA 3.14159, PI, 5E-30, ", "
COMMAS CANNOT OCCUR IN UNQUOTED STRINGS.
```

12.1.4 Semantics

Data from the totality of data-statements in each program-unit will behave as if collected into a single data sequence. The order in which data appear textually in the totality of all data-statements determines the order of the data in the data sequence .

If the execution of a program reaches a line containing a data-statement, then it will proceed to the next line with no further effect.

Execution of a read-statement will cause variables in the variable-list to be assigned values, in order, from the sequence of data in the program-unit containing the read-statement. A conceptual pointer is associated with this data sequence. At the initiation of execution of the program-unit, this conceptual pointer points to the first datum in the data sequence. Each time a read-statement is executed, each variable in the variable-list in sequence is assigned the value of the datum indicated by the pointer and the pointer advanced to point beyond that datum.

If an attempt is made to read data beyond the end of the data sequence, an exception will occur unless a missing-recovery is present in the read-statement. In that case, the specified io-recovery-action will be taken. If the io-recovery-action is an exit-do-statement or exit-for-statement, that statement will have its normal effect. If the io-recovery-action is a line-number, then execution will continue at the line having that line-number.

The type of a datum in the data sequence will correspond to the type of the variable to which it is to be assigned, i.e., numeric-variables require numeric-constants as data and string-variables require string-constants or unquoted-strings as data. An unquoted-string which is also a numeric-constant may be assigned to either a string- variable or a numeric-variable by a read-statement.

If the evaluation of a numeric datum causes an underflow, then its value will be replaced by zero.

Subscripts and substring-qualifiers in the variable-list will be evaluated after values have been assigned to the variables preceding them (i.e., to the left of them) in the variable-list.

Execution of a restore-statement resets the pointer for the data sequence in the program-unit containing the restore-statement to the beginning of the sequence, so that the next read-statement executed will read data from the beginning of the sequence. If a line-number is present, then the pointer for the data sequence in the program-unit containing the restore-statement is set to the first datum in the data-statement with the given line-number, so that the next read-statement executed will read data from the beginning of the designated data-statement.

12.1.5 Exceptions

- The variable-list in a read-statement requires more data them are present
- in the remainder of the data-list and a missing-recovery has not been specified (8001, fatal).
- An attempt is made to assign a value to a numeric-variable from a datum which is not a numeric-constant (8101, fatal).
- The evaluation of a numeric datum causes an overflow (1006, fatal).
- The assignment of a datum to a string-variable results in a string overflow (1053, fatal).

12.1.6 Remarks

Implementations may choose to treat underflows as exceptions (1506, nonfatal: supply zero and continue). In extended U/PL implementations, this permits interception by exception handlers.

12.2 Input

12.2.1 General Description

Input-statements provide for user interaction with a program by allowing variables to be assigned values supplied from a source external to the program. The input- statement enables the entry of mixed string and numeric data, with data items being separated by commas.

A prompt for input may be specified to replace the usual prompt supplied by the implementation.

The line-input-statement enables an entire line of input, including embedded spaces and commas, to be assigned as the value of a string-variable.

12.2.2 Syntax

1. input-statement = INPUT input-modifier-list? variable-list

2. input-modifier-list = input-modifier (comma input-modifier)* colon

3. input-modifier = prompt-specifier / timeout-expression / time-inquiry

4. prompt-specifier = PROMPT string-expression

5. timeout-expression = TIMEOUT numeric-time-expression

6. numeric-time-expression = numeric-expression

7. time-inquiry = ELAPSED numeric-variable

8. line-input-statement = LINE INPUT input-modifier-list? string-variable-list

9. input-prompt = (implementation-defined)

10. input-reply = data-list comma? end-of-line

11. line-input-reply = character* end-of-line

At most one prompt-specifier, one timeout-expression, and one time-inquiry will occur in an input-modifier-list. These may occur in any sequence.

12.2.3 Examples
```
INPUT X
INPUTA$ Y(2)
INPUT PROMPT "What is your name? N$
INPUT TIMEOUT 3*N, ELAPSED T, PROMPT Pstring$: N$
LINE INPUT A$
LINE INPUT PROMPT A$, B$
2, SMITH, -3
25, 0, -10.2
He said, "Don't".
```

12.2.4 Semantics

Execution of input-statement will cause execution of the program to be suspended until a valid input-reply, as specified below, has been supplied. An input-statement will cause variables in the variable-list to be assigned, in order, values from the input-reply.

In interactive mode, the user of the program will be informed of the need to supply data by the output of an input-prompt.

Input modifier list

If a prompt-specifier is present in the input-statement, then the implementation- defined input-prompt will not be output; instead, the value of the string-expression in the prompt-specifier will be output (unless the input-reply is terminated by a comma, see below). In Autorun mode, the input-reply will be requested from the external source by an implementation-defined means.

If a timeout-expression is present in an input-modifier-list, then the numeric-time- expression contained therein will be evaluated to obtain a (possibly fractional) number S of seconds. If no valid input-reply or line-input-reply has been supplied within S seconds, then an exception will occur. A time-inquiry returns the (possibly fractional) number of seconds elapsed between the issuance of the input-prompt and the reception of the end-of-line of the last input-reply for this input-statement. This value is assigned to the numeric-variable in the time-inquiry. If no clock is provided by an implementation, then a timeout-expression will have no effect. If a clock is provided, a time-inquiry result will always be positive. If no clock is provided, a time-inquiry result will be -1. The values (minimum and maximum) and resolution of both timeout expressions and time-inquiries are implementation-defined.

Assignment of Values

The assignment of a value from the input-reply to the corresponding variable will take place as soon as an item of data in the input-reply has been validated with respect to the type of the datum and the allowable range of values for that datum.

Subscripts and substring-qualifiers in a variable-list or string-variable-list will be evaluated after values have been assigned to the variables preceding them (i.e., to the left of them) in the variable-list or string-variable-list.

The type of each datum in the input-reply will correspond to the type of the variable to which it is to be assigned, i.e., numeric-constants will be supplied as input for numeric-variables, and either string-constants or unquoted-strings will be supplied as input for string-variables. An unquoted-string which is also a numeric- constant may be assigned to either a string-variable or a numeric-variable by an input-statement.

If the evaluation of a numeric datura causes an underflow, then its value will be replaced by zero.

If an input-reply supplied in response to a request for input does not end with a comma, then the number of data in all the input-replies submitted will equal the number of variables requiring values.

If the last character other than a space before the end-of-line in an input-reply is a comma, then this will be taken to signify that further data are to be supplied. As many values as are contained in that input-reply will be assigned to variables in the variable-list. The input-prompt (but not the string-expression of the prompt- specifier, if there is one) will then be reissued, and execution of the program will remain suspended until another valid input-reply has been supplied, from which further data will be obtained.

When a line-input-statement is executed, a line-input-reply will be requested for each string-variable in the string-variable-list in the same fashion as an input-reply is requested. That is, the value of the first line-input-reply will be assigned to the first variable in the variable-list. If there are further variables in the variable-list, the input-prompt (but not the string-expression of the prompt- specifier, if there is one) will then be reissued, and execution of the program will remain suspended until a second valid line-input-reply has been supplied and assigned to the second variable in the variable-list. This process continues until a valid line-input-reply has been supplied for each variable in the variable-list. The characters of each line-input-reply, including any leading and trailing spaces, will be concatenated to form a single string, which will become the value of the corresponding string-variable, except that the end-of-line, which terminates a line-input- reply, will not be included. Quotation marks within a line-input-reply are treated as actual characters. Thus, two adjacent quotation-marks are taken as two characters, not as one.

12.2.5 Exceptions

- The line supplied in response to a request for an input-reply is not a syntactically correct input-reply (8102, nonfatal: request that a new input-reply be supplied) .
- A datum supplied as input for a numeric-variable is not a numeric-constant (8103, nonfatal: request that the current input-reply be resupplied).
- There are insufficient data in an input-reply not containing a final comma (8002, nonfatal: request that the current input-reply be resupplied).
- There are too many data in an input-reply or there are just enough data, and the input-reply ends with a comma (8003, nonfatal: request that the current input- reply be resupplied).
- The evaluation of a numeric datum causes an overflow (1007, nonfatal: request that the current input-reply be resupplied).
- The assignment of a datum or a line-input-reply to a string-variable results in a string overflow (1054, nonfatal: request that the current input-reply or line- input-reply be resupplied).
- The value of a numeric-time-expression is less than zero (8402, fatal).
- A valid input-reply or line-input-reply has not been supplied within the number of seconds specified by a timeout-expression in an input-modifier-list (8401, fatal).

12.2.6 Remarks

This Standard requires that users in the interactive mode always be given the option of resupplying erroneous input-replies; in Autorun mode this may be treated as a fatal exception. This Standard does not require an implementation to provide facilities for correcting erroneous input-replies, though such facilities may be provided.

It is recommended that the default input-prompt consist of a question-mark followed by a single space.

This Standard does not require an implementation to output (i.e., echo) an input-reply or line-input-reply.

Implementations may choose to treat underflows as exceptions (1507, nonfatal: supply zero and continue). In Expanded U/PL implementation, this permits interception by exception handlers.

If an input datum is an unquoted-string, leading and trailing spaces are ignored. If it is a quoted-string, then all spaces between the quotation-marks are significant.

12.3 Output

12.3.1 General Description

The display-statement is designed for generation of tabular output in a consistent format. The set-statement with MARGIN can be used to specify the width of output-lines. The set-statement with ZONEWIDTH can be used to specify the width of display zones within a display-line. The ask-statement is used to inquire about the current MARGIN and ZONEWIDTH. Generalizations of the display-statement are described in 10.4, 10.5, and 11.3.

12.3.2 Syntax

1. display-statement = DISPLAY display-list

2. display-list = (display-item? display-separator)* display-item?

3. display-item = expression / tab-call

4. tab-call = TAB left-parenthesis index right-parenthesis

5. display-separator = comma / semicolon

6. set-statement = SET set-object

7. set-object > (MARGIN / ZONEWIDTH) index

8. ask-statement > ASK ask-io-list

9. ask-io-list = ask-io-item comma ask-io-item)*

10. ask-io-item = (MARGIN / ZONEWIDTH) numeric-variable

A given ask-io-item must appear at most once in an ask-statement.

12.3.3 Examples

```
DISPLAY X
DISPLAY X, Y
DISPLAY X, Y, Z,
DISPLAY ,,, X
DISPLAY
DISPLAY "X EQUALS", 10
DISPLAY X, (Y+Z)/2
DISPLAY TAB(IO); A$ "IS DONE."
SET MARGIN 120
SET ZONEWIDTH 20
```

12.3.4 Semantics

The execution of a display-statement will generate a string of characters and end-of- lines for transmission to an external device. This string of characters will be determined by the successive evaluation of each display-item and display-separator in the display-list.

If an expression in a display-list invokes a function which causes a display-statement to be executed which transmits characters to the same device as the original display- statement, then the effect is implementation-defined.

Printing numeric values

Numeric-expressions will be evaluated to produce a string of characters consisting of a leading space if the number is positive, or a leading minus-sign if the number is negative, followed by the decimal representation of the absolute value of the number and a trailing space. The possible decimal representations of a number are the same as those described for numeric-constants in 5.1 and will be used as follows.

Each implementation will define two quantities, a significance-width d to control the number of significant decimal digits displayed in numeric representations, and an exrad-width e to control the number of digits displayed in the exrad component of a numeric representation. The value of d will be at least six and the value of e will be at least two.

Each expression whose value is exactly an integer, and which can be represented with d or fewer decimal digits will be output using the implicit point unsealed representation.

All other values will be output using either explicit point unsealed representation or explicit point scaled representation. Values which can be represented with d or fewer digits in the unsealed representation no less accurately than they can in the scaled representation will be output using the unsealed representation. For example, if d = 6, then 1CT(-6) is output as .000001 and 10~(-7) is output as I.E-7.

Values represented in the explicit point unsealed representation will be output with up to d significant decimal digits and a period; trailing zeros in the fractional part may be omitted. A number with a magnitude less than 1 will be represented with no digits to the left of the period. This form requires up to d+3 characters counting the sign, the period and the trailing space. Values represented in the explicit point scaled representation will be output in the format:

significand E sign integer

where the value x of the significand is in the range $1 < x < 10$ and is to be represented with exactly d digits of precision, and where the exrad component has one to e digits. Trailing zeros may be omitted in the fractional part of the significand and 82 leading zeros may be omitted from the exrad. A period will be displayed as part of the significand. This form requires up to d+e+5 characters counting the two signs, the period, the "E" and a trailing space.

Printing string values

String-expressions will be evaluated to generate the corresponding string of characters.

Print separators and tabs

The evaluation of the semicolon separator will generate the null string, i.e., string of zero length. The evaluation of a tab-call or a comma separator depends upon the string of characters already generated by the current or previous display-statements. The "current line" is the (possibly empty) string of characters generated since the beginning of execution or since the last end-of-line was generated.

The "columnar position" of the current line is the display position that will be occupied by the next character output to that line. Print positions will be numbered consecutively from the left, starting with position one. Each time a character in positions 2/0 through 7/14 of the standard character set is generated, the columnar position will be increased by one. Each time an end-of-line is generated, the columnar position will be reset to one. The effect of other characters on the columnar position is implementation-defined.

The "margin" is the maximum columnar position in which a character may appear. Prior to execution of a set-statement with MARGIN, the margin will be implementation- defined, but must be not less than the default zone width. A margin of MAXNUM will indicate that the columnar position may be arbitrarily large.

Each display-line is divided into a fixed number of display zones where the number of zones and the length of each zone is implementation-defined. All display zones, except possibly the last one on a line, which may be shorter, will have the same width. The default width of a zone will be at least $d+e+6$ display positions. The zone width may be changed by the execution of a set-statement with ZONEWIDTH. ZONEWIDTH may be set to any value greater than zero, but not greater than the current margin.

The purpose of the tab-call is to set the columnar position of the current line to the specified value prior to displaying the next display-item. More precisely, the argument of the tab-call will be evaluated and rounded to the nearest integer n. If n is less than one, an exception will occur. If n is greater than the margin m, then n will be reduced by an integral multiple of m so that it is in the range 1 < n < m; i.e., n will be set equal to MOD(n-1,m) + 1.

If the columnar position of the current line is less than or equal to n, then spaces will be generated, if necessary, to set the columnar position to n; if the columnar position of the current line is greater than n, then an end-of-line will be generated followed by n-1 spaces to set the columnar position of the new current line to n.

The evaluation of the comma display-separator depends upon the columnar position. If this position is neither in the last display zone on a line nor beyond the margin, then one or more spaces will be generated to set the columnar position to the beginning of the next display zone on the line. If the initial columnar position is in the last display zone on a line, then an end-of-line will be generated. Finally, if the initial columnar position is beyond the margin (as it would be if evaluation of the last display-item exactly filled the line), then an end-of-line will be generated.

Overlength output lines

Whenever the columnar position is greater than one and the generation of the next display-item would cause a character to appear beyond the margin, then an end-of-line will be generated prior to the characters generated by that display-item.

During the generation of a display-item, whenever that generation would cause a character to appear beyond the margin, an end-of-line will be generated prior to that character, resetting the columnar position to one.

End of display-list

When evaluation of a display-list is completed, if that display-list did not end with a display-separator, then a final end-of-line will be generated; otherwise, no such final end-of-line will be generated.

A completely empty display-list will generate an end-of-line, thereby completing the current line of output. If this line contained no characters, then a blank line will result.

Setting the margin

Execution of a set-statement with a `MARGIN` will cause its index to be evaluated and to become the new margin. The change in the margin will take effect immediately, even if a line of output is partially filled. The set-statement with a `MARGIN` affects only unformatted output.

Setting the zone width

Execution of a set-statement with a `ZONEWIDTH` will cause its index to be evaluated and to become the new zone width. The change in the zone width will take effect immediately, even if a line of output is partially filled. The set-statement with a `ZONEWIDTH` affects only unformatted output.

Ask-statement

Execution of an ask-statement will cause the variables in the ask-io-list to be assigned values corresponding to the current margin, if `MARGIN` is present, or current zonewidth, if `ZONEWIDTH` is present. If the columnar position may be arbitrarily large, then the value `MAXNUM` will be returned to the numeric-variable in the ask- statement with `MARGIN`.

12.3.5 Exceptions
- The value of the index in a tab-call is less than one (4005, nonfatal: supply one and continue).
- The value of the index in a set-statement with a `MARGIN` is less than the current zonewidth (4006, fatal).
- The value of the index in a set-statement with a `ZONEWIDTH` is less than one or greater than the current margin (4007, fatal).

12.3.6 Remarks
The character string generated by displaying the value of a numeric-expression contains a single trailing space. If the generation of that space would cause the columnar position to exceed the margin by more than one, then implementations may choose not to generate that space, thereby allowing the number to be displayed in the final display zone on a line.

Implementations may choose to use a lower-case "e" in displaying numerical values using the explicit point scaled representation.

The display-separator following a tab-call is significant in the same manner that it is significant following an expression.

12.4 Formatted Output

12.4.1 General Description

A display-statement may control the format of output by specifying an image to which that output must conform. The image is specified either within the display-statement or in a separate image-line.

12.4.2 Syntax

    1. display-statement = DISPLAY formatted-display-list

    2. formatted-display-list = USING image (colon output-list)?

    3. image = line-number / string-expression

    4. output-list = expression (comma expression)* semicolon?

    5. image-line = line-number IMAGE colon format-string end-of-line

    6. format-string = literal-string (format-item literal-string)*

    7. literal-string = literal-item*

    8. literal-item = letter / digit / apostrophe / colon / equals-sign / exclamation-mark / left-parenthesis / question-mark / right-parenthesis / semicolon / slant / space / underline

    9. format-item = (justifier? floating-characters (i-format-item / f-format-item / e-format-item)) / justifier

    10. justifier = greater-than-sign / less-than-sign

    11. floating-characters = (plus-sign* / minus-sign) dollar-sign? / dollar-sign* (plus-sign / minus-sign)?

    12. i-format-item = digit-place digit-place* (comma digit-place digit-place*)*

    13. digit-place = asterisk / number-sign / percent-sign

    14. f-format-item = period number-sign number-sign* / i-format-item period number-sign*

15. e-format-item = (i-format-item / f-format-item) circumflex-accent circumflex-accent / circumflex-accent circumflex-accent*

An image which is a line-number will refer to an image-line in the same program-unit. Any leading spaces following the colon in an image-line are part of the format string.

All digit-places in an i-format-item will be the same character, i.e., all will be number-signs, all will be percent-signs, or all will be asterisks.

12.4.3 Examples

```
10 SET sum = 20
20 DISPLAY USING "The answer is ###.#": sum produces "The
answer is 20.0". 30 DISPLAY USING 40: 342, 42.021
40 IMAGE : RATE OF LOSS #### EQUALS ####.## POUNDS
produces "RATE OF LOSS 342 EQUALS 42.02 POUNDS".
10 SET A$ = "<##### ####.#### ####. #### "
20 DISPLAY USING A$: 1, 1, 1 produces " 1 1.0000 1000.
0000E-03".
60 DISPLAY USING 70: "ONE", "TWO", "THREE"
70 IMAGE : Z<«"«>»« ########Z produces "ZONE TWO THREE Z".
80 SET A$ = "Pay $**.## on ### %% 19%%"
90 DISPLAY USING A$: 1, "May", 2, 83 produces "Pay $*1.00
on May 02 1983".
10 DISPLAY USING "<%%.« >-$##.## $$$+***": 3.1, -1234.567,
2
produces "003.10 -$1234.57 $+**2".
10 DISPLAY USING "<$$$$.« $$$$.«#.-.02, -.02 produces " $-
.02 $-.200E-001".
10 DISPLAY USING : 1234.7777 produces "$**1,234.78".
```

12.4.4 Semantics

A display-statement with a formatted-display-list identifies a format-string to be used to control the output generated by the evaluation of the output-list. If the image is specified via a line-number, then the format-string is contained in the image-line with the indicated line-number; otherwise, it is the value of the string-expression.

Format string analysis

The selected format-string will be analyzed as a number of format-items separated by possibly zero-length literal-strings.

Format-items will be found within the format-string by scanning the latter from left to right. A search will be made for the first character which is the start of a syntactically correct format-item, and the longest such format-item starting at that character identified. The scan for format-items will continue in this way up to the end of the format-string, the search for the start of each new format-item beginning at the character immediately beyond the previously identified format-item. Corresponding to each format-item will be an output field whose length equals the number of characters in the format-item (including the justifier, floating-characters, digit-places, commas, period, number-signs, and circumflex-accents). Characters which are not part of any format-item will be 1iteral-items.

Format-strings which are defined in image-lines will be interpreted as ending with the last character in the line which is not a space or end-of-line.

Literal strings and output fields

A sequence of values to be output will be generated by evaluating each expression in the output-list in sequence. As each value is generated, the literal-string preceding the next format-item in the format-string will first be copied unchanged into the string of characters being generated. Then a number of characters equal to the length of the output field determined by that format-item will be generated, as follows.

Formatted numeric output

Numeric values will be rounded and represented in a manner corresponding to the format-item used. If a justifier is present in the format-item, it will be replaced by the character immediately to its right. If, however, the character to its right is a period, or if there is no character to its right, then the justifier will be replaced by a number-sign.

First, a representation for the magnitude of the value will be generated.

- For an i-format-item, the value will be rounded to the nearest integer and represented using implicit point unsealed notation.
- For an f-format-item, the value will be represented using explicit point unsealed notation, rounding the representation or extending it on the right with zeros in accordance with the number of number-signs following the period in the format- item.
- For both i-format-items and f-format-items, leading zeros to the left of the implicit or explicit decimal point will not be generated, unless this results in no digits being generated. In that case, the character "0" will be generated immediately to the left of the explicit or implicit decimal point. After this, if there remain unfilled digit-places, then leading zeros will be generated in the integer or to the left of the period when a percent-sign is used as a digit-place, leading asterisks when an asterisk is used as a digit-place, and leading spaces when a number-sign is used as a digit-place, such that the number of characters to the left of the implicit or explicit decimal point is equal to the number of digit- places in the format-item.
- For an e-format-item, the value will be represented using explicit or implicit point scaled notation, corresponding to the use of an f-format-item or i-format- item, respectively, within the e-format-item. The significand for nonzero values will be scaled by powers of ten such that the leftmost digit-place or number-sign position is occupied by a nonzero digit. In all other respects, the significand will be generated according to the above rules for i-format-items and f-format- items. The number of circumflex-accents in an e-format-item will determine the number of characters in the exrad. The first of these characters will be the letter E, the next a mandatory sign, and the remaining characters the representation of the magnitude of the exrad, with leading zeros being generated so that the number of characters in the exrad equals the number of circumflex-accents in the format-item. If the exponent is zero, the mandatory sign is positive; the exponent of zero is zero.

Second, commas will be inserted in the numeric representation wherever a comma occurs in the format-item, provided at least one digit has been generated to the left of the point of insertion; if no digit has been generated to the left of this point, then an asterisk will be inserted if the digit-place immediately to the left is an asterisk, and a space inserted if the digit-place immediately to the left is a number-sign.

Finally, the representation of the numeric value so generated will be extended by spaces on the left so that its length equals that of the format-item. This has the effect of right-justifying a numeric-representation in an output field.

Formatted string output

A string value may be output using any type of format-item. The string will be extended by spaces so that its length equals that of the format-item. These space will be added on the left (for right-justification) if the format-item begins with a greater-than-sign, on the right (for left-justification) if it begins with a less- than-sign, and equally on either side (for centering) otherwise; if the number of spaces required in the last case is odd, the extra space will be added on the right.

Formatted Output Completion

If the number of values to be output exceeds the number of format-items in the format-string, an end-of-line will be generated each time the end of the format-string is reached, and the format-string reused for the remaining expressions. If format-items remain in the format-string after all values have been output, then the next literal-string, if any, will be output. Generation of characters is always terminated beginning at the first unused format-item. Finally, an end-of-line will be generated after all other character generation is completed, unless the output-list ends with a semicolon, in which case no such end-of-line will be generated.

The current margin will not affect the output; in particular, no end-of-line will be generated upon formatted output just because the margin is exceeded. If the execution of a program reaches an image-line, it will proceed to the next line with no further effect.

12.4.5 Exceptions

- An invalid format-string is specified in a formatted-display-list (8201, fatal).
- A formatted-display-list contains an output-list, but there is no format-item in the format-string (8202, fatal).
- An output string, whether generated from a string-expression or a numeric- expression, is longer than its corresponding format-item (8203, nonfatal: fill the output field with asterisks, report the unformatted representation of the value on the next line, and continue displaying on the following line in a position identical to the position which would have resulted if no exception had occurred).
- The exrad for numeric output exceeds the space allocated by circumflex-accents in a format-item (8204, nonfatal: fill the output field with asterisks, report the unformatted representation of the value, and continue).

12.4.6 Remarks

Since format-strings may be evaluated dynamically, errors in them (even if occurring in an image-line and therefore statically determined) may be treated as exceptions.

Implementations may choose to use a lower case "e" in displaying numerical values using the explicit point scaled representation.

The integer part of a number generated with an i-format-item or f-format-item may validly contain more digits than there are digit-places in the format-item, as long as the floating-characters provide sufficient room.

Negative numeric values always generate a minus-sign. The corresponding format-item must provide room for this minus-sign with floating-characters, since digit-places are completely filled by digits, or by leading spaces, zeros, or asterisks. In particular, a format-item with no floating-characters, or with only a single dollar-sign as a floating-character, will cause exception 8203 if an attempt is made to fill that field with a negative value.

12.5 Array Input and Output

12.5.1 General Description

Statements are provided which enable entire arrays to be input or output. These statements generalize the input and output statements which manipulate single values.

12.5.2 Syntax

1. array-read-statement = MAT READ (missing-recovery colon)? redim-array-list

2. redim-array-list = redim-array (comma redim-array)*

3. redim-array = array-name redim?

4. array-input-statement = MAT INPUT input-modifier-list? (redim-array-list / variable-length-vector)

5. variable-length-vector = array-name left-parenthesis question-mark right-parenthesis

6. array-line-input-statement = MAT LINE INPUT input-modifier-list? redim-string-array-list

7. redim-string-array-list = redim-string-array (comma redim-string-array)*

8. redim-string-array = string-array redim?

9. array-display-statement = MAT DISPLAY (array-display-list / (USING image colon array-output-list))

10. array-display-list = array-name (display-separator array-name)* display-separator?

11. array-output-list = array-name (comma array-name)* semicolon?

A redim and the array in its redim-array will have the same number of dimensions.

A variable-length-vector must be one-dimensional.

12.5.3 Examples

```
MAT READ A
MAT READ A(M,N), B
MAT INPUT A$(3,4)
MAT INPUT X(?)
MAT INPUT PROMPT "Enter data: X(?)
MAT LINE INPUT A$
MAT DISPLAY A; B, C;
```

12.5.4 Semantics
The array read statement

Execution of an array-read-statement will cause arrays in the redim-array-list to be assigned, in order, values from the data sequence created by data-statements in the program-unit containing that statement. Values will be assigned to all elements in each array in row major order, (i.e., the last subscript varying most rapidly, then the next to last subscript, if any, etc.) with each successive value being obtained from the datum in the data sequence indicated by the pointer for the sequence and the pointer being advanced beyond that datum.

The type of each datum in the data sequence will correspond to the type of the array-element to which it is to be assigned.

If a redim is present then dynamic redimensioning will take place before values are assigned to the redimensioned array. The redimensioning will be done according to the rules for bounds in array-declarations. The values of the indices will be used as the new lower and upper bounds for the array. If an exception occurs when attempting to redimension an array, it will retain its old dimensions. Redims in the redim- array-list will be evaluated after values have been assigned to the arrays preceding them (i.e., to the left of them) in the redim-array-list.

If the evaluation of a numeric datum causes an underflow then its value will be replaced by zero.

The array input statement

Execution of an array-input-statement will cause execution of the program to be suspended until a valid input-reply, as specified below, has been supplied. An array- input- statement will cause arrays in the redim-array-list to be assigned, in order, values from the input-reply. Values will be assigned to all elements in each array in row major order.

In the interactive mode, the user of the program will be informed of the need to supply data by the output of an input-prompt. The prompt is identical to that of the input-prompt of the input-statement.

The type of each datum in the input-reply will correspond to the type of the array- element to which it is to be assigned.

If a redim is present then dynamic redimensioning will take place as described above for the array-read-statement before values are assigned to the redimensioned array. Redims in the redim-array-list will be evaluated after values have been assigned to the redim-arrays preceding them (i.e., to the left of them) in the redim-array-list.

If the recovery procedure for an input exception causes input data to be re-supplied to an array which was redimensioned after the original assignment of data to it, but before the exception occurred, the effect is implementation-defined. Data in response to a request for array input need not be supplied in a single input-reply. If the array-list has not been completely supplied with data and the input-reply contains a final comma, then the input-prompt will be issued, and a further input-reply will be requested to obtain more data.

If the evaluation of a numeric datum causes an underflow then its value will be replaced by zero.

Input of variable length vectors

If a variable-length-vector occurs in an array-input-statement, then as many data as are present in the input-reply (or sequence of input-replies up to and including the first which does not end with a comma) will be supplied as input for that vector. Assignment of data will begin with the current lower bound for the vector. After assignment, the vector will be redimensioned dynamically by setting the upper bound for its subscript equal to the subscript of the element receiving the last datum. The number of data values assigned to the variable-length-vector will not exceed the original size for that vector as specified in its array-declaration.

The type of each datum in the input-reply will correspond to the type of the array.

The array-line-input-statement

When an array-line-input-statement is executed, a line-input-reply will be requested for each element of each string-array in the string-array-list in the same fashion that an input reply is requested and will assign the entire contents of successive line-input-replies (excluding their end-of-lines) in row major order to elements of the string-arrays in the string-array-list. The number of line-input-replies requested will equal the number of elements requiring values. 90 In the interactive mode, the user of the program will be informed of the need to supply data by the output of an input-prompt.

If a redim is present then dynamic redimensioning will take place as described above for the array-read-statement before values are assigned to the redimensioned array. Redims in the redim-string-array-list will be evaluated after values have been assigned to the redim-string-arrays preceding them (i.e., to the left of them) in the redim-string-array-list.

The array display statement

Execution of an array-display-statement will cause the values of all elements in all arrays in the array-display-list to be displayed. An end-of-line will be generated prior to any characters generated by an array-display-statement if the current line of output is nonempty.

For an array-display-statement with an array-display-list, the characters generated for transmission to an external device by the displaying of a two-dimensional array are almost precisely those that would be generated if the elements in that array had been listed, row by row, in the display-list of a display-statement, separated by the separator which follows the array-name in the array-display-list (or separated by a comma if no separator follows the array name). The only additional characters generated will be an end-of-line each time a row of the array has been displayed (if such an end-of- line has not already been generated). A three-dimensional array will be displayed like a series of two-dimensional arrays, one for each value of the first subscript, with an extra end-of-line generated between each value of the first subscript. When a one-dimensional array is displayed, it will be treated like a row-vector, and displayed as if it were a 1 x N array.

Finally, an extra end-of-line will be generated between the output for successive arrays in an array-display-list.

For an array-display-statement with an array-output-list, the characters generated for transmission to an external device are exactly those that would be generated if the elements of each array had been listed array by array, in row-major order, in the output-list of a display-statement, using the same image as that in the array-display- statement. No additional end-of-lines will be generated. As with a display-statement using an image, if there is no trailing semicolon in the array-output-list, a final end-of-line will be generated after all other output from the array-display-statement. If there is such a semicolon, then this final end-of-line will not be generated.

12.5.5 Exceptions

- The redim-array-list in an array-read-statement requires more data than are present in the remainder of the data sequence and no missing-recovery has been specified (8001, fatal). - An attempt is made to assign a value to an element of a numeric-array from a datum in the data sequence which is not a numeric-constant (8101, fatal).
- The assignment of a datum during execution of an array-read-statement results in a string overflow (1053, fatal).
- The evaluation of a numeric datum in a data-list causes an overflow (1006, fatal).
- The line supplied in response to a request for array input is not a syntactically correct input-reply (8102, nonfatal: request that a new input-reply be supplied).
- A datum supplied as input for a numeric-array is not a numeric-constant (8103, nonfatal: request that the current input-reply be resupplied).
- There are insufficient data in an input-reply not containing a final comma (8002, nonfatal: request that the current input-reply be resupplied).

- There are too many data in an input-reply or there are just enough data, and the input-reply ends with a comma (8003, nonfatal request that the current input-reply be resupplied).
- The evaluation of a numeric datum in an input-reply causes an overflow (1007, nonfatal: request that the current input-reply be resupplied).
- The assignment of a string datum during execution of an array-input-statement or an array-line-input-statement causes a string overflow (1054, nonfatal: request that the current input-reply or line-input-reply be resupplied).
- The total number of elements required for a redimensioned array exceeds the number of elements reserved by the array's original dimensions (5001, fatal).
- The first index in a redim-bounds is greater than the second index (6005, fatal).
- A redim-bounds consists of a single index which is less than the default lower bound in effect (6005, fatal).
- A valid input-reply or line-input-reply has not been supplied within the number of seconds specified by a timeout-expression in an input-modifier-list (8401, fatal).
- The value of numeric-expression used as a time-expression is less than zero (8402, fatal).
- An invalid format-string is specified in an array-display-statement (8201, fatal).
- An array-display-statement contains an array-output-list, but there is no format-item in the format-string (8202, fatal).

12.5.6 Remarks

This Standard does not require an implementation to output (i.e., echo) the input- reply or line-input-reply.

This Standard does not require an implementation to provide facilities for correcting erroneous input-replies, though such facilities may be provided.

Implementations may choose to treat underflows as exceptions (1507, nonfatal: supply zero and continue). In Expanded U/PL implementations, this permits interception by exception handlers.

13. FILES

Two distinct levels of file processing are defined for U/PL and Expanded U/PL. The different combinations of file organization and record types permitted for the two levels are detailed below.

The construct rules permitted in Expanded U/PL only are so identified. In the text, the usage of indentation permits to distinguish the parts of the text valid for U/PL only or for Expanded U/PL only from the parts of text valid for both levels. Although the features permitted in U/PL are a true subset of those permitted in Expanded U/PL, when the identification of these features would be too difficult to present in a single text, this text is repeated for each of the two levels and so identified.

By convention, construct rules referring to U/PL and Expanded U/PL are called core rules and construct rules referring only to Expanded U/PL are called Expanded rules.

Files are organized collections of data external to U/PL programs. They provide the user with a means of saving data developed during execution of a program and then retrieving and modifying that data during subsequent execution of U/PL programs. The process by which external data is transferred to or from a program is called input or output, respectively. An implementation-defined means must be provided for the creation, preservation and retrieval of files. Input and output operations to these files must perform as specified in this section.

This section describes the logical appearance of files and devices to a U/PL program. In some cases, these attributes may reflect physical characteristics, but in general this Standard makes no presumptions concerning the physical representation or organization of files or devices.

The meaning of certain terms used throughout this section is as follows. A "file element" is an entity, a sequence of which constitutes a file. Thus, for keyed and sequential files, a file element is a record, for relative files it is a record area, for stream files, it is a value. Associated with each file during execution is a "file pointer", which always uniquely identifies a particular file element upon completion of any statement, or points to the end of file. If the pointer is at the beginning of the file, then it identifies the first file element, if any. If a file is an empty sequence, then the beginning and end of file are the same, and the pointer identifies this location. Whenever reference is made to the "next" file element, it is understood that if none such exists, the end of file is substituted. For sequential, stream and keyed files, the "end of file" is the location immediately following the last file element. For relative files, the "end of file" immediately follows the last existing record, and thus identifies an empty record area.

U/PL

There are two kinds of file-organization: sequential and stream. A sequential file is a sequence of records. A stream file is a sequence of values.

There are two kinds of record-type: display and internal. A display record is a sequence of characters. An internal record is a sequence of typed values. Display records provide for the exchange of data between systems employing different internal representations for numeric and string values, and also manipulate data in human-readable form. Internal records provide for efficient manipulation of data within a single system.

The following combinations of file-organization and record-type are supported:

- sequential display
- sequential internal
- stream internal

All other combinations of file-organization and record-type are

implementation- defined.

There are five statements which operate on the file as a whole and are thus called "file operations": OPEN, CLOSE, ERASE, SET and ASK. There are five statements which apply to individual file elements and are known as "record operations": INPUT, DISPLAY, READ, WRITE and SET with pointer-control, including the variations using MAT and LINE. References to "INPUT operations", "WRITE operations", and so forth should be understood to include any of the statements using the keyword in question, e.g., "WRITE operations" includes WRITE and MAT WRITE. The five record operations can affect data within a file, variables within the program and the file pointer.

DISPLAY and WRITE affect file data and the pointer, READ and INPUT affect program variables and the pointer. SET with pointer-items obviously affects only the pointer.

Expanded U/PL

There are four kinds of file-organization: sequential, stream, relative and keyed. Sequential and keyed files are sequences of records. A relative file is a sequence of record areas, each of which may or may not contain a record. A stream file is a sequence of values.

There are three kinds of record-type: display, internal and native. An internal record is a sequence of typed values. A native record is a sequence of fields, as described by a program-specified template. Display records provide for the exchange of data between systems employing different internal representations for numeric and string values, and also manipulate data in human-readable form. Internal records provide for efficient manipulation of data within a single system. Native records provide for the exchange of data among different language processors within a single system.

The following combinations of file-organization and record-type are supported:

- sequential display
- sequential internal
- stream internal
- relative internal (Expanded internal)
- keyed internal (Expanded internal)
- sequential native (Expanded native)
- relative native (Expanded native)
- keyed relative (Expanded native)

All other combinations of file-organization and record-type are implementation- defined.

Within each subsection, the syntax rules for sequential display, sequential internal and stream internal are presented first, followed by additional syntax constructs which pertain to Expanded files. Some of the Expanded constructs apply only to Expanded native files: these are preceded by an "N".

There are five statements which operate on the file as a whole and are thus called "file operations": OPEN, CLOSE, ERASE, SET and ASK. There are seven statements which apply to individual file elements and are known as "record operations": INPUT, DISPLAY, READ, WRITE, REWRITE, DELETE and SET with pointer- control, including the variations using MAT and LINE. References to "INPUT operations", "WRITE operations", and so forth should be understood to include any of the statements using the keyword in question, e.g., "WRITE operations" includes WRITE and MAT WRITE. The seven record operations can affect data within a file, variables within the program and the file pointer. DISPLAY, WRITE, REWRITE and DELETE affect file data and the pointer, READ and INPUT affect program variables and the pointer. SET with pointer-items affects only the pointer. Devices Not all input or output is to or from a file, as defined above. An implementation may allow file processing statements to apply as well to devices, such as a terminal, a line printer or communications line.

When the term "file" is used throughout chapter 11, it should generally be understood to mean any source or destination of external data, i.e., either a true file or a device. In certain contexts where it is necessary to distinguish between the two, the terms "true file" and "Device" will be used for emphasis.

Devices differ from files in the following ways:

- It is implementation-defined whether data written to any given device is stored there and may later be retrieved by input operations.
- It is implementation-defined whether a given device is erasable.
- RELATIVE and KEYED file-organizations are not allowed for devices (not relevant to U/PL).
- A device need not support all access modes.
- A device need not support the minimum record size of 132. However, the implementation must document the minimum record-size for each device supported.
- It is implementation-defined whether a given device has record-setter capability.

- It is implementation-defined what condition causes the data-found condition to be set true or false for a given device.
- For interactive terminal devices only, the semantics of the input-control-items prompt- specifier, timeout-expression, and time enquiry must be supported. The implementation must define which devices, if any, are interactive terminal devices. The effect of these input-control-items on other devices and on true files is implementation-defined.
- It is implementation-defined whether the following conditions are treated as fatal exceptions, as defined in 11, or as nonfatal, as defined in 10 (in which case the recovery procedure is applied), when these conditions occur within INPUT operations on a device.

13.1 File Operations

13.1.1 General Description

There are four statements which affect a file as an entity. The open-statement makes a file accessible to the program, establishing the connection between the file and the program. Since the format for identifying files may vary with the operating system, it is assumed only that with each file is associated a string of characters, called its name, which identifies the file to the operating system. A file is identified within a program by the number of a channel through which it is accessed. The close-statement terminates the accessibility effected by the open-statement. The erase-statement deletes all or part of the data within a true file but may have no effect on a device. The ask-statement is used to inquire about the current status of the file.

13.1.2 Syntax U/PL and Expanded U/PL

1. open-statement = OPEN channel-setter NAME file-name file-attribute-list

2. channel-setter = channel-expression colon

3. channel-expression = number-sign index

4. file-name = string-expression

5. file-attribute-list = (comma file-attribute)*

6. file-attribute > core-file-attribute

7. core-file-attribute = access-mode / file-organization / record-type / record-size

8. access-mode = ACCESS (INPUT / OUTPUT / OUTIN / string-expression)

9. file-organization = ORGANIZATION (file-organization-value /string expression)

10. file-organization-value > core-file-org-value

11. core-file-org-value = SEQUENTIAL / STREAM

12. record-type = RECTYPE (record-type-value / string-expression)

13. record-type-value > core-record-type-value

14. core-record-type-value = DISPLAY / INTERNAL

15. record-size = RECSIZE (VARIABLE / string-expression) (LENGTH index)?

16. close-statement = CLOSE channel-expression

17. erase-statement = ERASE REST ? channel-expression

18. ask-statement > ASK channel-setter ask-item-list

19. ask-item-list = ask-item (comma ask-item)*

20. ask-item = ask-attribute-name variable variable*

21. ask-attribute-name > core-attribute-name

22. core-attribute-name = ACCESS / DATUM / ERASABLE / FILETYPE / MARGIN / NAME / ORGANIZATION / POINTER / RECSIZE / RECTYPE / SET / ZONEWIDTH

Expanded U/PL only

23. file-organization-value > Expanded-file-org-value

24. Expanded-file-org-value = RELATIVE / KEYED

N25. record-type-value > Expanded-record-type-value

N26. Expanded-record-type-value= NATIVE

27. file-attribute > Expanded-file-attribute

28. Expanded-file-attribute = collate-sequence

29. collate-sequence = COLLATE (STANDARD / NATIVE / string-expression)

30. ask-attribute-name > Expanded-attribute-name

31. Expanded-attribute-name = RECORD / KEY / COLLATE

A given file-attribute must appear at most once in a file-attribute-list.

A given ask-attribute-name must appear at most once in an ask-item-list.

The number and types of variables in an ask-item must agree with the table below in Semantics.

13.1.3 Examples

```
OPEN #3: NAME "myfile"
OPEN #N: NAME A$, ACCESS OUTIN, ORGANIZATION STREAM, RECTYPE INTERNAL, RECSIZE
VARIABLE LENGTH N
OPEN #N+1: NAME "MY" & F$, ORGANIZATION ORG$
CLOSE #N
ERASE #3
ERASE REST #4
ASK #3: ACCESS AC$, DATUM DT$, NAME NM$, ORGANIZATION ORG$, POINTER P$, RECSIZE
RS$ NUMCHARS, RECTYP RT$
ASK #N: KEY K$
```

13.1.4 Semantics

Files are accessed through channels to which they may be assigned during execution of a program-unit. A channel is a logical path through which external data may be transferred to or from a U/PL program. Within a program-unit, a channel is identified by a channel number local to that program-unit. The channel number is an integer from 0 up to and including some implementation-defined maximum. This maximum must be at least 99. A file, identified by its file-name, is open if it is currently assigned to a channel and closed otherwise. A channel is active if it currently has some file assigned to it and inactive otherwise. At the initiation of execution of a program, all channels except channel zero will be inactive. Channel zero will always be active. Execution of the open-statement, close-statement, or erase-statement (see below) for channel zero will cause a nonfatal exception.

Input and output from and to channel zero will have the same source and destination as input-statements and display-statements which do not contain channel-expressions. Channel zero will behave as a device with the file-attributes sequential, display, and outin, and without record-setter or erase capability.

Open-statement

The open-statement makes the file identified by the file-name accessible to the program through the channel number specified in the channel-expression. It is implementation-defined whether file names differing only in the case of the letters (upper or lower) denote the same file or different files. Following a successful open-statement, the associated channel will be active and the file open. An attempt to open a file on a channel which is already active causes an exception. The effect of attempting to open a file which is already open is implementation-defined. The number of channels other than channel zero which may be active simultaneously is at least one.

After a successful open, a true file will be accessible in accordance with the associated file-attributes, whether explicitly specified or in effect by default. This accessibility consists of the ability to perform certain operations and manipulate the file pointer in certain ways. See the preceding section for an overview of which statements are allowed under which attributes. If an attempt is made to OPEN a file which cannot be made accessible with the requested attributes (i.e., if not all the associated operations can be successfully executed for this file), then an exception results. 100 For a device, a successful open guarantees that, with two exceptions, all the file processing statements will have the same effects as for a true file. In particular, on output, the same data will be generated, and on input, values and characters will be interpreted and assigned to variables in the same way. A device, however, might not support the semantics associated with the recorder-setter or the erase-statement (below). The ask-statement may be used to determine whether a particular device supports these capabilities.

Minimum U/PL

If a file is opened successfully with a given file-organization, record-type, and record-size, then closed, and then opened at a later time with a different value for one of these file-attributes, then it is implementation-defined whether the file is thus accessible. Also, for files with record-type INTERNAL, if a different ARITHMETIC option is in effect for the two executions, it is implementation-defined whether the file is thus accessible. Conversely, if a true file is reopened at a later time with the same values for the file-attributes mentioned and, for files with record-type INTERNAL, the same ARITHMETIC option is in effect, and the user has employed the implementation- defined means to preserve the file unchanged in the interim, then the file must be accessible, and the contents of the file faithfully preserved. Devices are not required to preserve data. In the foregoing, "same ARITHMETIC option" refers to DECIMAL or NATIVE.

If a file with record-type INTERNAL opened in one program-unit is accessed by another program-unit with a different ARITHMETIC option, the results are implementation-defined.

Implementations must provide true files for which all access-modes are available. Implementations may also support true files for which some access-modes are not available. A device need not support all access-modes.

Implementations conforming to this standard need only to accept and process the following combinations of file-organization-value and record-type-value:

- sequential display,
- sequential internal,
- stream internal.

The effect of the other combination is implementation-defined.

When a string-expression is used as an attribute value, its value must be one of the associated keywords for that attribute. Upper-case-characters and lower- case-characters will be treated as equivalent within such string values. Implementations may define additional file attribute values.

Expanded U/PL

If a file is opened successfully with a given file-organization, record-type, and record-size, then closed, and then opened at a later time with a different value for one of these file-attributes, then it is implementation-defined whether the file is thus accessible. Also, for files with record-type INTERNAL or NATIVE, if a different ARITHMETIC option is in effect for the two executions, it is implementation-defined whether the file is thus accessible. Conversely, if a true file is re-opened at a later time with the same values for the file- attributes mentioned and, for files with record-type INTERNAL or NATIVE, the same ARITHMETIC option is in effect, and the user has employed the implementation-defined means to preserve the file unchanged in the interim, then the file must be accessible, and the contents of the file faithfully preserved. Devices are not required to preserve data. In the foregoing, "same ARITHMETIC option" refers to DECIMAL, NATIVE or FIXED, not to the default specification in the FIXED option. If a KEYED file is re-opened with a different collate-sequence, an exception results.

If a file with record-type INTERNAL or NATIVE opened in one program-unit is accessed by another program-unit with a different ARITHMETIC option, the results are implementation-defined.

Implementations must provide true files for which all access-modes are available. Implementations may also support true files for which some access-modes are not available. A device need not support all access-modes.

Implementations conforming to this standard need only to accept and process the following combinations of file-organization-value and record-type-value:

- sequential display
- sequential internal
- stream internal
- relative internal
- keyed internal
- sequential native
- relative native
- keyed relative

The effect of the other combinations is implementation-defined.

When a string-expression is used as an attribute value, its value must be one of the associated keywords for that attribute. Upper-case-characters and lower-case-characters will be treated as equivalent within such string values. Implementations may define additional file attribute values.

Access-mode

An access-mode specifies the direction in which data may be transferred from and to a file, either by one of the keywords INPUT, OUTPUT, or OUTIN, or by a string-expression whose value is one of these keywords.

If access-mode is INPUT, then it will be possible to read data from the file, but not to change the file. In particular, READ, SET with pointer-items, and INPUT statements (including variations with MAT and LINE) are allowed, but not DISPLAY, WRITE, REWRITE or DELETE. REWRITE and DELETE apply only to Expanded U/PL.

If the access-mode is OUTPUT, then it will be possible to add new data to the file, but not to change existing data in it, nor to retrieve data from it. In particular, DISPLAY, SET with pointer-items, and WRITE are allowed, but not READ, INPUT , REWRITE or DELETE. REWRITE or DELETE apply only to Expanded U/PL.

If the access-mode is OUTIN, then all record-operations (including REWRITE and DELETE for Expanded U/PL) are allowed for the file.

The erase-statement will be allowed only for a file with an access-mode of OUTIN.

If no access-mode is specified explicitly in the file-attribute-list, then the access-mode will be OUTIN if the file can be both read and written INPUT if it can only be read, and OUTPUT if it can only be written. Channel zero will behave as if opened with OUTIN.

For a file opened with access-mode OUTPUT, the pointer will be set to the end of the file following the OPEN, otherwise, it will be set to the beginning of file.

File-organization

The file-organization specifies the logical relationship between file elements, and the means by which the file pointer can be manipulated to identify the elements. The organization is specified with one of the keywords SEQUENTIAL, STREAM, RELATIVE or KEYED, or with a string-expression whose value is one of these keywords. Devices are accessed as either SEQUENTIAL or STREAM, RELATIVE and KEYED are allowed only for true files. RELATIVE and KEYED apply only to Expanded U/PL.

If no file-organization is explicitly specified in the open-statement, then the organization will be determined from available system information about the file. If such information is insufficient, the system will attempt to open the file as SEQUENTIAL. Channel zero will behave as if opened with SEQUENTIAL.

- A sequential file is a sequence of records. The order of the records is established by the order in which they were written. Records can be added only to the end of the file. The only means for identifying records with the file pointer is relative to the current position of the pointer, and the two special locations BEGIN (which identifies the first record in the sequence, if any), and END, immediately following the last record (the only location where it is possible to add records). A single record operation may affect several DISPLAY records, but only one INTERNAL or, for Expanded U/PL, NATIVE record.
- A stream file is much like a sequential file, except that it is a sequence of individual values, rather than of records. The order of values is established by the order in which they were written. Values

can be added only to the end of the file. The only means for identifying values is relative to the current pointer position, or BEGIN and END (specifying respectively, the first value, if any, in the sequence, and the location immediately following the last value). One record operation may typically read or write a contiguous series of values within a stream file.

Expanded U/PL only

- A relative file is a sequence of record-areas, each of which may or may not contain a record. The record-areas are numbered sequentially beginning with 1. This sets the order of the record-areas and the records within them is established by the identifying integer associated with each. The file pointer may be manipulated with the use of this record number as well as by those means provided for sequential files. For relative files, the beginning of file is the first record-area, regardless of whether it contains a record. The end of file immediately follows the last existing record. So, if the highest existing record number is 44, end of file refers to record-area 45. If there are no records in the file, end of file refers to record-area number 1. Records within a relative file may not only be read and written, but also changed (with REWRITE) and deleted (with DELETE). Moreover, records may be added, not only at the end of file, but also at any empty record-area, including those past the end of file. A record operation processes at most one record.

- A keyed file is a sequence of records, each of which is identified by a string called a key. The logical sequence of records is established by the collating order of their keys. (See collate-sequence, below.) The file pointer may be manipulated with respect to the keys, as well as by the means provided for sequential files. As with sequential files, beginning of file refers to the first existing record in the sequence (if any), and end of file refers to the location immediately following the last record. Records may be added anywhere within the sequence. An exact key, however, must always be specified for record creation, and no duplicate keys are allowed. Records may also be read, changed or deleted. A record operation processes at most one record.

Record-types

A record-type specifies the logical representation of data within a record or as an individual file element. The record-type affects how data is interpreted and transformed when being transferred between a program and a file. A record-type is specified with one of the keywords DISPLAY, INTERNAL or NATIVE or with a string-expression whose value is one of these keywords. NATIVE apply only for Expanded U/PL.

If no record-type is explicitly specified on the OPEN, the record-type is determined from available system information about the file. If such information is insufficient, then the file will be opened as DISPLAY. Channel zero behaves as if opened with DISPLAY.

- The display type specifies that a record is a sequence of characters. On output, the characters are processed in accordance with the semantics of the DISPLAY statement, and on input with those of the INPUT statement. READ and WRITE are also allowed for display records; they follow the semantic rules for INPUT and DISPLAY, respectively.
- The internal type specifies that a record is a sequence of typed values (or that each file element is a value), in the same sense that a program variable contains a value. The essential aspect of internal format is that (for a true file) values are preserved and retrievable. Thus, if a numeric or string value is written from a program variable, and later read into another variable, the two variables must be strictly equal (assuming the original variable to be unchanged). Since INPUT and DISPLAY statements are essentially character-oriented, they cause an exception when used on a file opened as internal.

Expanded U/PL only

The native type specifies that a record is a sequence of fields, as described by a program-specified TEMPLATE. This TEMPLATE, in conjunction with the list of operands of the associated record operation, specifies the size, type, number, and order of fields within the record. This allows data in a file to be put in a form suitable for exchange with other language processors which have similar record specification capabilities. Values are preserved subject to certain restrictions regarding the size of the fields in the record. As with the internal type, INPUT and DISPLAY cause an exception when used on a file opened as native.

Record-size

A record-size specifies the maximum length of records in a file. It is specified explicitly with the keyword LENGTH.

Unless an enhancement to this Standard provides for fixed-length records, all files will be composed of variable-length records, i.e., of records whose lengths are independent of each other. The length of a record of type DISPLAY will be the number of characters in that record. The length of records of other types (INTERNAL or, for Expanded U/PL only, NATIVE) will be implementation-defined. An attempt to perform a record operation for a record whose length exceeds the maximum set (either explicitly or by default) in the OPEN operation will use an exception. A specified LENGTH index must be greater than zero.

If no record-size is explicitly specified in the open-statement, then the record-size is determined from available system information about the file. If such information is insufficient, then the file will be opened as VARIABLE. If the index is omitted, then the maximum length of records will be implementation-defined. Channel zero will behave as if opened with VARIABLE and the length index omitted.

Implementations must support record-sizes of at least 132 for true files. Collate-sequence (Expanded U/PL only)

The collate-sequence specifies, for a KEYED file, the collating sequence of the record keys. A collate-sequence is specified with one of the keywords STANDARD or NATIVE, or with a string-expression whose value is one of these keywords. Collate- sequence has meaning only for a KEYED file. For other file-organizations, it has no effect.

The collate-sequence of a file governs all record operations for that file and the file-operation ERASE. Thus, the logical appearance of the file, when operated on by READ, WRITE, REWRITE, DELETE, SET with pointer-control,

ERASE and ASK must be in accordance with the specified collate-sequence (see file-organization, above).

The collate-sequences STANDARD and NATIVE imply exactly the same ordering as in the option-statement. Thus, if the collate-sequence associated with a file and a program-unit agree, it follows that an earlier key in the file will always compare as less than a later key. When the sequences disagree, this relationship may not hold. Nonetheless, it must be possible for a program-unit with a different collate- sequence to access a KEYED file; the collate-sequence affects only the logical order of the records, not their contents. Implementations with KEYED files must support both collate-sequences.

If no collate-sequence is specified in the open-statement, then the collate-sequence will be determined from available system information about the file. If such information is insufficient, the system will attempt to open the file with the same collate-sequence as that in effect for the program-unit containing the open- statement. Since channel zero has file-organization SEQUENTIAL (not KEYED), it has no associated collate-sequence.

Close-statement

Execution of a close-statement will close the file assigned to the specified channel, causing the channel to become inactive. If no file is assigned to the channel, no action occurs. Upon exit from an external-sub-def or external-function-def, any files opened by such a procedure whose channels are not formal parameters will be closed. Upon program termination, any files still open will be closed.

Erase-statement

For a true file, execution of an erase-statement will delete all or part of the data within the file assigned to the specified channel. The file-attributes associated with the file are not changed. If the REST option is omitted, then all file elements are deleted, the file becomes empty, and the file pointer points to the end of file (which is the same as the beginning file).

If the REST option is specified, then all file elements at or beyond the current location of the file pointer are deleted. All file elements preceding it are left unchanged. The file pointer is then set to end of file.

The erase-statement may not be effective for a device. The ask-statement can be used to determine if a device supports this capability.

An erase-statement executed for channel zero will cause an exception, but no other effect will occur.

An erase-statement is allowed only for a file opened with access-mode OUTIN. For other access-modes, there is no effect on the file and an exception results.

Ask-statement

Execution of an ask-statement will cause the variables in the ask-item-list to be assigned values corresponding to the attributes of the file currently assigned to the specified channel, as indicated in the following table. If the channel is inactive, then all such string-variables will be assigned the null string, and all such numeric variables will be assigned 0. In all cases below, A$ represents a string- variable and N represents a numeric-variable.

In *Expanded U/PL* the following responses can be expected:

ACCESS A$
The access-mode of the file, i.e., ,, INPUT M , "OUTPUT", or "OUTIN".

COLLATE A$
The collate-sequence associated with a KEYED file, i.e., "STANDARD" or "NATIVE". For file-organizations other than KEYED, the null string is assigned.

DATUM A$
The type of the next datum in the file following the current pointer position, i.e., "NUMERIC", "STRING", "NONE" (if no data follow), or "UNKNOWN" (if it is impossible to determine the type or whether more data follow). DATUM is well-defined only for STREAM INTERNAL files. For other file organizations, it is implementation-defined.

ERASABLE A$
"YES" or "NO" depending on whether or not this file is erasable, i.e., if the ERASE statement can delete file elements.

FILETYPE A$
"FILE" or "DEVICE" depending on whether this is a true file capable of preserving data or is a device.

KEY A$

The key associated with the record identified by the file pointer in a keyed file. If the pointer is at the end of file or if this is not a keyed file, the null string is assigned.

MARGIN N
The current margin for a display file (MAXNUM if the record may be of arbitrary length). If the file is not DISPLAY, zero is assigned.

NAME A$
The name of the file assigned to the channel.

ORGANIZATION A$
The file-organization of the file, i.e., "SEQUENTIAL", "STREAM", "RELATIVE"

or "KEYED".

POINTER A$
The current pointer position for the file, i.e., "BEGIN", "MIDDLE", or "END", where MIDDLE will mean neither BEGIN nor END, and END will be the pointer position for a file, or a position beyond the end, in the case of a RELATIVE file. UNKNOWN may be returned in the case of devices for which an implementation cannot determine which of the above values is correct.

RECORD N

The number of the record-area identified by the file-pointer. For non-relative files, zero is assigned.

RECSIZE A$ N
The record-size of the file, i.e., "VARIABLE" and the maximum length for its records (MAXNUM if there is no effective limit on record-length, e.g., a communication line).

RECTYPE A$
The record-type for the file, i.e., "DISPLAY", "INTERNAL" or "NATIVE".

SETTER A$
"YES" or "NO" depending on whether or not this file has record-setter capability.

ZONEWIDTH N
For DISPLAY files, the current zonewidth. For non-DISPLAY files, zero is returned.

13.1.5 Exceptions

- The value of a channel-expression is not between 0 and the implementation-defined maximum (7001, fatal).
- Channel zero is specified in an open-statement, a close-statement, or an erase- statement (7002, nonfatal do nothing and continue).
- A nonzero channel specified in an open-statement is already active (7003, fatal).
- A string-expression used to specify a file-attribute does not have a recognizable value (7100, fatal).
- Access to a file in an open-statement is not possible in accordance with the specified or default file-attributes (71xx fatal: the values and meanings for xx are implementation-defined).
- A KEYED file is re-opened with a different collate-sequence from that of an earlier open (7050, fatal). (Expanded U/PL only)
- A LENGTH index is not greater than zero (7051, fatal).
- A device is opened as RELATIVE or KEYED (7052, fatal). (Expanded U/PL only)
- A nonzero channel specified in an erase-statement is inactive (7004, fatal).
- An erase-statement is used on a file which has not been opened as OUTIN (7301, fatal).
- An erase-statement is used on a device without erase capability which has been opened with OUTIN (7311, nonfatal: do nothing and continue).

13.1.6 Remarks

It is recommended that implementations recognize as file-names at least those strings of characters consisting of an upper-case-letter followed by at most three more upper-case-letters or digits. It is also recommended that information required by the operating system, for the purpose of protecting the security of files be considered part of the file-name.

It is recommended that implementations use the file-name to distinguish between the opening of a true file, and opening of non-file devices, such as a communications line or a line printer.

It is recommended that the number of channels which may be active simultaneously be at least four in addition to channel zero.

It is recommended that the default maximum length of records in a file be infinite, i.e., that records be allowed to be of any length.

It is also recommended that record-size for INTERNAL and, for Expanded U/PL only, NATIVE files has a meaning comparable to that for DISPLAY, i.e., that it specifies the maximum number of characters or bytes within the record.

Additional values may be returned by an ASK statement if an implementation supports access-modes, file-organizations, record-types, record-sizes and collate-sequences in addition to those specified in this Standard.

If implementations return a status code following various file operations, it is recommended that this be made accessible through an additional ASK attribute to be called IOSTAT which returns a single string value, e.g., "ASK IOSTAT S$" returns a value in S$ reflecting the status of the file following the last attempted operation.

The maximum length of a KEY is implementation-defined. (Expanded U/PL only)

13.2 File Pointer Manipulation
13.2.1 General Description
The pointer for an open file can be altered in certain ways, without also performing any data transfer. The rules for pointer manipulation with the set-statement with pointer-items also apply when used in conjunction with other record operations.

13.2.2 Syntax
U/PL and Expanded U/PL

    1. set-object > channel-setter pointer-items

    2. pointer-items = (pointer-control / io-recovery / pointer-control comma io-recovery)

    3. pointer-control > POINTER core-record-setter

    4. record-setter > core-record-setter

    5. core-record-setter = BEGIN / END / SAME

    6. io-recovery = missing-recovery / not-missing-recovery

    7. not-missing-recovery = IF THERE THEN io-recovery-action

Expanded U/PL only (Expanded Files constructs):

    8. pointer-control > Expanded-record-setter

    9. record-setter > Expanded-record-setter

    10. Expanded-record-setter = RECORD index / KEY (exact-search / inexact-search) string-expression

    11. exact-search = equals-sign?

    12. inexact-search = greater-than-sign / not-less

13.2.3 Examples
```
SET #N: POINTER BEGIN, IF MISSING THEN EXIT DO
SET #3: RECORD N+1, IF MISSING THEN 1200
SET #4: KEY "Jones", IF THERE THEN EXIT DO
```

13.2.4 Semantics
Execution of a set-statement with pointer-items will set the pointer for the file assigned to the specified channel. After the pointer has been set, an optional io- recovery may take effect. The semantics associated with the record-setter and when the io-recovery takes effect are uniform for all the record operations. If any of the exceptions listed below in occurs, the file

pointer remains unchanged from its state before the SET with pointer-control. A device may not be able to achieve the effect of a record-setter. The ask- statement may be used to determine whether a device has record-setter capability.

Record-setters U/PL

An absent record-setter leaves the file pointer unchanged from its previous state. The io-recovery (see below), if present, still has its usual effect.

A record-setter of NEXT indicates that the pointer is to be set to the next record (for SEQUENTIAL files) or value (for STREAM files) at or beyond the current location. For a SEQUENTIAL file, the only case in which NEXT would have some effect is if there were a partial record pending. In this case, an end-of-record will be generated, and the pointer left at end of file. Expanded U/PL

An absent record-setter leaves the file pointer unchanged from its previous state. The io-recovery (see below), if present, still has its usual effect.

A record-setter of NEXT indicates that the pointer is to be set to the next existing record (for non-STREAM files) or value (for STREAM files) at or beyond the current location. In the case of a RELATIVE file, NEXT will therefore cause the pointer to skip over any empty record areas to the next existing record. If the pointer is already at or beyond the end of file, or is pointing to an existing record, NEXT will leave the pointer unchanged. This capability allows RELATIVE files to be processed as if they were SEQUENTIAL. In the case of STREAM and KEYED files, the pointer is always pointing to an existing file element or end of file and so is left unchanged. For a SEQUENTIAL file, the only case in which NEXT would have some effect is if there were a partial record pending. In this case, an end-of-record will be generated, and the pointer left at end of file.

A record-setter of BEGIN causes the pointer to be set to the beginning of file, i.e., to the first file element. If the file is empty, the location is also the end of file.

A record-setter of END causes the pointer to be set to end of file, defined as immediately beyond the last file element (if any) in the case of SEQUENTIAL,

STREAM, and KEYED files, and as immediately beyond the last existing record in the case of a RELATIVE file (or at record-area number 1, if no records exist).

A record-setter of SAME allows the user to access the same file-element(s) that have most recently been processed since the OPEN for that channel. Its use is valid only if the most recently executed record operation which accessed the channel meets these conditions : it was not a delete-statement, and no exception occurred during its execution at least until after the file pointer had been set.

If these conditions are not met, no pointer manipulation takes place and an exception results. If they are met and the most recent operation was a READ, INPUT, SET with pointer-items, or REWRITE, then the file pointer is reset to the same file element it was just set to by the record-setter of that operation. If this operation had no record-setter, then SAME resets the pointer to the same location it had at the beginning of that operation. If the most recent operation was a WRITE or DISPLAY, then SAME sets the pointer to the first file element created by that operation.

A record-setter with RECORD is valid only for use with RELATIVE files. If an attempt is made to use this record-setter on a file not opened as RELATIVE, the pointer is left unchanged and an exception results. The index is evaluated by rounding to an integer, and the pointer set to the corresponding record-area, whether or not it contains a record. If the index evaluates to an integer less than one, the pointer is left unchanged, and an exception is generated.

A record-setter with KEY is valid only for use with a KEYED file. If an attempt is made to use this record-setter on a file not opened as KEYED, the pointer is left unchanged and an exception results. For an exact-search the pointer is set to the record whose key equals that of the string-expression; if none such exists, the pointer is set to the first record whose key is greater than the ring-expression. If there is no such record, the pointer is set to end of file. For an inexact-search with not-less, the pointer is set exactly as for an exact-search, except for the setting of the data-found condition (see below). For an inexact-search with greater- than-sign, the pointer is set to the first record whose key is strictly greater than the string-expression; if none exists, it is set to end of file.

Io-recovery

At the completion of pointer manipulation there will be set a condition called data- found, which is either true or false. If data-found is true, and if a not-missing- recovery has been specified, then the io-recovery-action takes effect. If the data- found condition is false and a missing-recovery has been specified, then the io- recovery-action also takes effect. Except for these two cases, the io-recovery- action, if any, is ignored. The data-found condition is false if:

- in Expanded U/PL only, an exact-search has been specified, but no record was found whose key was equal to the string-expression, or
- after the pointer is set, it points to end of file, or
- in Expanded U/PL only, after the pointer is set, it points to an empty record-area, or
- for a device, there is an implementation-defined condition signifying that no data is available for input; otherwise, the data-found condition is true.

If the io-recovery-action is an exit-do-statement or exit-for-statement, the statement will have its normal effect. If the io-recovery-action is a line-number then execution will continue at the specified line.

13.2.5 Exceptions

- A set-statement with pointer-items is executed for an inactive channel (7004, fatal).
- A record-setter is used with channel zero (7002, nonfatal: do nothing and continue).
- A record-setter is used on a device without record-setter capability (7205, nonfatal: do nothing and continue).
- The record-setter SAME is used, and the most recently executed operation for the channel was a delete-statement (7204, fatal). (Expanded U/PL only)
- The record-setter SAME is used, and the most recently executed operation for the channel caused an exception before pointer manipulation took place (7204, fatal).
- The record-setter SAME is used, and no record operation has been executed on that channel since the OPEN (7204, fatal).

- The record-setter RECORD is used on a file opened with a file-organization other than RELATIVE (7202, fatal). (Expanded U/PL only)
- The record-setter KEY is used on a file opened with a file-organization other than KEYED (7203, fatal). (Expanded U/PL only)
- The index of a RECORD record-setter evaluates to an integer less than one (7206, fatal). (Expanded U/PL only)
- A record-setter specifies an exact-search for the null string (7207, fatal). (Expanded U/PL only)

13.2.6 Remarks

For devices, data-found could be set false by such conditions as no more files on an SD Card reader, control-Z sent from a terminal (which signifies end-of-file for some systems), or that the device is for output only, e.g., a line printer

13.3 File Data Creation

13.3.1 General Description

Statements are provided to allow the user to send data developed within the program to an external destination. In the case of true files, such data can be retrieved and modified by later programs. The facilities generalize the output capabilities presented in Section 10 to files. New facilities are also defined to allow output to the various record-types. The set-objects MARGIN or ZONEWIDTH are not part of a data creation statement but are included in this section because of their interaction with display records.

13.3.2 Syntax

U/PL and Expanded U/PL

    1. display-statement > DISPLAY channel-expression display-control (colon (display-list / output-1ist))?

    2. array-display-statement > MAT DISPLAY channel-expression display-control colon (array-display-list / array-output-list)

    3. display-control =(comma display-control-item)*

    4. display-control-item = core-record-setter / not-missing-recovery / USING image

5. set-object > channel-setter (`MARGIN` / `ZONEWIDTH`) index

6. write-statement = `WRITE` channel-expression write-control colon expression-list

7. array-write-statement = `MAT WRITE` channel-expression write-control colon array-list

8. write-control = (comma write-control-item)*

9. write-control-item > record-setter / not-missing-recovery

10. expression-list = expression (comma expression)*

11. array-list = array-name (comma array-name)*

Expanded U/PL only (Expanded Files construct):

N12. write-control-item > template-identifier

N13. template-identifier = `WITH` (line-number / string-expression)

N14. declarative-statement > template-statement

N15. template-statement = `TEMPLATE` colon template-element-list

N16. template-element-list = template-element (comma template-element)*

N17. template-element = fixed-field-count (field-specifier / left-parenthesis template-element-list right-parenthesis) / variable-field-count field-specifier

N18. fixed-field-count = `SKIP`? (integer OF)?

N19. variable-field-count = question-mark OF

N20. field-specifier = numeric-specifier / string-specifier

N21. numeric-specifier = `NUMERIC` asterisk numeric-field-size

N22. numeric-field-size = fixed-point-size / E

N23. fixed-point-size = integer-size period? / integer-size? period fraction-size

N24. integer-size = integer

N25. fraction-size = integer

N26. string-specifier = STRING asterisk string-field-size

N27. string-field-size = integer

Within a display-statement or array-display-statement, an image must not be used with a display-list, i.e., only an output-list may be used when an image is present as a display-control. The line-number of a temp late-identifier must refer to a temp late-statement in the same program-unit. (Expanded U/PL only)

The integer in a fixed-field-count must be greater than zero. (Expanded U/PL only) In a fixed-point-size, the integer-size or fraction-size must be greater than zero.(Expanded U/PL only)

String-field-size must be greater than zero. (Expanded U/PL only)

The record-setter in a write-control must not specify an inexact-search. (Expanded U/PL only) A given display-control-item must appear at most once in display-control. A given write-control-item must appear at most once in write-control.

13.3.3 Examples

```
DISPLAY #3: A, B, C
DISPLAY #3, END, USING 123: A$, B+C;
MAT DISPLAY #N, SAME, IF THERE THEN EXIT FOR: A$, B$, C
//3: MARGIN N+1
WRITE #3, RECORD 47, IF THERE THEN 666: A+B, C$ & D$
WRITE #X+Y WITH TEMPLATES3$: X, Y, Z + W
MAT WRITE #3, KEY "Whoever", IF THERE THEN 666,
WITH 111: A, B$
TEMPLATE: STRING*5, 2 OF NUMERIC*
TEMPLATE: ? OF NUMERIC*5.2, ? OF STRING*5
5 OF STRING*22, 3 OF NUMERIC*E, ? OF NUMERIC*.6
```

13.3.4 Semantics

All data creation statements follow a general pattern which will be described here. In all cases, the function of a data creation statement is to add one or more new file elements to a file. Previously existing file elements are not affected. Details 113 on aspects peculiar to each of the various forms are presented below, under the headings of each statement type.

First, the channel to which the data will be sent is determined from the channel- expression. The file-attributes are checked against the intended operations. All data creation statements require an access-mode of OUTPUT or OUTIN. If the channel is active and the file-attributes are compatible with the data creation statement, then the next phase begins. Otherwise, an exception results and the file, the file pointer, and all program variables remain unchanged.

The second phase of processing involves setting the file pointer, based on the record-setter (or its absence). This is done exactly as described in 11.2. The data- found condition is now set, again as described in 11.2. If data-found is true and a not-missing-recovery is present, then the io-recovery-action is taken. If data-found is true, and a not-missing-recovery is absent, then an exception results. In either case, no further change is made to the pointer position or the file.

If data-found is false, then the third phase begins, the actual output of data at the location indicated by the pointer. The operands are evaluated in succession from left to right until enough data to fill a file-element has been generated. Only then is the file-element actually added to the file and the pointer advanced immediately beyond the file-element just created. In particular, this means that an exception during data transfer will never result in a partial file-element being added to the file. However, if a statement can create several file-elements, those which have already been created before the exception occurs continue to exist in the file. Following the completion of data transfer, the file pointer is always left pointing at the next file-element (or end of file if none such exists) beyond the last one created. If an exception prevented the creation of any file elements, the pointer is left as it was set in the second phase.

Print-statement

The transfer of data with the display-statement works just as described in 10.3 and 10.4, except that the sequence of characters generated constitutes a record of a DISPLAY file, rather than current line, and end-of-record is generated in place of end-of-line. Note that it is possible to create records containing zero characters. End-of-record is the implementation-defined means whereby it is indicated that the storage of a file-element in a file is completed, i.e., no change or addition to this record is possible with a data creation statement. Except for the special case discussed below, no data is actually added to the file until a valid end-of-record has been generated, i.e., partial records are not added to the file. The effective margin for the file, which is used to control when end-of-record is generated, is taken from the value of RECSIZE established when the file was opened, or from a set-statement with MARGIN for this channel executed since the open (see below).

In one special case, a partial record is added to a file. If the display-list or output-list contains a trailing display-separator, then upon successful completion of the statement, a partial record has been created at the end of file, with the pointer left at end of file, i.e., just beyond the partial record. Note that if there is an exception before completion of the statement, then the partial record is not added to the file, as would also be true of a complete record. If and only if the next operation for the channel is a display-statement with an absent record-setter, then the sequence of characters it generates is appended to the end of the partial record, in accordance with the usual rules regarding the margin. If the next operation for that channel is anything other than such a display-statement, then before any other processing takes place, an end-of-record is added to complete the partial record, and the pointer left at end of file.

Array-display-statement

The transfer of data with the array-display-statement works just as described in 10.5, except that the sequence of characters generated constitutes a record of a DISPLAY file, rather than the current line, and end-of-record is generated in place of end- of-line. Note that by the rules of 10.5, a partial record is never created by the array-display-statement with an array-display-list but may be created with an array- output- list containing a trailing semicolon. Since an array-display-statement always starts a new line, it may not be used to complete a partial record. The effective margin is controlled as described under display-statement and "Setting the margin" (below).

Setting the margin

Associated with each open `DISPLAY` file is a margin, the maximum number of characters which a record can contain. The margin is used by display-statement and array-display- statement to determine when an end-of-record should be generated. Upon open, the effective margin is the `LENGTH` index in `RECSIZE`, or the implementation-defined length, which must be not less than the default zone width, if `LENGTH` is not specified explicitly. The set-statement with a `MARGIN` changes the margin for the active channel to the specified index. If a partial record exists in the file affected by the margin, the new margin is used when subsequently attempting to complete the partial record. A margin of `MAXNUM` indicates that a record may be arbitrarily large. The margin index must evaluate to greater than zero. The effect of a set-statement with `MARGIN` ends when the file is closed.

The maximum margin supported is implementation-defined.

Setting the zone width

Associated with each open `DISPLAY` file is a zone width, which controls the effect of `DISPLAY` as described in 10.3. Upon open, the zone width for a file is set to the implementation-defined default value, which will be at least $d+e+6$. The set- statement with `ZONEWIDTH` changes the zone width for the active channel to the specified index.

All zones are the same width, except possibly the last, which may be shorter. If a partial record exists in the file affected by the set-statement with `ZONEWIDTH`, the new zone width is used when subsequently attempting to complete the partial record. In a set-statement with `ZONEWIDTH` the index must evaluate to greater than zero. The effect of the set-statement with `ZONEWIDTH` ends when the file is closed.

The maximum zone width is implementation-defined.

Display record-type

DISPLAY records are sequences of characters; the characters generated by the DISPLAY operations are as described in Section 10. The accuracy of numeric values is limited only by the implementation-defined significance-width or length of the format-item, and by the ARITHMETIC option in effect.

Channel zero

DISPLAY to channel zero works in accordance with the semantics for a device without record-setter or erase capability. The destination of the output data is the same as if the channel-expression had been omitted. Also, if there is an exception for which a different recovery procedure is specified in Section 10 than in 11, the procedure of Section 10 will be used. A set-statement with MARGIN or ZONEWIDTH specifying channel zero has the same effect as if the channel-setter were omitted.

Write operation

The write-statement and array-write-statement are used to create records of any type. Successive expression values are arranged in corresponding sequences of values or fields or characters and written out to the file. Partial records are never created.

File organization

For STREAM files, one statement may create several file-elements, specifically one file-element is created for each expression or array-element evaluated. If an exception occurs during internal evaluation, previously created values remain in the file, the pointer is left at end of file, and any remaining values are ignored.

For INTERNAL SEQUENTIAL or NATIVE files, the values or fields generated by the expressions or arrays form one record. Thus, if an exception occurs before the statement is completed, no record is added to the file, and the file pointer is left unchanged from phase two. NATIVE files apply only to Expanded U/PL.

Expanded U/PL only

Since records in a KEYED file are identified by their keys, it is necessary when creating a new record that an explicit key be associated with it; so, when attempting to write to a KEYED file, sin exact-search must always be specified in the record-setter. If data-found is false, then a new record is inserted into the file, with a key equal to the string-expression of the exact-search.

Display record-type

A WRITE operation type on a display record generates exactly the same sequence of records and characters as would a DISPLAY operation with the same expression-list or array-list. Note, however, that not all DISPLAY facilities are available for WRITE, which is record-oriented, rather than line-oriented.

For DISPLAY files, one statement may create several file-elements in the case of margin overflow. If a fatal exception occurs during generation of an element, any elements previously created by that statement remain in the file, the pointer is left at the end of the file, and any remaining expressions are ignored.

Internal record-type

An internal record (of a STREAM file) is a sequence of values. There are two types of values, numeric and string. The sequence of values and their types are determined by the sequence and types of the expressions and array-elements from which the values are generated. When a value stored in a file is later retrieved, the effect is as if the expression or array-element with which it was created were assigned to the input variable with a let-statement. The length and content of string values are preserved. Numeric values are also preserved consistent with the usual limitations on precision associated with the prevailing ARITHMETIC option.

Native record-type (Expanded U/PL only)

The TEMPLATE describes the location, size, and type of fields within a record. When writing to a native file, a TEMPLATE must always be used. It must not be used with any other record-type. A TEMPLATE is associated with a particular data creation statement by means of the template-identifier in the statement which specifies the template-statement to be used or a string-expression whose value must be a syntactically correct template-element-list. The string-expression is evaluated before the expression-list or array-list of the write-statement or array-write-statement. Several statements may use the same template-statement.

When generating data for a native record, each expression within the expression-list is associated with a numeric-specifier or string-specifier within a TEMPLATE; the specifier is then used to transform the value of the expression into a field within a 116 record. The association takes place from left to right within the expression-list and the templates-element-list, each expression using the next available field-specifier. If the type of the expression (numeric or string) disagrees with the type of the specifier, an exception results. The number of expressions must not be greater than the number of specifiers. Extra specifiers beyond the last expression are ignored. The contents of the field are determined by the value of the expression and the size characteristics of the specifier.

For string values, the string-field-size is the number of characters in the field. The string value is left-justified within the field. If the value's length exceeds that of the field, an exception results. If shorter, the field is padded on the right with spaces.

Numeric fields are used to retain numeric values (both magnitude and sign). The sign is always stored in the field, but the numeric-field-size explicitly describes only the storage of the number's magnitude. For a numeric-field-size of E, the value is retained with the implementation-defined number of significant digits for the prevailing ARITHMETIC option. For a fixed-point-size, the integer-size describes the number of available digit places to the left of the decimal point, and the fraction- size, to the right of the decimal point. An omitted integer-size or fraction-size is treated as equivalent to zero. The numeric value is stored in accordance with these sizes. If the value contains significant digits to the right of the available field positions, the value is rounded when stored. This may result in a field with a value of zero. If the value contains significant digits to the left of the available field positions, an exception results.

The fixed-field-count in a template-statement indicates skipping and/or repetition for individual specifiers or a series of specifiers. The integer of the fixed-field- count indicates the number of repetitions and the keyword SKIP indicates that the affected specifiers will generate skipped fields. A field-count applies to the entity (either a field-specifier or a parenthesized template-element-list) in the same template-element. For an integer field-count (indicating repetition) the effect is just as if the entity governed by the field-count had been written out explicitly the equivalent number of times. When SKIP is used within a field-count, it indicates that the specifiers governed by it are not associated with values from the expression-list or array-list. Rather, as the record is being generated, fields within the record are assigned the value zero if numeric and spaces if string, corresponding to the usual size and type of the field-specifier in question. If a field-specifier is governed by several SKIPs (from various levels above it) the effect is just as if it were governed by only one, as described above. For example, given the following expression- lists and templates-element-lists,

```
A, B, C and NUMERIC*4, NUMERIC*5, NUMERIC*6
D, E and NUMERIC*4, SKIP NUMERIC*5, NUMERIC*6
```

A and D will occupy equivalent field locations, as will C and E. The second field in the second record will be the same size as occupied by B in the first record, with a value of zero.

As an illustration of the preceding description, equivalent pairs of template-element- lists are shown below:

```
1 - STRING*4, STRING*4, STRING*4
2 - 3 OF STRING*4
1 - STRING*5, STRING*4, NUMERIC*2, NUMERIC*2, NUMERIC*2, STRING*4, NUMERIC*2, NUMERIC*2, NUMERIC*2
2 - STRING*5, 2 OF (STRING*4, 3 OF NUMERIC*2)
1 - SKIP NUMERIC*3, SKIP NUMERIC*3, NUMERIC*4, SKIP STRING*5, SKIP STRING*6
2 - SKIP 2 OF NUMERIC*3, NUMERIC*4, SKIP (STRING*5, SKIP STRING*6)
```

Note that in 2 of the last example, the SKIP immediately in front of STRING*6 is superfluous. A variable-field-count is used only in conjunction with arrays (see below).

If execution reaches a temp late-statement, it proceeds to the next line with no further effect.

Array-write-statement

An array-write-statement behaves just like the write-statement would if the arrays were written out explicitly as array-elements in row major order (the last subscript varying most rapidly). Thus, for example, if "DIMA (3), B(2,2) M and OPTION BASE 1 are in effect, the following two statements are equivalent:

```
MAT WRITE #3: A, B
WRITE #3: A(1),A(2),A(3), B(1,1),B(1,2),B(2,1),B(2,2)
X. 7
```

Expanded U/PL only

When writing to a NATIVE record, arrays in an array-list can use the variable-field-count. If a fixed-field-count is used, then the number and type of the specifiers must match the array-elements as with WRITE. When the first element of an array is to be associated with a field-specifier, and if a template- element has just been completed (or if this is the first array in the list), and if the next template-element has a variable-field-count, then the field- specifier is used for all the elements of the array. When evaluation of the array is complete, the next array, if any, uses the next temp late-element which may or may not also have a variable-field-count. An array must use either a template-element with a variable-field-count or template-elements with fixed- field-counts, but not both.

13.3.5 Exceptions

- The value of the index in a set-statement with MARGIN is less than the current zonewidth for that file (4006, fatal).
- The value of the index in a set-statement with a ZONEWIDTH is less than one, or greater than the current margin for that file (4007, fatal).
- A set-statement with MARGIN or ZONEWIDTH specifies an inactive channel (7004, fatal).
- A set-statement with MARGIN or ZONEWIDTH specifies a file not opened as DISPLAY (7312, fatal).
- A set-statement with a MARGIN or ZONEWIDTH specifies a file opened as INPUT (7313, fatal).

The following exceptions for data creation statements are grouped according to the phase of processing during which they are detected. Phase 1 exceptions imply no change to the file or file pointer. Phase 2 exceptions imply no change to the file.

Phase 3 exceptions imply that some file-elements may have been created.

Phase 1 Exceptions:

- A data creation statement attempts to access an inactive channel (7004, fatal).
- A display-statement or array-display-statement attempts to access a file opened as INTERNAL or, for Expanded U/PL only, NATIVE (7317, fatal). 118 - The record-setter cannot be processed correctly, as described in 11.2.5, exceptions 7002 and 7202-7207 (use the procedure of 11.2.5).
- A data creation statement attempts to access a file opened as INPUT (7302, fatal).
- A write-statement or array-write-statement attempts to access a KEYED file but does not specify an exact-search in its record-setter (7314, fatal). (Expanded U/PL only)
- The string-expression of a template-identifier is not a syntactically correct template-element-list (8251, fatal). (Expanded U/PL only)
- A template-identifier is used on a file opened as DISPLAY or INTERNAL (7315, fatal). (Expanded U/PL only)

- A write-statement or array-write-statement does not have a template-identifier when attempting to access a file opened as NATIVE (7316, fatal). (Expanded U/PL only)

Phase 2 Exceptions:

- For a data creation statement, the condition data-found is true, and a not-missing- recovery has not been specified (7308, fatal).

Phase 3 Exceptions:

- An attempt is made to create a record larger than the value of RECSIZE (8301, fatal).
- An expression or array-element does not agree in type (numeric or string) with its associated TEMPLATE field-specifier (8252, fatal). (Expanded U/PL only)
- A template-element with a variable-field-count does not coincide with the first element of an array (8253, fatal). (Expanded U/PL only)
- There are not enough field-specifiers in a template-statement for all the expressions or array-elements (8254, fatal). (Expanded U/PL only)
- A numeric value has significant digits to the left of the available digit places in the field of a template (8255, fatal). (Expanded U/PL only)
- A string value is longer than the length of its field in the template (8256, fatal). (Expanded U/PL only)

13.3.6 Remarks (Expanded U/PL only)

Implementations may provide syntactic enhancements to template-element-list, e.g., to allow for additional data types. The exception for incorrect syntax then applies to the Expanded definition of template-element-list.

The variable-field-count is especially useful when writing an array whose size may change in the program, since the use of the fixed-field-count implies knowing the exact size in advance.

13.4 File Data Retrieval

13.4.1 General Description

Statements are provided to allow the program to retrieve data from a file to which it has previously been written or from a device. The facilities generalize the input capabilities presented in Section 10 to files. New facilities are also defined to allow input from the various record-types.

13.4.2 Syntax

U/PL and Expanded U/PL

1. input-statement > INPUT channel-expression input-control colon variable-list (comma SKIP REST)?

2. array-input-statement > MAT INPUT channel-expression input-control colon (redim-array-list / variable-length-vector)

3. line-input-statement > LINE INPUT channel-expression input-control colon string-variable-list

4. array-line-input-statement > MAT LINE INPUT channel-expression input-control colon redim-string-array-list

5. input-control = (comma input-control-item)*

6. input-control-item = core-record-setter / missing-recovery / prompt-specifier / timeout-expression / time-inquiry

7. read-statement > READ channel-expression read-control colon variable-list (comma SKIP REST)?

8. array-read-statement > MAT READ channel-expression read-control colon redim-array-list

9. read-control > (comma read-control-item)*

10. read-control-item > record-setter / missing-recovery

Expanded U/PL only (Expanded Files constructs):

1. Nil. read-control-item > template-identifier
2. A given input-control-item must appear at most once in input-contro1. (Expanded U/PL only)

3. A given read-control-item must appear at most once in read-control. (Expanded U/PL only)
4. A variable-length-vector must be declared as one-dimensional. (Expanded U/PL only)

13.4.3 Examples

```
INPUT #3: A, B, C, A$
MAT INPUT #W, BEGIN, IF MISSING THEN EXIT DO: A, B$
LINE INPUT #G, NEXT: A$, B$, C$
MAT LINE INPUT #4, IF MISSING THEN 1234: A$, B$(N), C$(8)
MAT LINE INPUT #4, IF MISSING THEN 1234: A$, B$(N), C$(8)
READ #3, SAME, WITH 333: W$, SKIP REST
MAT READ #N, RECORD W+2, IF MISSING THEN 111, WITH 222: N, W(Q)
```

13.4.4. Semantics

All data retrieval statements follow a general pattern, which will be described here. Details on the aspects peculiar to each of the various forms are presented below, under the headings for each statement type.

First, the channel from which data will be retrieved is determined from the channel- expression. Then, the file-attributes are checked against the intended operation. All data retrieval statements require an access-mode of INPUT or OUTIN. If the channel is active and the file-attributes are compatible with the data retrieval statement, then the next phase begins. Otherwise, an exception results and the pointer and all program variables remain unchanged. The second phase of processing involves setting the file pointer, based on the record-setter if present. In the absence of a record-setter the file pointer does not change. This is done exactly as described in 11.2. The data-found condition is now set, again as described in 11.2. If data-found is false and a missing-recovery is present, then the io-recovery-action is taken, otherwise an exception results. In either case, no further change is made to the pointer position.

If data-found is true, then the third phase begins, the actual input of data from the element indicated by the pointer. Data is transferred from the file element(s) to each of the operands (variables or arrays), from left to right, with successive data or values or fields from the file being assigned to successive variables or arrays. Note in particular that evaluation of subscripts, substring-qualifiers, and redims is delayed until after assignment of data to previous operands but occurs before assignment of data to the operand to which they apply. Note also that assignment of a string value to a string variable with a substring-qualifier takes place in accordance with the usual semantics of string assignment described in 6.5. If an exception occurs during data transfer, variables and array-elements for which a legal assignment has been made retain their new values, but all subsequent variables and array- elements retain their original values. Following a successful data retrieval operation, the pointer is advanced to the next file element, i.e., the next record, record-area, or value in the file.

One data retrieval operation usually affects only one file element. The three cases in which several file elements may be processed are:

- LINE or MAT LINE INPUT,
- READ from a STREAM file, and
- INPUT or READ from a DISPLAY file with records with trailing commas (indicating continuation of data).

The SKIP REST option is allowed only for non-stream files. It causes the remainder of the record from which the last datum or value or field was taken to be ignored. It is still mandatory that the record contain enough data to satisfy the variables or arrays in the list.

During this third phase of processing, a number of exception conditions may arise. Each such exception is associated with a particular file element. In all cases, the pointer is advanced to the file element immediately following the one with which the exception is associated. The following table summarizes these exceptions and which file-element they apply to.

Exception	**Associated file-element**
File-element larger than `RECSIZE`	The oversize file-element
Invalid redim, subscript, substring-qualifier, redim too large.	The file-element from which data would have been taken
Bad `TEMPLATE`: wrong type, field-count of "?" on other than first element of an array, too few specifiers (Expanded U/PL only)	The file-element from which data would have been taken
Bad data: wrong type, syntax, overflow	File-element containing the bad data
Insufficient data in file-element	The file-element with insufficient data
Insufficient data in file	End of file (i.e., no associated file-element)
Excess data in file-element	The file-element with excess data

Input-statement

The effect of a prompt-specifier, timeout-expression, and time-enquiry is as described in 10.2. These input-control-items apply only to interactive terminal devices. For other devices and true files, their effect is implementation-defined. The transfer of data with the input-statement also works just as described in 10.2, except that records are treated like input-replies, and end-of-record is treated like end-of-line. Each datum (as defined in 10.1) is assigned in order to a variable in the variable-list. All the `INPUT` operations (as opposed to the `READ` operations) are valid only for a file opened as `DISPLAY`. For any other record-type, an exception results. The input-statement may process several records if the last non-blank character in a record is a comma. If, following a record with a trailing comma, end of file is encountered before all variables have been assigned values, then the remaining variables will retain their old values, the file pointer will be positioned to end of file, and an exception will result.

When any of the INPUT statements is executed for a device and a phase 3 exception occurs, implementations may use the recovery procedures specified for true files in this section, or, if an equivalent exception is specified in Section 10, that recovery procedure may be used instead. This is to allow input from several interactive devices to use the nonfatal recovery procedures.

Array-input-statement

The array-input-statement behaves just like the input-statement would if the arrays were written out explicitly as array-elements in row major order (the last subscript varying most rapidly). The only additional capability is that of allowing a redim to change the dimensions of the array in accordance with the redim rules for the array- input- statement without a channel-expression. Thus, for example, if "DIM A(3)" and OPTION BASE 1 are in effect, the following two statements are equivalent:

```
MAT INPUT #N: A
INPUT #N: A(1), A(2), A(3)
```

The following two statements are also equivalent:

```
MAT INPUT #N: A$(2,2), C(2)
INPUT #N: A$(1,1), A$(1,2), A$(2,1), A$(2,2), C(1), C(2)
```

However, the effect of

```
MAT INPUT #N: A(1), B(A(1))
```

depends on the first datum encountered, since it controls the effective size of array B. Nonetheless, it behaves exactly as would an input-statement for which the appropriate number of array-elements for B had been coded. If an array is encountered whose redim yields a size less than 1 in any dimension, then it, and all subsequent arrays, will retain their old values, and an exception will result.

Variable-length-vectors

The transfer of data and consequent redimensioning of the array of a variable-length- vector takes place just as described in 10.5.

Line-input-s statement

The line-input-statement behaves exactly as described in 10.2, except that records are treated like input-replies, and end-of-record like end-of-line. The content of each successive record is assigned as the value of successive string-variables, including any leading or trailing spaces. A record may contain a null string, and it will be assigned in the normal way. If end of file is encountered before all variables have been assigned values, then the remaining variables will retain their old values, the file pointer will be positioned to end of file, and an exception will result.

Array-line-input-statement

The array-line-input-statement behaves just as would a line-input statement for which the array-elements had been coded out explicitly, instead of as arrays. See semantics above for array-input-statements. Note that here too, the size of a later array may depend on the value assigned to an earlier array, e.g.:

```
MAT LINE INPUT #N: A$(1), B$(VAL(A$(1)))
```

If the first record contained the string " 12 ", then twelve subsequent records would be read into the array B$. If an array is encountered whose redim yields a size less than 1 in either dimension, then it, and all subsequent arrays, will retain their old values, and an exception results.

Input-statements for channel zero

Input from channel zero works in accordance with the semantics for non-file devices. For those exceptions for which a different recovery procedure is specified in Section 10 than in 11, the procedure of Section 10 will be used.

Read-operation

The read-statement and array-read-statement are used to retrieve data from files with records of any type. Successive data or values or fields are assigned to successive variables or arrays in the operand list. READ may access several file elements for SEQUENTIAL or STREAM files, but only one for RELATIVE and KEYED files. RELATIVE or KEYED files are provided only in Expanded U/PL.

File organizations

For non-STREAM files (SEQUENTIAL files in U/PL and RELATIVE and KEYED files in Expanded U/PL), the variables receive values from the sequence of data or values or fields within a record. There must be just enough data within the record (or records in the case of DISPLAY records with trailing commas) to satisfy the variable-list (except for SKIP REST, see above). For STREAM files, the variables receive their values directly from the sequence that constitutes the file, beginning with the file-element indicated by the pointer, and so file-element boundaries are insignificant. If end of file is encountered before all variables have been assigned values, then the remaining variables will retain their old values, the file pointer will be positioned to end of file, and an exception will result.

Display record-type

Records in DISPLAY files are sequences of characters. The retrieval of string data will take place as described in 10.2. Note that retrieving data from a record created with DISPLAY does not necessarily preserve the same value, since, for instance, leading and trailing spaces are not saved in unquoted strings n input. For numeric data, the accuracy will be consistent with the usual semantics for assignment of a numeric-constant to a numeric-variable, i.e., at least six significant digits for OPTION ARITHMETIC NATIVE and at least ten digits for OPTION ARITHMETIC DECIMAL. For a numeric-constant with no more significant digits than the implementation-defined precision, the exact value is assigned with OPTION ARITHMETIC DECIMAL.

A `READ` operation on a `DISPLAY` record assigns values exactly as would an `INPUT` operation with the same variable-list or redim-array-list. Note, however, that not all the `INPUT` facilities are available for `READ`, which is record-oriented.

Internal record-type

An internal record (and a stream file) is a sequence of values. There are two types of value, numeric and string. For `INTERNAL` file elements, the values must be retrieved with a variable of the same type as that of the value, otherwise an exception results. Thus, the contents of an `INTERNAL` file element are self-typed. The sequence of values and their types are determined by the record operation which created or modified the file-element(s). When a value is retrieved, the effect is as if the expression with which it was created were assigned to the input variable with a let-statement. The length and content of string values are preserved. Numeric values are also preserved, consistent with the usual limitations on precision and type associated with the prevailing `ARITHMETIC` option.

Native record-type (Expanded U/PL only)

The `TEMPLATE` describes the location and type of fields within the record. When reading from a native record, a `TEMPLATE` must always be used. It must not be used with any other record-type. A `TEMPLATE` is associated with a particular data retrieval statement by means of the template-identifier in the statement, which specifies the template-statement to be used, or a string-expression whose value must be a syntactically correct template-element-list. The string-expression is evaluated before any input takes place and before any redims, substring qualifiers, or subscripts are evaluated. Several statements may use the same template-statement.

When retrieving data from a native record, each variable within the variable-list is associated with a field-specifier within a template; the specifier is then used to return data from a field within a record. This association takes place from left to right, within the variable-list and template-element-list, each variable using the next available field-specifier. A variable is associated with a specifier after a value has been assigned to the previous variable, and any subscripts, substring- qualifiers, or redims for this variable have been evaluated. If the type of the variable (numeric or string) disagrees with the type of the specifier, an exception results. The number of specifiers must not be less than the number of variables. Extra specifiers beyond the variables are ignored. The contents of the next field in the record is interpreted according to the specifier, and the resulting value placed in the variable.

When retrieving data, the specifiers of all fields within a record must be compatible with the specifiers with which they were created, otherwise the results are implementation-defined. In order to be compatible, the creating and retrieving specifiers for a field must both be of type STRING, with equal string-field-sizes, or both NUMERIC with a numeric-field-size of E, or both NUMERIC with equal integer-sizes and fraction-sizes. An omitted integer-size or fraction-size is treated as equivalent to zero.

When the TEMPLATE specifiers are compatible with the record, then the values are retrieved in accordance with the field sizes. For strings, a value is assigned with length equal to the string-field-size, and contents as originally stored in the record, including any spaces used for padding. For numbers, a value is assigned whose accuracy is limited only by the numeric-field-size and ARITHMETIC option. For numbers stored with a field size of E, or with a fixed-point-size and with no more significant digits than the implementation-defined precision, the exact value is retained under OPTION ARITHMETIC DECIMAL. Otherwise, the numbers are rounded according to the OPTION in effect and stored in the variable.

Section describes how values are stored in the fields of native records and the effect of field-counts. The only difference upon retrieval is that SKIP specifiers do not generate fields of zero or spaces but cause the affected fields simply to be skipped over. As before, such specifiers are not associated with variables.

Array-read-statement

In general, an array-read-statement behaves just like the read-statement would if the arrays were written out explicitly as array-elements. As with INPUT, there is delayed evaluation of redims.

Expanded U/PL only

For this reason, when reading from a native record, a variable-field-count is provided. If a fixed-field-count is used, then the number and types of the specifiers must match the array-elements, as with READ. When the first element of an array is to be associated with the next specifier, however, and if a temp late-element has just been completed (or if this is the first array in the list), and the next template-element is a variable-field-count, then the associated specifier is used for all the elements of the array. When the array has been filled, the next array, if any, uses the next temp late-element, which may or may not also have a variable-field-count. An array must either use a template-element with a variable-field-count or template-elements with fixed- field-counts, but not both.

13.4.5 Exceptions

The exceptions are grouped according to the phase of processing during which they are detected. Phase 1 exceptions imply no change to the file pointer or variables. Phase 2 exceptions -imply no change to the variables. Phase 3 exceptions imply that some variables may have received values from the file.

Phase 1 Exceptions:

- A data retrieval attempts to access an inactive channel (7004, fatal).
- An input-statement, array-input-statement, line-input-statement, or array-line- input-statement attempts to access a file opened as INTERNAL or, in Expanded U/PL only, NATIVE (7318, fatal).
- The record-setter cannot be processed correctly, as described in 11.2.5, exceptions 7002 and 7202-7207 (use the procedure of 11.2.5).
- A data retrieval statement attempts to access a file opened as OUTPUT (7303, fatal).
- The string-expression of a template-identifier is not a syntactically correct template-element-list (8251, fatal). (Expanded U/PL only)
- A temp late-identifier is used on a file opened as DISPLAY or INTERNAL (7315, fatal). (Expanded U/PL only)
- A read-statement or array-read-statement does not have a template-identifier when attempting to access a file opened as NATIVE (7316, fatal). (Expanded U/PL only)

- The `SKIP REST` option is used on a file opened as `STREAM` (7321, fatal).

Phase 2 Exceptions:

- For a data retrieval statement, the condition data-found is false and a missing-recovery has not been specified (7305, fatal).

Phase 3 Exceptions:

- An attempt is made to access a record larger them the value of `RECSIZE` (8302, fatal).
- The first index in a redim-bounds is greater than the second (6005, fatal).
- A single index used in redim bounds is less than the default lower bound in effect for the program unit (6005, fatal). 125 " The total number of elements required for a redimensioned array exceeds the number of elements reserved by the array's original dimensions (5001, fatal).
- A variable or array-element does not agree in type (numeric or string) with its associated `TEMPLATE` specifier (8252, fatal). (Expanded U/PL only)
- A variable-field-count in a temp late-element does not coincide with the first element of an array (8253, fatal). (Expanded U/PL only)
- There are not enough `TEMPLATE` specifiers for all the variables or array-elements (8254, fatal). (Expanded U/PL only)
- A data retrieval statement, other than a line-input-statement or an array-line- input- statement, attempts to access a `DISPLAY` record that is not a syntactically legal input-reply (8105, fatal).
- The datum of a `DISPLAY` record to be assigned to a numeric variable is not a numeric-constant (8101, fatal).
- A value in an `INTERNAL` record does not agree in type (numeric or string) with the variable to which it is to be assigned (8120, fatal).

- A value, datum, or field (for Expanded U/PL only) in a file causes numeric overflow upon assignment to the variable (1008, fatal).
- A value, datum, or field (for Expanded U/PL only) in a file causes string overflow upon assignment to a variable (1105, fatal).
- There are not enough data, values, or fields (for Expanded U/PL only) within a record of a non-STREAM file for the operands of a data retrieval statement and the record is not DISPLAY with a trailing comma (8012, fatal).
- End of file is encountered while seeking further data for the operands of a data of a data retrieval statement (8011, fatal).
- There are too many data in a record for the operands of a data retrieval statement and SKIP REST is not specified (8013, fatal).
- There is just enough data in a DISPLAY record with a trailing comma to satisfy a request for input, and SKIP REST is not specified (8013, fatal).

13.4.6 Remarks

Implementations may choose to treat underflows as exceptions (1508, nonfatal: supply zero and continue). In Expanded U/PL, this permits interception by exception handlers.

13.5 File Data Modification (Expanded U/PL only)

13.5.1 General Description

Statements are provided to allow the user to modify data previously stored in a file. Such data can either be changed or deleted. The modifications are always done at the record level.

13.5.2 Syntax

Core constructs :

None.

Expanded U/PL only (Expanded Files constructs):

    1. imperative-statement > rewrite-statement / array-rewrite-statement / delete-statement

    2. rewrite-statement = REWRITE channel-expression rewrite-control colon expression-list

3. array-rewrite-statement = MAT REWRITE channel-expression rewrite-control colon array-list

4. rewrite-control = (comma rewrite-control-item)*

5. rewrite-control-item > missing-recovery / record-setter

6. delete-statement = DELETE channel-expression delete-control

7. delete-control = (comma delete-control-item)*

8. delete-control-item = missing-recovery / record-setter

N9. rewrite-control-item > template-identifier

The line-number of a template-identifier must refer to a template-statement in the

same program-unit. A given rewrite-control-item must appear at most once in rewrite-control. A given delete-control-item must appear at most once in delete-control.

13.5.3 Examples
```
REWRITE #N, KEY = B$, IF MISSING THEN 666: A,B,C$
MAT REWRITE #3, RECORD N-1, WITH 111: X,Y,Z
DELETE #3, KEY "JONES"
```

13.5.4 Semantics

The data modification statements are modeled closely on certain aspects of data retrieval statements and data creation statements. Like the data retrieval statements, they operate on existing records. Like the data creation statements, they can alter the state of a file. The data modification statements are specified only for file- organizations RELATIVE and KEYED. For other file-organizations, their effect is implementation-defined. The data modification statements may be used only with access-mode OUTIN. Except for access-mode, the first and second phase of processing (i.e. checking of file attributes and setting the file pointer) for these statements is exactly like that for the data retrieval statements, because they operate on existing records. The third phase of processing, undertaken only if the operation is legal, the file pointer successfully set, and data-found is true, is described below under the individual headings.

Rewrite-statement

The rewrite-statement generates exactly one record, and that record is identical to the one that would be generated by a write-statement with the same expression-list or array-list and temp late-identifier, if any, with one exception : for a `NATIVE` record, fields governed by SKIP are not filled with zero or spaces, but rather the previous contents of the fields are left unchanged. This effect of SKIP occurs only if the `TEMPLATE` used by the `REWRITE` is compatible with `TEMPLATE` last used to alter the record. The result of using an incompatible `TEMPLATE` containing SKIP is implementation-defined. The use of an incompatible `TEMPLATE` without SKIP is defined above since the entire record is replaced.

If no exceptions occur during the generation of data to be used for modification of existing data, then the record pointed to by the file pointer is replaced by the record just generated, and the file pointer advanced to the next file-element. This 127 implies that the identifying record-number in a `RELATIVE` file, or identifying key in a `KEYED` file is not changed. If there is an exception, the pointer is left as it was set in the second phase and the data in the file is unchanged .

Array-rewrite-statement

An array-rewrite-statement behaves just like rewrite-statement would if the array- elements were written out explicitly. The rules for matching arrays and specifiers in a `TEMPLATE` are exactly the same as for the array-write-statement.

Delete-statement

The delete-statement causes the record indicated by the file pointer to be deleted, and the file pointer advanced to the next file-element. This implies that for a `RELATIVE` file, the affected record-area no longer contains a record, and for a `KEYED` file, the affected record is eliminated from the sequence of records constituting the file.

13.5.5 Exceptions

The following exceptions are grouped according to the phase of processing during which they are detected. Phase 1 exceptions imply no change to the file or file pointer. Phase 2 exceptions imply no change to the file. Phase 3 exceptions also imply no change to the file.

Phase 1 Exceptions:

- A data modification statement attempts to access an inactive channel (7004, fatal).

- A data modification statement attempts to access channel zero (7320, fatal).

- The record-setter cannot be processed correctly, as described in 11.2.5, exceptions 7002 and 7202-7207 (use the procedure of 11.2.5).

- A data modification statement attempts to access a file opened as INPUT or as OUTPUT (7322, fatal).

- The string-expression of a template-identifier is not a syntactically correct template-element-list (8251, fatal).

- A temp late-identifier is used on a file opened as INTERNAL or DISPLAY (7315, fatal).

- A rewrite-statement or array-rewrite-statement does not have a template-identifier when attempting to access a file opened as NATIVE (7316, fatal).

Phase 2 Exceptions:

- For a data modification statement, the condition data-found is false, and a missing-recovery has not been specified (7305, fatal).

Phase 3 Exceptions:

- An attempt is made to rewrite a record larger than the value of RECSIZE (8301, fatal).

- An expression or array-element does not agree in type (numeric or string) with its associated TEMPLATE specifier (8252, fatal).

- A template-element with a variable-field-count does not coincide with the first element of an array (8253, fatal). 128 - - There are not enough TEMPLATE specifiers for all the expressions or array-elements (8254, fatal).

- A numeric value has significant digits to the left of the available digit places in the field of a template (8255, fatal).

- A string value is longer than the length of its field in the template (8256, fatal)

13.5.6 Remarks

Note that the DELETE and REWRITE will affect the record indicated by the file pointer, even if the pointer is set with NEXT or left as is from previous operation (i.e. if the record-setter is absent).

14. EXCEPTION HANDLING AND DEBUGGING

14.1 Exception Handling (Expanded U/PL only)

14.1.1 General Description

Exception handling facilities provide a means of regaining control of a program after an exception has occurred.

14.1.2 Syntax

Expanded U/PL only

    1. protection-block = when-use-block / when-use-name-block

    2. when-use-block = when-line when-block use-line exception-handler end-when-line

    3. when-line = line-number WHEN EXCEPTION IN tail

    4. when-block = block*

    5. use-line = line-number USE tail

    6. exception-handler = block*

    7. end-when-line = line-number END WHEN tail

    8. when-use-name-block = when-use-name-line when-block- end-when-line

    9. when-use-name-line = line-number WHEN EXCEPTION USE handler-name tail

    10. handler-name = routine-identifier

    11. handler-return-statement = RETRY / CONTINUE

    12. exit-handler-statement = EXIT HANDLER

    13. cause-statement = CAUSE EXCEPTION exception-type

    14. exception-type = index

    15. detached-handler = handler-line exception-handler end-handler-line

16. handler-line = line-number HANDLER handler-name tail

17. end-handler-line = line-number END HANDLER tail

18. numeric-supplied-function > EXLINE / EXTYPE

19. string-supplied-function > EXTEXT dollar-sign

Handler-return-statements and exit-handler-statements will only occur within exception-handlers. The no-argument numeric-supplied-functions EXLINE and EXTYPE will be invoked only within exception-handlers. EXTEXT$ takes a single numeric argument, which is an index.

No line-number in a control-transfer outside a protection-block will refer to a line in that protection-block other than its when-line or when-use-name-line. No line- number in a control-transfer inside an exception-handler will refer to a line outside that exception-handler other than its own end-handler-line or end-when-line, nor will a line-number in a control-transfer outside an exception-handler refer to a line inside that exception-handler or to its end-handler-line or end-when-line.

A detached-handler referred to in a when-use-name-line within an internal-proc-def must be defined in the same internal-proc-def. A detached-handler referred to in a when-use-name-line that is not within an internal-proc-def must be defined in the same program-unit but not within an internal-proc-def. No two handler-lines in the same program unit will have the same handler-name. A detached-handler may not appear within a protection-block.

A protection-block may not appear within an exception-handler.

14.1.3 Examples

Example 1 : handling errors in input-replies by allowing the input-reply to be resupplied after issuing a suitable message

```
100 WHEN EXCEPTION IN
110 DISPLAY "Enter your age and weight' 131 120 INPUT a, w
130 IF a > 10 THEN
140 DISPLAY "What is your height"
150 INPUT h
160 END IF
170 USE
180 DISPLAY "Please enter numbers only"
190 RETRY
200 END WHEN
```

Example 2 : dynamic file opening 100 HANDLER file_trouble

```
110 SET file_ok$ = "false"
120 IF EXTYPE = 7107 THEN
130 SET message$ = "doesn't exist"
140 ELSEIF EXTYPE = 7102 THEN
150 SET message$ = "is the wrong type"
160 ELSE
170 SET message$ = "couldn't be used"
180 END IF
190 DISPLAY "file"; filenameS; messageS; "try again"
200 END HANDLER
500 DO
510 INPUT filenameS
520 SET file_ok$ = "true"
530 WHEN EXCEPTION USE file-trouble
540 OPEN #n: NAME filenameS I other parameters omitted
550 END WHEN
560 LOOP UNTIL file_ok$ = "true"
```

Example 3: Nested handlers

```
100 WHEN EXCEPTION IN
110 DO
120 READ #1, IF MISSING THEN EXIT DO: A
130 SET I = 1+1 ! I initialized outside loop
140 WHEN EXCEPTION IN
150 SET B(I) = 1000*A*A
160 USE
170 ! Assume it is numeric overflow
180 SET B(I) = MAXNUM
190 CONTINUE
200 END WHEN
210 LOOP
220 USE
230 IF EXTYPE = 8101 THEN ! non-numeric data
240 RETRY ! get next data item
250 ELSE ! give up
260 DISPLAY "Unable to process file"
270 STOP
280 END IF
290 END WHEN
```

14.1.4 Semantics

When an exception occurs during the execution of a program-unit, the action taken will depend upon whether or not the exception occurs within a when-block. If the exception occurs outside a when-block, then the default exception handling procedures specified in this Standard will be applied. If the exception occurs within a when-block, then the default exception handling procedures, which require that an exception be reported, will not be applied; instead, control will be transferred to the exception-handler associated with the inner-most protection-block within which the exception occurred.

When the protection-block is a when-use-block, the associated exception-handler is that which follows the use-line of the protection-block. When the protection-block is a when-use-name-block, the associated exception-handler is the detached-handler named in the when-use-name-line of the protection-block. In all respects, a detached- handler behaves semantically as though it were an exception-handler in the when-use- block of the when-block with the exception.

Within an exception-handler, the type of the exception which caused that handler to be executed will be obtainable as the value of the parameterless function EXTYPE. The values of EXTYPE for all exceptions defined in this Standard are specified in Table 2, along with the description of each exception in this Standard. The line-number of the line whose execution caused the exception will be obtainable as the value of the parameterless function EXLINE.

There are four means of exiting from an exception-handler:

- Execution of the handler-return-statement CONTINUE will cause control to be transferred to the statement lexically following that which caused the exception. If the exception occurred in a line which begins or is part of a structure (such as a do-line, loop-line, for-line, if-then-line, elseif-then-line, select-line, or case-line), then control will be transferred to the statement lexically following the entire structure of which the line is a part.

- Execution of the handler-return-statement RETRY will cause control to be transferred to the statement or line which caused the exception, causing the statement or line to be re-executed; if that statement was performing data retrieval, then the previous input-reply or line-input-reply will be discarded and a new one requested .

- If control reaches an end-when-line which terminates an exception-handler or reaches an end-handler-line, then control will be transferred to the line following the end-when-line of the protection-block within which the exception occurred with no further effect.

- Execution of an exit-handler-statement will cause the exception to be propagated to the lexical environment surrounding the innermost protection-block containing the exception (also note the effect of calls and function invocations - see below); i.e. the effect on handling the exception is as if the exception-handler did not exist (except for the effect of any statements already executed in the handler), and the rules for handling the original exception depend upon whether or not the exception occurs within some outer when-block.

If execution reaches a use-line in a when-use-block, or an end-when-line in a when- use-name-block, then control will be transferred to the line following the protection-block of which the use-line or end-when-line is a part. If execution reaches an end-handler-line of a detached-handler, control will continue at the line following the end-when-line of the when-use-name-block causing the exception. If execution reaches a handler-line of a detached-handler other than by the occurrence of an exception, control will then continue at the line immediately following the end- handler- line.

A separate GOSUB stack is associated with each exception-handler so RETURN never attempts to transfer control into or out of an exception handler.

Execution of a cause-statement will result in the occurrence of a fatal exception and the setting of EXTYPE to the rounded value of the exception-type.

If an exception is caused by a statement lexically within an exception-handler, then this new exception will be handled by the default exception-handling procedures.

If a fatal exception occurs in a procedure-part or internal-proc-def and either:

- the line causing the fatal exception is not contained in a when-block and therefore no exception-handler is entered, or

- an exception-handler is entered, an exit-handler-statement is executed with the handler, and there is no lexically surrounding when-block to intercept the exception, then the fatal exception will be propagated back to the line that invoked the procedure-part or internal-proc-def. This propagation will continue to occur until either:

- a user-defined exception-handler resolves the exception by execution of a handler- return- statement o by causing control to pass to an end-handler-line or to an end- when-line which terminates the exception-handler, or

- the main program or a parallel-section is reached, in which case the default exception-handling procedures are applied.

If an exception-handler is invoked as a result of this process, then the value returned by the EXTYPE function will be 100000 plus the value that would have been returned by EXTYPE in the procedure-part or integral-proc-def in which the exception originally occurred. The value of EXLINE will be the line-number of the most recent line to which the exception was propagated, i.e., the line lexically within the when- block associated with the exception-handler, not the line of the original exception.

The default exception-handling procedures will always report the EXTYPE and EXLINE of the original exception.

The value of EXTYPE for exceptions defined by local enhancements to this Standard will be negative. When negative values of EXTYPE are propagated, the value will be -100000 plus the value that would have been returned by EXTYPE for the original exception.

Values of EXTYPE from 1 to 999 will not be used by future enhancements to this Standard, nor will they be used by local enhancements to this Standard.

The value of EXTEXT$ will be the text part of the error message provided by the system for the exception number obtained by rounding its argument to an integer. If its argument is not the exception number of a standard system exception, the value of EXTEXT$ will be the null string.

If the main-program is reached and no exception-handler is invoked there as a result of the original exception, then the exception will be handled by the default exception handling procedures specified in this Standard.

12.1.5 Exceptions
A cause-statement is executed (exception-type, fatal).

12.1.6 Remarks
Users should note that there are two kinds of exception propagation specified in this section. First, there is "lexical" propagation, outward to surrounding protection- blocks within a program-unit or internal-proc-def. If

this process propagates the exception outside of any such protection-block, "invocation" propagation takes effect, passing the exception back to invoking statements.

The function EXLINE should be used with caution, as the use of editing facilities which renumber lines in a program may invalidate computations involving EXLINE. For example, the program fragment:

```
1000 SELECT CASE INT(EXLINE/100)
1010 CASE 1, 2
1100 CASE 3 TO 7
```

would probably behave differently if lines 100 through 800 were renumbered.

When a fatal exception is propagated back to invoking statements and the default exception-handling procedure is applied as a result, only the original exception's EXTYPE and EXLINE must be reported. Implementations may, however, also report the line-numbers of the lines through which the exception was propagated, or any other information deemed useful.

It is not possible to pass a nonfatal exception back to a calling routine since it will be handled either by an exception-handler in the called routine or by the system handler. An exception handler may, however, cause a fatal exception with a cause- statement .

The cause-statement is not intended actually to simulate any given exception, but rather to raise a fatal exception with a specified value of EXTYPE. In particular, if the specified EXTYPE is the same as for some nonfatal exception, implementations need not apply the recovery procedure as though that nonfatal exception had actually occurred. It is presumed that a program will normally contain an exception-handler to receive and process the exception.

All positive values of EXTYPE are reserved for future versions of this Standard. Exceptions defined by local enhancements to this Standard should be identified by negative values for EXTYPE, following the categories established in Table 2. The value returned by EXTYPE for an exception defined in a local enhancement and occurring in a procedure-part or internal-proc-def should be -100000 plus the negative value identifying that exception. For example, if an implementation chose an EXTYPE value of -4029 for an invalid argument in a new built-in function, and if that exception occurred in a subprogram, but was not handled there, then the value of EXTYPE in an exception-handler in a calling program should be -104029.

It is recommended that implementations use the "zero-th" value in a class of EXTYPE values to represent "other exceptions of this type". For example, an EXTYPE value of 1000 might represent all overflows not defined in this Standard.

Values of EXTYPE from 1 to 999 may only occur from cause-statements in application programs. These values should be encouraged for use, since they will not be assigned standard meanings in future enhancements to this Standard.

CONTINUE should be used with caution. For instance, if an exception occurs within a def-statement, on-gosub-statement, on-goto-statement, or if-statement, CONTINUE will transfer control to the lexically following line. Such action may not be equivalent to resumption of normal flow of control.

The following example illustrates the effect of CONTINUE with control structures:

```
100 WHEN EXCEPTION IN
120 INPUT PROMPT "enter your age and weight": a, w
130 DO WHILE a > 1
140 IF a < 9999999999 THEN
150 INPUT PROMPT "What is your height ": h
160 DISPLAY "Check the following:"
170 DISPLAY "Age:"; a, "Weight:"; w, "Height:";
200 INPUT PROMPT "Enter your age": a
210 END IF
220 DISPLAY "Lexically following IF"
230 LOOP
240 DISPLAY "Lexically following DO WHILE"
```

For exception in line :	CONTINUE transfers control to line:
120	130
130	240
140	220
150	160

The precise format of the values of the EXTEXT$ function is implementation-defined. In particular, implementations may choose to omit, or to mark in a special way, those fields in an error message that are specific to a particular instance of an exception, such as the line number at which the exception occurred or the value of an out-of-range subscript.

14.2 Debugging (U/PL and Expanded U/PL)

14.2.1 General Description

Debugging facilities are provided by language statements in order to allow test points to be built into a program. These statements allow the user to set break points, to trace the action of the program, and to turn the debugging system on and off within each program-unit.

14.2.2 Syntax

    1. debug-statement = DEBUG (ON / OFF)

    2. break-statement = BREAK

    3. trace-statement = TRACE ON (TO channel-expression)? / TRACE OFF

14.2.3 Examples

TRACE ON

TRACE ON TO #3

14.2.4 Semantics

Each program-unit will have a debugging status, which is either active or inactive at any given time. The debugging status of a program-unit will persist between invocations of that program-unit (with the exception of the main program). Changes in the debugging status of one program-unit will not affect the debugging status of any other program-unit. At the beginning of execution of the program, debugging will be inactive for all program-units.

Execution of the debug-statement DEBUG ON will cause debugging to become active for the program-unit in which that debug-statement occurs. Debugging will remain active for the remainder of that invocation of that program-unit, and for each subsequent invocation of that program-unit, until the debug-statement DEBUG OFF is executed in that program-unit. Execution of the debug-statement DEBUG OFF will cause debugging to become inactive for the remainder of that invocation of that program-unit, and for each subsequent invocation of that program unit, until the debug-statement DEBUG ON is executed in that program-unit.

The execution of a break-statement when debugging is active will cause an exception. The standard recovery procedure from this exception will be to report the line- number of the break-statement and to signify to the user that interaction with the debugging system is possible. The actions allowed by the debugging system, including the method for continuing execution or terminating execution of the program, are implementation-defined. If the execution of a program reaches a line containing a break-statement, and debugging is inactive, then it will proceed to the next line with no other effect.

The execution of a trace-statement when debugging is active will turn tracing on (if ON is specified) or off (if OFF is specified) in the program-unit containing the trace-statement. Prior to the execution of any trace-statement upon each separate entry to a program-unit, tracing will be off. If the execution of a program reaches a line containing a trace-statement, and debugging is inactive, then it will proceed to the next line with no other effect.

The execution of a trace-statement will not affect the debugging status, nor will the execution of a debug-statement affect the tracing status (ON or OFF).

Whenever tracing is on and debugging is active in a program-unit, the following actions will occur each time a line of the specified type is executed :

- for any line which interrupts the sequential order of execution of lines in a program, both the line-number of that line and the line-number of the next line to be executed will be reported; and

- for any line which assigns a value to a variable or to an element of an array, both the line-number of that line and any values assigned by execution of that line will be reported. Whenever tracing has been turned on via a trace-statement with a channel-expression, trace reports will be directed to the (display format) file assigned to the specified channel. If no channel-expression has been specified, the trace report will be directed to the device associated with channel zero.

The contents of the trace report are implementation-defined, but will include at least the name of the variable traced, as that name lexically appears in the statement causing the TRACE report, and its value; if the variable is an array element, the value(s) of its subscripts will also be included.

14.2.5 Exceptions

- A break-statement is executed when debugging is active (10007, nonfatal: the recovery procedure is to report the line-number of the statement and to permit interaction with the debugging system).

- An attempt is made to direct a trace report to an inactive channel. (7401, fatal).

- An attempt is made to direct a trace report to a file which is not display format opened with access OUTPUT or OUTIN (7402, fatal).

14.2.6 Remarks

Since an array-assignment assigns a value to each element of an array, tracing an array-assignment causes reporting of all new array element values.

The form of all trace reports is implementation-defined.

Implementations may provide debugging facilities through commands in addition to statements. It is recommended that such commands use the same keywords as the statements.

15. GRAPHICS

The facilities provided in section 15.1 through 15.3 are a subset of those provided by level 0b of the Graphical Kernel System (GKS) as defined in ISO 7942. The values of the EXTYPE function for exceptions defined in GKS are 11000 plus the value of the GKS error number. In GKS terms, any program that includes statements from Section 15 of this Standard has implied calls to the functions OPEN GKS, OPEN WORKSTATION (#0, "Maindev", 1), and ACTIVE WORKSTATION #0 before any graphics statements are executed, and calls to the functions DEACTIVE WORSTATION #0, CLOSE WORKSTATION #0 and CLOSE GKS as the program terminates.

15.1 Coordinate Systems

15.1.1 General Description

The coordinates used to produce graphic output may be chosen to suit the application. The range of this system of "problem coordinates" (world coordinates) is established by a SET WINDOW statement. This range is mapped into a rectangular portion of an abstract viewing surface which can be specified by a SET VIEWPORT statement. It is possible to specify what part of this abstract viewing surface will be presented to the user on the display surface by a SET DEVICE WINDOW statement. This rectangle, in turn, may be located on the display surface by a SET DEVICE VIEWPORT statement.

No output will be produced outside the device viewport. It is possible to guarantee that all graphic output which lies outside the viewport will be eliminated by enabling clipping.

Ask statements are provided to determine the current values for the parameters established by execution of one of the set statements or by default.

15.1.2 Syntax

> 1. set-object > WINDOW boundaries / VIEWPORT boundaries / DEVICE WINDOW boundaries / DEVICE VIEWPORT boundaries / CLIP string-expression

2. boundaries = boundary comma boundary comma boundary comma boundary

3. boundary = numeric-expression

4. ask-statement > ASK ask-object status-clause?

5. status-clause = STATUS numeric-variable

6. ask-object > WINDOW boundary-variables / VIEWPORT

boundary-variables / DEVICE WINDOW

boundary-variables / DEVICE VIEWPORT

boundary-variables / DEVICE SIZE

numeric-variable comma numeric-variable comma

string-variable / CLIP string-variable

7. boundary-variables = numeric-variable comma numeric-variable comma

numeric-variable comma numeric-variable

15.1.3 Examples

```
WINDOW 0, PI*2, -1, 1
VIEWPORT .5*width, width, .5*height, height
DEVICE WINDOW 0, .8, 0, 1
DEVICE VIEWPORT .3, .5, .1, 1
CLIP "Off"
ASK WINDOW X1, X2, Y1, Y2
ASK VIEWPORT L, R, B, T
ASK DEVICE WINDOW XMIN, XMAX, YMIN, YMAX
ASK DEVICE VIEWPORT LEFT, RIGHT, BOTTOM, TOP
ASK DEVICE SIZE Width, Height, Unit$
ASK CLIP CLIP_STATE$
```

15.1.4 Semantics

Graphic output is specified in problem coordinates. A normalization transformation defines the mapping from the problem coordinate system onto the normalized device coordinate (NDC) space which can be regarded as an abstract viewing surface.

The normalization transformation is specified by defining the limits of a rectangular area, called a window, in problem coordinates. The window is mapped linearly onto a specified rectangular area, called a viewport, in NDC space.

Execution of a set-statement with the keyword WINDOW will establish the boundaries of the window. The parameters represent the problem coordinates of the left, right, bottom, and top edges, in that order, of the window rectangle. At the start of program execution the window values are (0, 1, 0, 1).

Execution of a set-statement with the keyword VIEWPORT will establish the viewport boundaries. The parameters represent the normalized device coordinates of the left, right, bottom, and top edges, in that order, of the viewport rectangle. Viewport coordinates must not be less than zero not more than one. The value of the left coordinate will be less than the right, and the bottom less than the top. At the start of program execution the viewport values are (0, 1, 0, 1).

The viewport may also be used to define a clipping rectangle. Execution of a set- statement with the keyword CLIP will enable or disable clipping to the viewport boundary depending on whether the value of the string-expression is "ON" or "OFF". The letters in the value of the string-expression may be any combination of upper-case and lower-case. At the start of program execution, clipping will be enabled.

A device transformation is used to map a rectangle in NDC space called a device window uniformly onto a rectangle on a physical surface called a device viewport. This transformation will perform equal scaling with a positive scale for both axes. To ensure equal scaling, the device transformation maps the device window onto the largest rectangle that can fit within the device viewport such that the aspect ratio of the device window is preserved and the lower-left corner of the device window is mapped onto the lower-left corner of the device viewport.

Execution of a set-statement with the keyword DEVICE WINDOW will establish the boundaries of the device window. The parameters represent the normalized device coordinates of the left, right, bottom, and top edges, in that order, of the device widow rectangle. These coordinates will not be less than zero not greater than one. The value of the left coordinate will be less than the right, and the bottom less than the top. At the start of program execution, the device window values are (0, 1, 0, 1). To ensure that no output outside the device window is displayed, clipping takes place at the device window boundaries. This clipping may not be disabled. Execution of a set-statement with the keywords DEVICE WINDOW will cause the display surface to be cleared if it is not already clear.

Execution of a set-statement with the keywords DEVICE VIEWPORT will establish the boundaries of the device viewport. The parameters represent the coordinates of the left, right, bottom, and top edges, in that order of the device viewport rectangle. Units for the device viewport will be meters on a device capable of producing a precisely scaled image and appropriate device dependent coordinates otherwise. The left and bottom edges of a display surface are represented by the coordinate value zero. At the start of program execution, the device viewport is the entire screen. Execution of a set-statement with the keywords DEVICE VIEWPORT will cause the display surface to be cleared if it is not already clear.

If a status-clause is included in an ask-statement, a status associated with the execution of the ask-statement will be returned in the numeric-variable. If the statement returned meaningful values for the ask-object, a value of zero will be returned in the status-clause. If the ask-statement could not return meaningful values for the ask-object a nonzero value will be returned in the status-clause that is defined with the semantics of the particular ask-object. If an ask-statement with a particular ask-object is always expected to return meaningful values, the semantics for that ask-object do not specify alternate status values and zero will always be returned.

Execution of an ask-statement with one of the keywords WINDOW, VIEWPORT, DEVICE WINDOW, or DEVICE VIEWPORT will provide the current values for the specified rectangle. Values for the left, right, bottom and top sides, respectively, will be assigned to the boundary-variables equal to the values last established by a set- statement, or, if no appropriate set-statement has been executed, equal to the default value.

Execution of an ask-statement with the keywords DEVICE SIZE will assign to the first numeric variable the size in the horizontal direction and will assign to the second numeric variable the size in the vertical direction of the available display surface. The string-variable will be assigned the value "METERS" if the sizes are in meters or the value "OTHER" if the units of measure are device coordinates of other units. The values "METERS" and "OTHER" will consist of upper-case-letters.

Execution of an ask-statement with the keyword CLIP will assign the value "ON" to the string-variable if clipping is enabled and the value "OFF" if it is disabled. The values returned will be all upper-case-letters.

15.1.5 Exceptions

- The boundaries in a set-statement specify a rectangle of zero width or height (11051, nonfatal: continue with current values).
- The boundaries in a set-statement with the keywords VIEWPORT, DEVICE WINDOW, or DEVICE VIEWPORT specify a rectangle of negative width or height (11051, nonfatal: continue with current values).
- A boundary of the viewport is not in the range [0, 1] (11052 nonfatal: continue with current values).
- A boundary of the device window is not in the range [0, 1] (11053, nonfatal: continue with current values).
- A boundary of the device viewport is not in the display space (11054, nonfatal: continue with current values).
- The value of the string-expression in a set-statement with the keyword CLIP is neither M ON M nor "OFF" after conversion to upper-case (4101, nonfatal: continue with current value).

15.1.6 Remarks

The manner in which a particular graphic display device is selected by a program is implementation-defined.

The meaning of a window with the left edge greater than the right or the bottom edge greater than the top is implementation-defined. If possible, implementations should provide appropriately inverted images. The effect of all graphic output is defined in terms of the abstract problem space, in which lower values are to the left and down, and higher values to the right and up. When this problem space is mapped to NDC, it may be inverted as indicated by the order of the WINDOW boundaries. This relaxes the GKS rule that states that reversal window coordinates causes an error.

SET WINDOW, SET VIEWPORT, SET DEVICE WINDOW, and SET DEVICE VIEWPORT correspond to the GKS functions SET WINDOW, SET VIEWPORT, SET WORKSTATION WINDOW, and SET WORKSTATION VIEWPORT, respectively. The GKS transformation number is one in these statements as defined above. The GKS workstation number is #0 in these statements.

SET CLIP corresponds to the GKS function SET CLIPPING INDICATOR.

ASK WINDOW and ASK VIEWPORT correspond to the GKS function INQUIRE NORMALIZATION TRANSFORMATION for normalization transformation one.

ASK CLIP corresponds to the GKS function INQUIRE CLIPPING INDICATOR.

ASK DEVICE WINDOW and ASK DEVICE VIEWPORT correspond to the current workstation window and current workstation viewport parameters, respectively, of the GKS function INQUIRE WORKSTATION TRANSFORMATION with a workstation identifier of one.

ASK DEVICE VIEWPORT before any SET DEVICE VIEWPORT may be used to find the device coordinates of the full available device surface.

ASK DEVICE SIZE corresponds to the device coordinate units and maximum display surface size in device coordinate units parameters of the GKS function INQUIRE MAXIMUM DISPLAY SURFACE SIZE.

15.2 Attributes and Screen Control

15.2.1 General Description

A graphical display device may possess several styles of lines or points, each with a particular width or texture. A particular style may be selected for graphic output. A graphic device also may be able to draw lines and/or fill areas in a variety of colors. Particular colors may be selected for line drawing and screen background.

The current style and color of the geometric object may be determined by ask- statements. The number of colors and the number of line or point styles available may also be determined by ask-statements.

The clear-statement clears the entire screen, returning it to its background color. For hard-copy devices, the clear-statement causes the paper to advance, the pen to move aside, or similar action.

This Standard provides text of one style and size that will be output horizontally with the initial-point at the left.

15.2.2 Syntax

1. imperative-statement > clear-statement

2. clear-statement = CLEAR

3. set-object > primitive-1 STYLE index / primitive-2 COLOR index

4. primitive-2 = primitive-1 /TEXT / AREA

5. primitive-1 = POINT / LINE

6. rgb-list > [removed]

7. ask-object > primitive-1 STYLE numeric-variable / primitive-2 COLOR numeric-variable/ MAX primitive-1 STYLE numeric-variable / MAX COLOR numeric-variable

8. mix-list = [removed]

9. text-facet = [removed]

15.2.3 Examples

```
LINE STYLE 2
TEXT COLOR 5
Max color color__max
Max point style PtStyles
```

15.2.4 Semantics

Execution of a clear-statement will clear the graphic display if not already clear. For soft-copy devices, it will erase the screen. For hard-copy devices, it will advance the medium or allow the device operator to change it.

Execution of a set-statement with the keywords LINE STYLE or POINT STYLE will cause the index to be evaluated by rounding to obtain an integer N and will establish the style for subsequent lines or points to be the Nth one of the set of available line or point styles. The number of line styles available is implementation-defined, but will be at least three. A line style of one must correspond to drawing of solid lines. A line style of two will correspond to drawing of dashed lines. A line style of three will correspond to dotted lines. All other values for line style are implementation-defined. At the initiation of program execution, the line style will be one.

Point styles produce centered symbols. The number of point styles is implementation- defined, but will be at least three. A point style of one must correspond to a dot (.), a point style of two to a plus sign (+), a point style of three to an asterisk (*)• All other values for point-style are implementation-defined. At the start of program execution, the point style will be three.

Execution of an ask-statement with the keywords LINE STYLE or POINT STYLE will assign the number of the actual current line style or point style to the numeric- variable.

Execution of an ask-statement with the keywords MAX LINE STYLE or MAX POINT STYLE will assign to the numeric-variable the largest value of LINE STYLE or POINT STYLE, respectively, available.

All values for style will be valid from one to the number returned by ASK MAX POINT STYLE or ASK MAX LINE STYLE.

Execution of a set-statement with the one of the keyword pairs POINT COLOR, LINE COLOR, TEXT COLOR, or AREA COLOR will cause the index to be evaluated by rounding to obtain an integer N and will establish the color index of subsequent points, lines, text, or filled areas to be the Nth one of the set of colors, if possible with the current graphics device. This color is called a foreground color. At the initiation of execution, the color associated with each index is implementation-defined, and the foreground color indices will all have the value one. The number of colors available is implementation-defined.

Execution of an ask-statement with one of the keyword pairs POINT COLOR, LINE COLOR, TEXT COLOR, or AREA COLOR will assign to the numeric-variable the current value of the color index for points, lines, text or filled areas, as appropriate.

Execution of an ask-statement with the keywords MAX COLOR will assign to the numeric-variable the largest distinct value available as an index for SET POINT COLOR, SET LINE COLOR, SET TEXT COLOR, or SET AREA COLOR. All values for color index from zero to this value should be valid.

15.2.5 Exceptions

- A color index in a set-statement with the keywords POINT COLOR, LINE COLOR, TEXT COLOR, or AREA COLOR is less than zero or greater than the maximum color index for the implementation (11085, nonfatal: use the implementation default).

- The value of the numeric-expression in a set-statement with the keywords LINE STYLE is less than or equal to zero or greater than the maximum style available (11062, nonfatal: use the value one).

- The value of the numeric-expression in a set-statement with the keywords POINT STYLE is less than or equal to zero or greater than the maximum style available (11056, nonfatal: use the value three).

15.2.6 Remarks

It is recommended that implementations make the value returned by ASK MAX COLOR the same as the number of colors (not counting background color) available for simultaneous display, not the total number of distinct colors available on the device.

The CLEAR statement corresponds to the GKS function CLEAR WORKSTATION (#0, CONDITIONALLY). SET LINE STYLE and SET POINT STYLE corresponds to the GKS functions SET LINETYPE and SET MARKER TYPE, respectively. SET LINE COLOR, SET POINT COLOR, SET TEXT COLOR, and SET AREA COLOR correspond to the GKS functions SET POLYLINE COLOUR INDEX, SET POLYMARKER COLOUR INDEX, SET TEXT COLOUR INDEX, and SET FILL AREA COLOUR INDEX, respectively.

The following ask-objects correspond to various parameters of the GKS function INQUIRE CURRENT INDIVIDUAL ATTRIBUTE VALUES: LINESTYLE is linetype, POINSTYLE is marker type, LINE COLOR is polyline color index, POINT COLOR is polymarker color index, TEXT COLOR is text color index and AREA COLOR is fill area color index.

15.3 Graphic Output

15.3.1 General Description

The statements described in this section are used to generate various kinds of graphic output. The user may cause points, line segments, or filled-in areas to be 144 drawn on the screen. There is a facility for including text within the drawing. The effect of the graphic output statements depends on the current values of the various

set-objects described in section 13.1 and 13.2.

15.3.2 Syntax

    1. imperative-statement > graphic-output-statement

    2. graphic-output-statement > geometric-statement / graphic-text-statement

    3. geometric-statement > graphic-verb geometric-object colon point-list

4. graphic-verb > GRAPH

5. geometric-object = POINTS / LINES / AREA

6. point-list = coordinate-pair (semicolon coordinate-pair)*

7. coordinate-pair = numeric-expression comma numeric-expression

8. array-geometric-statement = [removed]

9. size-select = [removed]

10. array-point-list = [removed]

11. graphic-text-statement = graphic-verb TEXT initial-point (comma USING image colon expression-list / colon string-expression)

12. initial-point = comma AT coordinate-pair

13. array-cells-statement = [removed]

14. point-pair = [removed]

A graphic-output-statement with LINES as the geometric-object must contain at least two coordinate-pairs in its point-list. A graphic-output-statement with AREA as the geometric-object must contain at least three coordinate-pairs in its point-list.

15.3.3 Examples
```
GRAPH LINES: 3,4; 5,6; 66.66,77.77
GRAPH TEXT, AT XP, YP: "here is the label: " & TEXT$
GRAPH TEXT, AT 0,Y_VALUE, USING "##. ## ": Y_VALUE
```

15.3.4 Semantics
The graphic-output-statement

Graphic-output-statements are the means by which the user generates all graphic output. The geometric-statement is used to draw a series of marked points, a contiguous set of line segments, or a filled polygon area. The graphic-text-statement produces alphanumeric labels.

The geometric-statement

The geometric-statement makes use of a sequence of points specified in problem coordinates. That sequence is determined by the coordinate-pairs in the point-list, the first coordinate-pair designating the first point and so on through the end of the point-list.

If the geometric-object is POINTS, then a point marker of the style and color indicated by the current value of POINT STYLE and POINT COLOR will be drawn at each point in the sequence. If the geometric-object is LINES, then a line segment will be drawn connecting each successive pair of points in the sequence, the first to the second, the second to the third, and so on. Thus, the number of line segments will be one fewer than the number of points in the sequence. The style and color of the segments are determined by the current value of LINE STYLE and LINE COLOR. If the geometric-object is AREA, then a filled polygon is drawn whose edges consist of the sequence of line segments as described above for LINES. If the first and last points in the sequence are not coincident, then the line segment joining them completes the outline. The color of the interior and edge is determined by the current value of AREA COLOR. The interior of the polygon is defined as the set of all points (pixels) such that any line segment beginning at that point and extended indefinitely in any direction will cross the polygon boundary an odd number of times. The fill pattern will be solid on devices where this is possible.

The graphic-text-statement

The graphic-text-statement draws a label consisting of the string of characters generated by its string-expression, or by its image and expression-list. The characters used for labels will have an implementation-defined size and style. The effect of clipping on characters which lie partly in and partly out of the viewport on the screen is implementation-defined.

15.3.5 Exceptions
- A graphic-output-statement with `LINES` as the geometric-object specifies fewer than two points (11100, fatal)
- A graphic-output-statement with `AREA` as the geometric-object specifies fewer than three points (11100, fatal)

15.3.6 Remarks

The graphic-text-statement is designed to give easy access to a device's hardware generated character set.

Text is described with respect to problem coordinates and may become distorted when the aspect ratio of the window and viewport differ.

If a device is unable to fill a polygon, it is recommended that the outline of the polygon be drawn and the interior be hashed or shaded in a manner corresponding to the current color number.

It is recommended that the result of filling an area consisting solely of colinear points be a line segment through those points, that filling or drawing a line through a set of coincident points result in a dot being drawn.

`GRAPH POINTS` correspond to the `GKS` function `POLYMARKER`. `GRAPH LINES` correspond to the `GKS` function `POLYLINE`. `GRAPH AREA` correspond to the `GKS` function `FILL AREA`. `GRAPH TEXT` is an extension of the `GKS` function `TEXT` in that it allows formatting of text with `USING`.

APPENDIX 1

ORGANIZATION OF THE U/PL STANDARD

This Standard is organized into a number of sections, each of which covers a group of related features of . Each section is divided further to treat particular features of U/PL . The final subdivisions of each section are used as follows:

Subsection 1- General Description
This subsection briefly describes the features of to be treated.

Subsection 2 - Syntax
The exact syntax of features of the language is describes in a modified context-free grammar or Backus-Naur Form. The details of this method of syntax specification are described in 3.1.

In order to keep the syntax reasonably simple the syntax specification will allow some constructions which, strictly speaking, are not legal according to this Standard; e.g., it will allow the generation of the statement

```
SET X = A(+1) + A(1,2)
```

in which the array A occurs with differing numbers of subscripts. Rather than ruling such constructions out by a more complicated formal syntax, this Standard instead rules them out by placing restrictions on that syntax.

The primary goal of the syntax is to define the notion of a program and its constituent parts. In addition, the syntax defines several other items which are not needed for the definition of a program. These include the input-prompt, which is output to request input, the input-reply and line-input-reply, which are strings supplied in response to a request for input.

Subsection 3 - Examples
A short list of valid examples that can be generated by the constructs in Subsection 2 is given. Examples are not given for all constructs as many are self-evident.

Subsection 4 - Semantics

The semantic rules in this Standard assign a meaning to the constructions generated according to the syntax.

Subsection 5 Exceptions

This subsection contains a list of those exception conditions which a standard-conforming implementation must recognize. Exception numbers (values of the EXTYPE function) are also given.

Subsection 6 - Remarks

This subsection contains remarks which point out certain features of this Standard as well as remarks which make recommendations concerning the implementation of a language processor in an operating environment.

APPENDIX 2

COMBINED LIST OF CONSTRUCT RULES

access-mode = ACCESS (INPUT / OUTPUT / OUTIN / string-expression)

actual-array = array-name

array-assignment = numeric-array-assignment / string-array-assignment

array-declaration = numeric-array-declaration / string-array-declaration

array-input-statement = MAT INPUT input-modifier-list? (redim-array-list / variable-length-vector) / MAT INPUT channel-expression input-control colon (redim-array-list / variable-length-vector)

array-line-input-statement = MAT LINE INPUT input-modifier-list? redim-string-array-list / MAT LINE INPUT channel-expression input-control colon redim-string-array-list

array-list = array-name (comma array-name)*

array-name = numeric-array / string-array

array-output-list = array-name (comma array-name)* semicolon?

array-display-list = array-name (display-separator array-name)* display-separator?

array-display-statement = MAT DISPLAY (array-display-list / (USING image colon array-output-list) / MAT DISPLAY channel-expression display-control colon (array-display-list / array output-list)

array-read-statement = MAT READ (missing-recovery colon)? redim-array-list / MAT READ channel-expression read-control colon redim-array-list

array-rewrite-statement = MAT REWRITE channel-expression rewrite-control colon array-list

array-write-statement = MAT WRITE channel-expression write-control colon array-list

ask-attribute-name = core-attribute-name / expanded-attribute-name

ask-io-item = (MARGIN / ZONEWIDTH) numeric-variable

ask-io-list = ask-io-item (comma ask-io-item)*

ask-item = ask-attribute-name variable variable*

ask-item-list = ask-item (comma ask-item)*

ask-object = WINDOW boundary-variables / VIEWPORT boundary-variables / DEVICE WINDOW boundary-variables / DEVICE VIEWPORT boundary-variables / CLIP string variable / DEVICE SIZE numeric-variable comma numeric-variable comma string-variable / primitive-1 STYLE numeric-variable / primitive-2 COLOR numeric-variable / MAX COLOR numeric-variable

ask-statement = ASK ask-io-list / ASK channel-setter ask-item-list / ASK ask-object status-clause?

block = statement-line / loop / if-block / select-block / image-line

bound-argument = left-parenthesis actual-array (comma index)? right-parenthesis

boundaries = boundary comma boundary comma boundary comma boundary

boundary = numeric-expression

boundary-variables = numeric-variable comma numeric-variable comma numeric-variable comma numeric-variable

bounds = left-parenthesis bounds-range (comma bounds-range)* right-parenthesis

bounds-range = signed-integer TO signed-integer / signed-integer

break-statement = BREAK

call-statement = CALL subprogram-name procedure-argument-list?

case-block = case-line block*

case-else-block = case-else-line block*

case-else-line = line-number CASE ELSE tail

case-item = constant / range

case-line = line-number case-statement tail

case-list = case-item (comma case-item)*

case-statement = CASE case-list

cause-statement = CAUSE EXCEPTION exception-type

channel-expression = number-sign index

channel-number = number-sign integer

channel-setter = channel-expression colon

character = quotation-mark / non-quote-character

clear-statement = CLEAR

close-statement = CLOSE channel-expression

collate-sequence = COLLATE (STANDARD / NATIVE / string-expression)

comparison = numeric-expression relation numeric-expression / string-expression relation string-expression

concatenation = ampersand

conditional-statement = if-statement / on-gosub-statement / on-goto-statement

conjunction = relational-term (AND relational-term)*

constant = numeric-constant / string-constant

control-transfer = gosub-statement / goto-statement / if-statement / io-recovery / on-gosub-statement / on-goto-statement

control-variable = simple-numeric-variable

coordinate-pair = numeric-expression comma numeric-expression

core-attribute-name = ACCESS / DATUM / ERASABLE / FILETYPE / MARGIN / NAME / ORGANIZATION / POINTER / RECSIZE / RECTYPE / SETTER / ZONEWIDTH

core-file-attribute = access-mode / file-organization / record-type / record-size

core-file-org-value = SEQUENTIAL / STREAM

core-record-setter = BEGIN / END / NEXT / SAME

core-record-type-value = DISPLAY / INTERNAL

data-list = datum (comma datum)*

data-statement = DATA data-list

datum = constant / unquoted-string

debug-statement = DEBUG (ON / OFF)

declarative-statement = data-statement / declare-statement / dimension-statement / null-statement / option-statement / remark-statement / template-statement

declare-statement = DECLARE type-declaration

def-statement = numeric-def-statement / string-def-statement

def-type = DEF function-list

defined-function = numeric-defined-function / string-defined-function / fixed-defined-function

delete-control = (comma delete-control-item)*

delete-control-item = missing-recovery / record-setter

delete-statement = DELETE channel-expression delete-control

detached-handler = handler-line exception-handler end-handler-line

digit = 0/1/2/3/4/5/6/7/8/9

digit-place = asterisk / number-sign / percent-sign

dimension-list = array-declaration (comma array-declaration)*

dimension-statement = DIM dimension-list

disjunction = conjunction (OR conjunction)*

do-body = block* loop-line

do-line = line-number do-statement tail

do-loop = do-line do-body

do-statement = DO exit-condition?

double-quote = quotation-mark quotation-mark

e-format-item = (i-format-item / f-format-item) circumflex-accent circumflex-accent circumflex-accent circumflex-accent*

else-block = else-line block*

else-line = line-number ELSE tail

elseif-block = elseif-then-line block*

elseif-then-line = line-number ELSEIF relational-expression THEN tail

end-function-line = line-number END FUNCTION tail

end-handler-line = line-number END HANDLER tail

end-if-line = line-number END IF tail

end-line = line-number end-statement tail

end-of-line = (implementation-defined)

end-select-line = line-number END SELECT tail

end-statement = END

end-sub-line = line-number end-sub-statement tail

end-sub-statement = END SUB

end-when-line = line-number END WHEN tail

Expanded-attribute-name = RECORD / KEY / COLLATE

Expanded-file-attribute = collate-sequence

Expanded-file-org-value = RELATIVE / KEYED

Expanded-record-setter = RECORD index / KEY (exact-search / inexact-search) string-expression

Expanded-record-type-value = NATIVE

equality-relation = equals-sign / not-equals

erase-statement = ERASE REST? channel-expression

exception-handler = block*

exception-type = index

exit-condition = (WHILE / UNTIL) relational-expression

exit-do-statement = EXIT DO

exit-for-statement = EXIT FOR

exit-function-statement = EXIT FUNCTION

exit-handler-statement = EXIT HANDLER

exit-sub-statement = EXIT SUB

expression = numeric-expression / string-expression

expression-list = expression (comma expression)*

exrad = E sign? integer

external-function-def = external-function-line unit-block* end-function-line

external-function-line = line-number EXTERNAL FUNCTION (numeric-defined-function / (string-defined-function length-max?)) function-parm-list? tail / line-number EXTERNAL FUNCTION fixed-defined-function function-parm-list? tail

external-function-type = EXTERNAL FUNCTION function-list

external-sub-def = external-sub-line unit-block* end-sub-line

external-sub-line = line-number EXTERNAL sub-statement tail

external-sub-type = EXTERNAL SUB sub-list

f-format-item = period number-sign number-sign* / i-format-item period number-sign*

factor = primary (circumflex-accent primary)*

field-specifier = numeric-specifier / string-specifier

file-attribute = core-file-attribute

file-attribute-list = (comma file-attribute)*

file-name = string-expression

file-organization = ORGANIZATION (file-organization-value / string-expression)

file-organization-value = core-file-org-value / expanded-file-org-value

fixed-declaration = simple-numeric-variable fixed-point-type? / numeric-array-declaration fixed-point-type?

fixed-defined-function = numeric-defined-function

fixed-field-count = SKIP? (integer OF)?

fixed-formal-array = formal-array fixed-point-type

fixed-point-size = integer-size period? / integer-size? period fraction-size

fixed-point-type = asterisk fixed-point-size

floating-characters = (plus-sign* / minus-sign*) dollar-sign? / dollar-sign* (plus-sign / minus-sign)?

for-body = block* next-line

for-line = line-number for-statement tail

for-loop = for-line for-body

for-statement = FOR control-variable equals-sign initial-value TO limit (STEP increment)?

formal-array = array-name left-parenthesis comma* right-parenthesis

format-item = (justifier? floating-characters (i-format-item / f-format-item / e-format-item)) / justifier

format-string = literal-string (format-item literal-string)*

formatted-display-list = USING image (colon output-list)?

fraction = period integer

fraction-size = integer

function-arg-list = left-parenthesis function-argument (comma function-argument)* right-parenthesis

function-argument = expression / actual-array

function-def = internal-function-def / external-function-def

function-list = defined-function (comma defined-function)*

function-parameter = simple-variable / formal-array / numeric-fixed-parameter

function-parm-list = left-parenthesis function-parameter (comma function-parameter)* right-parenthesis

geometric-object = POINTS / LINES / AREA

geometric-statement = graphics-verb geometric-object colon point-list

gosub-statement = (GOSUB / GO SUB) line-number

go to-statement = (GOTO / GO TO) line-number

graphic-output-statement = geometric-statement / graphic-text-statement

graphic-text-statement = graphic-verb TEXT initial-point (comma USING image colon expression-list / colon string-expression)

graphic-verb = GRAPH

handler-line = line-number HANDLER handler-name tail

handler-name = routine-identifier

handler-return-statement = RETRY / CONTINUE

i-format-item = digit-place digit-place* (comma digit-place digit-place*)*

identifier = numeric-identifier / string-identifier / routine-identifier

identifier-character = letter / digit / underline

if-block = if-then-line then-block elseif-block* else-block? end-if-line

if-clause = imperative-statement / line-number

if-statement = IF relational-expression THEN if-clause (ELSE if-clause)?

if-then-line = line-number IF relational-expression THEN tail

image = line-number / string-expression

image-line = line-number IMAGE colon format-string end-of-line

imperative-statement = array-assignment / array-input-statement / array-line-input-statement / array-display-statement / array-read-statement / array-write-statement / ask-statement / break-statement / call-statement / cause-statement / close-statement / debug-statement / erase-statement / exit-do-statement / exit-for-statement / exit-function-statement / exit-sub-statement / gosub-statement / goto-statement / input-statement / let-statement / line-input-statement / link-statement / numeric-function-set-statement / open-statement / display-statement / randomize-statement / read-statement / restore-statement / return-statement / set-statement / stop-statement / string-function-let-statement / trace-statement / write-statement / rewrite-statement / array-rewrite-statement / delete-statement / clear-statement / graphic-output-statement

increment = numeric-expression

index = numeric-expression

initial-number = line-number

initial-point = comma AT coordinate-pair

initial-value = numeric-expression

input-control = (comma input-control-item)*

input-control-item = core-record-setter / missing-recovery / prompt-specifier / timeout-expression / time-inquiry

input-modifier = prompt-specifier / timeout-expression / time-inquiry

input-modifier-list = input-modifier (comma input-modifier)* colon

input-prompt = [implementation-defined]

input-reply = data-list comma? end-of-line

input-statement = INPUT input-modifier-list? variable-list / INPUT channel-expression input-control colon variable-list (comma SKIP REST)?

integer = digit digit*

integer-size = integer

internal-def-line = line-number def-statement tail

internal-function-def = internal-def-line / internal-function-line block* end-function-line

internal-function-line = line-number FUNCTION (numeric-defined-function / (string-defined-function length-max?)) function-parm-list? tail / line-number FUNCTION fixed-defined-function function-parm-list? tail

internal-function-type = FUNCTION function-list

internal-proc-def = internal-function-def / internal-sub-def / detached-handler

internal-sub-def = internal-sub-line block* end-sub-line

internal-sub-line = line-number sub-statement tail

internal-sub-type = SUB sub-list

io-qualifier = INPUT / OUTPUT / OUTIN

io-recovery = missing-recovery / not-missing-recovery

io-recovery-action = exit-do-statement / exit-for-statement / line-number

justifier = greater-than-sign / less-than-sign

length-max = asterisk integer

letter = upper-case-letter / lower-case-letter

limit = numeric-expression

line = case-line / case-else-line / do-line / else-line / elseif-then-line / end-function-line / end-handler-line / end-if-line / end-line / end-select-line / end-sub-line / end-when-line / external-function-line / external-sub-line / for-line / handler-line / interna1-def-line / internal-function-line / internal-sub-line / if-then-line / image-line / loop-line / next-line / program-name-line / remark-line / select-line / statement-line / use-line / when-use-name-line

line-continuation = ampersand space* tail ampersand

line-input-reply = character* end-of-line

line-input-statement = LINE INPUT input-modifier-list? string-variable-list / LINE INPUT channel-expression input-control colon string-variable-list

line-number = digit digit*

link-statement = LINK program-designator (WITH function-arg-list)?

literal-item = letter /digit / apostrophe / colon / equals-sign / exclamation-mark / left-parenthesis / question-mark / right-parenthesis / semicolon /slant / space / underline

literal-string = literal-item*

loop = do-loop / for-loop

loop-line = line-number loop-statement tail

loop-statement = LOOP exit-condition?

lower-case-letter = a / b / c / d / e / f / g / h / I / j / k / l / m / n / o / p / q / r / s / t / u / v / w / x / y / z

main-program = unit-block* end-line

maxsize-argument = left-parenthesis actual-array right-parenthesis

missing-recovery = IF MISSING THEN io-recovery-action

multiplier = asterisk / slant

next-line = line-number next-statement tail

next-statement = NEXT control-variable

non-quote-character = ampersand / apostrophe / asterisk / circumflex-accent / colon / comma / dollar-sign / equals-sign / exclamation-mark / greater-than-sign / left-parenthesis / less-than-sign / number-sign / percent-sign / question-mark / right-parenthesis / semicolon / slant / underline / unquoted-string-character

not-equals = less-than-sign greater-than-sign / greater-than-sign less-than-sign

not-greater = less-than-sign equals-sign / equals-sign less-than-sign

not-less = greater-than-sign equals-sign / equals-sign greater-than-sign

not-missing-recovery = IF THERE THEN io-recovery-action

numeric-array = numeric-identifier

numeric-array-assignment = MAT numeric-array equals-sign numeric-array-expression

numeric-array-declaration = numeric-array bounds

numeric-array-element = numeric-array subscript-part

numeric-array-expression =(numeric-array numeric-array-operator)? numeric-array / scalar-multiplier numeric-array / numeric-array-value / numeric-array-function-ref

numeric-array-function-ref = (TRN / INV) left-parenthesis numeric-array right-parenthesis

numeric-array-operator = sign / asterisk

numeric-array-value = scalar-multiplier? (CON / IDN / ZER) redim?

numeric-constant = sign? numeric-rep

numeric-declaration = simple-numeric-variable / numeric-array-declaration

numeric-def-statement = DEF numeric-defined-function function-parm-list? equals-sign numeric-expression / DEF fixed-defined-function function-parm-list? equals-sign numeric-expression

numeric-defined-function = numeric-identifier

numeric-expression = sign? term (sign terra)*

numeric-field-size = fixed-point-size / E

numeric-fixed parameter = simple-numeric-variable fixed-point-type / fixed-formal-array

numeric-function = numeric-defined-function / numeric-supplied-function

numeric-function-set-statement= SET numeric-defined-function equals-sign numeric-expression

numeric-function-ref = numeric-function function-arg-list? / MAXLEN left-parenthesis (simple-string-variable / string-array) right-parenthesis / MAXSIZE maxsize-argument / SIZE bound-argument / LBOUND bound-argument / UBOUND bound-argument / DET (left-parenthesis numeric-array right-parenthesis) / DOT left-parenthesis numeric-array comma numeric-array right-parenthesis

numeric-identifier = letter identifier-character*

numeric-set-statement = SET numeric-variable-list equals-sign numeric-expression

numeric-rep = significand exrad?

numeric-specifier = NUMERIC asterisk numeric-field-size

numeric-supplied-function = ABS / ACOS / ANGLE / ASIN / ATN / CEIL / COS / COSH / COT / CSC / DATE / DEG / EPS / EXP / FP / MAXNUM / INT / IP / LOG / LOGIO / L0G2 / MAX / MIN / MOD / PI / RAD / REMAINDER / RND / ROUND / SEC / SGN / SIN / SINH / SQR / TAN / TANH / TIME / TRUNCATE / LEN / ORD / POS / VAL / EXLINE / EXTYPE

numeric-time-expression = numeric-expression

numeric-type = NUMERIC numeric-declaration (comma numeric-declaration)* / NUMERIC fixed-point-type? fixed-declaration (comma fixed-declaration)*

numeric-variable = simple-numeric-variable / numeric-array-element

numeric-variable-list = numeric-variable (comma numeric-variable)*

on-gosub-statement = ON index (GOSUB / GO SUB) line-number (comma line-number)* ELSE imperative-statement)?

on-goto-statement = ON index (GOTO / GO TO) line-number (comma line-number)* (ELSE imperative-statement)?

open-statement = OPEN channel-setter NAME file-name file-attribute-list

option = ARITHMETIC (DECIMAL / NATIVE / FIXED) / ANGLE (DEGREES / RADIANS) / COLATE (NATIVE / STANDARD) / BASE (0 / 1) / ARITHMETIC FIXED fixed-point-type

option-list = option (comma option)*

option-statement = OPTION option-list

other-character = [implementation-defined]

output-list = expression (comma expression)* semicolon?

plain-string-character = digit / letter / period / plus-sign / minus-sign

point-list = coordinate-pair (semicolon coordinate-pair)*

pointer-items = (pointer-control / io-recovery / pointer-control comma io-recovery)

primary = numeric-rep / numeric-variable / numeric-function-ref / left-parenthesis numeric-expression right-parenthesis

primitive-1 = POINT / LINE

primitive-2 = primitive-1 / TEXT / AREA

display-control = (comma display-control-item)*

display-control-item = core-record-setter / expanded-record-setter / not-missing-recovery / USING image

display-item = expression / tab-call

display-list = (display-item? display-separator)* display-item?

display-separator = comma / semicolon

display-statement= DISPLAY display-list / DISPLAY formatted-display-list / DISPLAY channel-expression display-control (colon (display-list / output-list))?

procedure = external-function-def / external-sub-def

procedure-argument = expression / actual-array / channel-expression

procedure-argument-list = left-parenthesis procedure-argument (comma procedure-argument)* right-parenthesis

procedure-parameter = simple-variable / formal-array / channel-number / numeric-fixed-parameter

procedure-parm-list = left-parenthesis procedure-parameter (comma procedure-parameter)*

procedure-part = remark-line* procedure

program = program-name-line? main-program procedure-part*

program-designator = string-expression

program-line = line-number (character / line-continuation)* end-of-line

program-name = routine-identifier

program-name-line = line-number PROGRAM program-name function-parm-list? tail

program-unit = main-program / procedure

prompt-specifier = PROMPT string-expression

protection-block = when-use-block / when-use-name-block

quoted-string = quotation-mark quoted-string-character* quotation-mark

quoted-string-character = double-quote / non-quote-character

randomize-statement = RSEED

range = (constant TO / IS relation) constant

read-control = (comma read-control-item)*

read-control-item = record-setter / missing-recovery / template-identifier

read-statement = READ (missing-recovery colon)? variable-list / READ channel-expression read-control colon variable-list (comma SKIP REST)?

record-setter = core-record-setter / expanded-record-setter

record-size = RECSIZE (VARIABLE / string-expression) (LENGTH index)?

record-type = RECTYPE (record-type-value / string-expression)

record-type-value = core-record-type-value / expanded-record-value

redim = left-parenthesis redim-bounds (comma redim-bounds)* right-parenthesis

redim-array = array-name redim?

redim-array-list = redim-array (comma redim-array)*

redim-bounds = (index TO)? index

redim-numeric-array = numeric-array redim?

redim-string-array = string-array redim?

redim-string-array-list = redim-string-array (comma redim-string-array)*

relation = equality-relation / greater-than-sign / less-than-sign / not-greater / not-less

relational-expression = disjunction

relational-primary = comparison / left-parenthesis relational-expression right-parenthesis

relational-term = NOT? relational-primary

remark-line = line-number (null-statement / remark-statement) end-of-line

remark-statement = REM remark-string

remark-string = character*

restore-statement = RESTORE line-number

return-statement = RETURN

rewrite-control = (comma rewrite-control-item)*

rewrite-control-item = missing-recovery / record-setter / template identifier

rewrite-statement = REWRITE channel-expression rewrite-control colon expression list

routine-identifier = letter identifier-character*

scalar-multiplier = primary asterisk

select-block = select-line remark-line* case-block case-block* case-else-block? end-select-line

select-line = line-number select-statement tail

select-statement = SELECT CASE expression

set-object = (MARGIN / ZONEWIDTH) index / channel-setter pointer-items / channel-setter (MARGIN / ZONEWIDTH) index / WINDOW boundaries / VIEWPORT boundaries / DEVICE WINDOW boundaries / DEVICE VIEWPORT boundaries / CLIP string-expression / primitive-1 STYLE index / primitive-2 COLOR index

set-statement = numeric-set-statement / string-set-statement

sign = plus-sign / minus-sign

signed-integer = sign? integer

significand = integer period? / integer? fraction

simple-numeric-variable = numeric-identifier

simple-string-declaration = simple-string-variable length-max?

simple-string-variable = string-identifier

simple-variable = simple-numeric-variable / simple-string-variable

statement = declarative-statement / imperative-statement / conditional-statement

statement-line = line-number statement tail

status-clause = STATUS numeric-variable

stop-statement = STOP

string-array = string-identifier

string-array-assignment = MAT string-array substring-qualifier? equals-sign string-array-expression

string-array-declaration = string-array bounds

string-array-element = string-array subscript-part

string-array-expression = string-array-primary (concatenation string-array-primary)? / string-primary concatenation string-array-primary / string-array-primary concatenation string-primary / string-array-value

string-array-primary = string-array substring-qualifier?

string-array-value = (string-primary concatenation)?

string-constant = quoted-string

string-declaration = simple-string-declaration / string-array-declaration length-max?

string-def-statement = DEF string-defined-function length-max? function-parm-list? equals-sign string-expression

string-defined-function = string-identifier

string-expression = string-primary (concatenation string-primary)*

string-field-size = integer

string-function = string-defined-function / string-supplied-function

string-function-set-statement = SET string-defined-function equals-sign string-expression

string-function-ref = string-function function-arg-list?

string-identifier = letter identifier-character* dollar-sign

string-set-statement = SET string-variable-list equals-sign string-expression

string-primary = string-constant / string-variable / string-function-ref / left-parenthesis string-expression right-parenthesis

string-specifier = STRING asterisk string-field-size

string-supplied-function = (CHR / DATE / LCASE / LTRIM / REPEAT / RTRIM / STR / TIME / UCASE / USING) dollar-sign / EXTEXT dollar-sign

string-type = STRING length-max? string-declaration (comma string-declaration)*

string-variable = (simple-string-variable / string-array-element) substring-qualifier?

string-variable-list = string-variable (comma string-variable)*

sub-list = subprogram-name (comma subprogram-name)*

sub-statement = SUB subprogram-name procedure-parm-list?

subprogram-def = internal-sub-def / external-sub-def

subprogram-name = routine-identifier

subscript = index

subscript-part = left-parenthesis subscript (comma subscript)* right-parenthesis

substring-qualifier = left-parenthesis index colon index right-parenthesis

tab-call = TAB left-parenthesis index right-parenthesis

tail = tail-comment? end-of-line

template-element = fixed-field-count (field-specifier / left-parenthesis template-element-list right-parenthesis) / variable-field-count field-specifier

template-element-list = template-element (comma template-element)*

template-identifier = WITH (line-number / string-expression)

template-statement = TEMPLATE colon template-element-list

term = factor (multiplier factor)*

then-block = block*

time-expression = numeric-time-expression / string-time-expression

time-inquiry = ELAPSED numeric-variable

timeout-expression = TIMEOUT numeric-time-expression

trace-statement = TRACE ON (TO channel-expression)?

type-declaration = numeric-type / string-type / def-type / internal-function-type / external-function-type / internal-sub-type / external-sub-type

unit-block = internal-proc-def / block

unquoted-string = plain-string-character / plain-string-character unquoted-string-character* plain-string-character

unquoted-string-character = space / plain-string-character

upper-case-letter = A/ B/ C/ D/ E/ F/ G/ H/ I/ J/ K/ L/ M/ N/O/P/Q/R/S/T/U/V/W/X/ Y / Z

use-line = line-number USE tail

variable = numeric-variable / string-variable

variable-field-count = question-mark OF

variable-length-vector = array-name left-parenthesis question-mark right-parenthesis

variable-list = variable (comma variable)*

when-block = block*

when-line = line-number WHEN EXCEPTION IN tail

when-use-block = when-line when-block use-line exception-handler end-when-line

when-use-name-block = when-use-name-line when-block end-when-line

when-use-name-line = line-number WHEN EXCEPTION USE handler-name tail

write-control = (comma write-control-item)*

write-control-item = record-setter / not-missing-recovery / template-identifier

write-statement = WRITE channel-expression write-control colon expression-list

APPENDIX 3

COMMON KEYWORDS, COMMANDS AND FUNCTIONS

ABS — The ABS function determines the absolute value of a number or numeric variable. A number's absolute value is its value without a + or - sign.

```
10 DISPLAY ABS(-435.28)
```

ACS - The ACS(n) function is used to compute the ARCCOS of the ratio n in radians (not in degrees). A radian is approximately 57 degrees.

```
10 A=ACS(N)
```

AND — AND may be used in several variations depending on the design of the U/PL implementation. Care should be taken when developing documentation to ensure that appropriate usage is defined:

- It is used in IF-THEN statements as a "logical math" operator.
- It may also be used to "logically" compare strings.
- It may be used to determine if the conditions specified by two relational operators are met.
- It may be used to compute the binary logical AND of two numbers using Boolean Algebra.

```
10 IF A=8 AND B=6 THEN 70
```

APPEND - APPEND is a command to combine a program from external storage (e.g. disk or SD card) with one already in memory. The line numbers of the program being brought in from "outside" must be larger than the last line number of the program already in memory.

ASC - The ASC function converts a character or string variable to its corresponding ASCII decimal number.

```
10 DISPLAY ACS("A")
```

ASET – The ASET(Pin#) Writes an analog value (PWM wave) to the assigned pin. Can be used to light a LED at varying brightness or drive a motor at various speeds. After a call to the ASET(Pin#), the pin will generate a steady rectangular wave of the specified duty cycle until the next call to the ASET(Pin#) or a call to DSET(Pin#) on the same pin.

```
10 ASET(5, HIGH)
```

ASN - The ASN(n) function is used to compute the ARCSIN in Radians (not in degrees) of the ratio n. A radian is approximately 57 degrees.

```
10 A=ACS(N)
```

AT - The AT function is used with DISPLAY statements to specify the DISPLAY statement's starting location. The AT function value may be a number, numeric variable, or mathematical operation. A comma or semi-colon must be inserted between the AT value and the string.

```
10 DISPLAY AT 40, "HELLO"
```

ATN - The ATN(n) function computes Arctangent in Radians (not in degrees) of the ratio n. A radian is approximately 57 degrees.

```
10 A=ACS(N)
```

AUTO - The AUTO command provides automatic insertion of program line numbers. The starting line number and the incremental value between lines can be specified in the AUTO command. For example, AUTO 100*5 sets the first line number at 100 and increments each successive line number by 5. This feature is very convenient when writing new programs. If the starting line number and increment value are not specified in the AUTO command, the system automatically sets the first line number at 10 and increments the line numbers by 10. If the AUTO command generates a line number that is already in use, an asterisk may appear following the number. This cautions the programmer that information typed into the system at that Line number will erase existing statements. The AUTO feature may be turned off to prevent this from happening. To turn off the AUTO feature, some systems require pressing the BREAK key, while others require typing a control C.

BASE - The BASE statement is used in some U/PL implementations to define the BASE (lowest) variable array element value as or 1.

        10 BASE 0

BEEP – The BEEP command plays a 1200Kz tone for 500 milliseconds from the system piezo-buzzer. The command may be used in immediate mode or as part of a program statement.

BLINKING – The BLINKING(Pin#, Duration) function sets an alternating digital HIGH and LOW signal at the supplied pin number for the supplied duration.

        10 BLINKING (4, 500)

BREAK - BREAK is used to direct one or more program lines to stop execution and place the system in the monitor or immediate mode, similar to a STOP statement. The BREAK statement can be used to cause any line number (or line numbers) to stop program execution by placing each line number (separated by a comma) after the BREAK statement.

        10 BREAK 10, 40, 50

CDBL - CDBL is used to change numbers or numeric variables from regular "single-precision" to "double-precision". Variables used in the CDBL function return to their original single-precision status if they are used again without the CDBL. Double-precision variables are capable of storing numbers containing 17 digits (only 16 digits are displayed). Single-precision variables are accurate to 6 digits. Great care must be used to ensure that the numbers which are used to create a double-precision answer are also double precision. If not, the answer will be a big long lie.

        10 DISPLAY "CDBL CHANGES X/Y FROM" ;X/Y;"TO ";CDBL(X)/CDBL(Y)

CHR$ - The CHR$ function is used to retrieve the single character represented by the decimal ASCII number code enclosed in parentheses.

        10 DISPLAY CHR$(X)

CINT - CINT is used to convert individual numbers or numeric variables to their integer value. Variables used in the CINT function return to their original precision if they are used again without the CINT function. Numbers are always rounded down — that is, the whole number remains the same regardless of the value of numbers removed to the right of the decimal point. When a negative number is integered, the resultant number will be rounded off to the next smaller whole number.

    10 CINT(N)

CLEAR — CLEAR is used to remove the resident program from RAM, reset all numeric variables to zero and erase data assigned to string variables.

    10 CLEAR

CLG - The CLG function is used to compute the value of the common (base 10) logarithm of any number (n) whose value is greater than 0.

    10 X=CLG(Y)

CLS - The CLS (clear screen) command is used to erase the entire screen instantly without disturbing the program. CLS can also be used as a program statement to clear the screen before starting a graphics display or a new "page" of displayed information.

10 CLS

COMMON - The COMMON statement is used to transfer values from one program to another. If each of two (or more) programs contains similar COMMON statements, when the second program is LINK-ed to the first, the current values stored in the variables named in COMMON will be available to the second program.

CONT - The CONTINUE command restarts program execution after it was "broken" due to a STOP statement, or use of a keyboard BREAK key. Unlike the RUN command, which causes execution to start at the program's beginning, CONT resumes execution at the line following the break and variables are not reset to zero. CONT has no application as a program statement since it is only used when the program has Stopped.

COS - The COS(A) function computes the COSINE of the angle A, when that value is expressed in Radians (not in degrees). One radian = approximately 57 degrees.

```
10 A=COS(N)
```

COSH - COSH(N) is a function that calculates the hyperbolic cosine of a number.

```
10 A=COSH(N)
```

DATA - A DATA statement contains data to be read by a READ statement. The items in the DATA statement must be separated by commas and may include both positive and negative numbers.

DEF - The DEF statement allows the user to define (create) new functions (most systems have some built in functions) which can then be used the same as any intrinsic (built in) function. The operation stored in the FN (variable) function by the DEF statement can be used to manipulate any number or numeric variable.

```
10 DEF FNA(N)=3*N-1
```

DEG - DEG is used as a command which causes the system to execute trigonometric functions in degrees (rather than in radians). One degree = approximately .02 radians.

DELAY - DELAY is used to suspend program execution for a specified time. In most U/PL implementations the time will be specified in milliseconds following execution of the DELAY command statement.

```
10 DELAY(500)
```

DIM - The dimension statement is used to establish the number of elements allowed in a numeric or string array. An array dimension is established by placing the array variable after the DIM statement, followed by the array size enclosed in parentheses. When the DIM statement is executed, the system sets the values stored in each designated array element to zero.

```
10 DIM A(10)
```

DISPLAY - DISPLAY has a wide range of uses. The most common is in program statements used to display variable values or whatever may be enclosed in quotes. For example, DISPLAY X displays the numeric value of the variable X, while DISPLAY "X" displays the letter X.

DRAW - DRAW is used to draw a pre-defined shape (numbered N) starting at location X,Y.

DSET - The DSET(Pin#) Writes an digital HIGH or LOW value to the assigned pin.

```
10 DSET(10,LOW)
```

EDUMP — The EDUMP(bytes) command is used to display the indicated number of bytes currently saved to the systems onboard EEPROM.

```
10 EDUMP(256)
```

ELIST - The ELIST command lists the program currently stored in the system EEPROM.

```
10 ELIST
```

ELOAD — The ELOAD command loads the program from the system EEPROM into the system RAM.

```
10 ELOAD
```

ELSE — ELSE is used to execute an alternate statement when the condition of an IF-THEN statement is not met.

```
10 IF X < 5 THEN 60 ELSE GOTO 90
```

END - The END statement is used to terminate execution of the program.

```
99 END
```

EQ – May be used as an alternate for the "=" as a relational operator. It may not be used as a variable assignment operator.

```
10 IF A EQ 10 THEN GOTO 60
```

ERASE – May be used to delete the resident program or data from the system EEPROM.

ERROR - ERROR ## is used to intentionally cause the system to report an ERROR. The nature of the error is specified by an error code in the ERROR statement. The ERROR statement is commonly used in programs to execute error trapping routines, or to DISPLAY a specified error message. Variables cannot be used as ERROR codes. Each code must be specified by an actual integer error code number.

ERUN – The ERUN command will cause the system to execute the program stored in the EEPROM. This may be used in immediate mode or as a system call from a program resident in RAM.

ESAVE – The ESAVE command copies the current program resident in RAM to the system EEPROM. If the program size exceeds the amount of EEPROM available in the system, the U/PL implementation must generate an error code to alert the user.

EXCHANGE - EXCHANGE is a statement that switches the values of two variables or array elements. For example, EXCHANGE A >B results in the original value of A being stored in B and the former value of B being stored in A. EXCHANGE is very useful for arranging values of an array in ascending or descending order.

```
50 EXCHANGE A,B
```

EXIT - EXIT is a statement to EXIT from a FOR-NEXT loop before that loop has completed the specified number of cycles. EXIT transfers program control to the line number designated and cancels the FOR-NEXT loop. The value of the loop counter at that time continues available for use in the rest of the program.

EXP - The EXP(n) function computes the natural logarithm's base value e (2.718282...) raised to the power of (n). This function is the opposite of the LOG function.

    10 X=EXP(N)

FILES — The FILES function lists all programs saved on a disk or SD Card available to the system. Depending on the U/PL implementation design, this may be a list of file names only or may include additional information such as file size, date created, date modified or last date accessed.

    10 FILES

FN - FN is a function that allows a "user-defined" process to be used as if it were a built-in function. The user-defined function is named by a letter following FN and accompanied by one or more values enclosed in parentheses, such as FNA(X,N). The DEF statement defines the process that will be executed when FN is used later.

    10 DEF FNA(X)=1/X

FNEND - The FNEND statement is used in systems which have the capability of defining and redefining a function at different points throughout a program. It ENDs the function's defining process. Each DEF statement which is spread out over more than one line must end with a FNEND statement, and the system cannot branch out of or into these DEF statements before the FNEND statement is executed.

FOR - The FOR statement is part of a FOR-TO-NEXT statement and is used to assign numbers to numeric variables within the range specified by FOR-TO. The first number immediately following the FOR is incremented by 1 each time its corresponding NEXT statement is executed. When the number following TO is exceeded, program execution continues at the line following the corresponding NEXT statement.

    10 FOR X=1 TO 5

GET - GET is a statement used to accept a single character from the keyboard without displaying it on the screen and without waiting for the RETURN key to be pressed. Its use is similar to INKEY$. With a numeric variable such as

GET A, GET accepts only numeric input. A string variable (e.g. GET A$) will accept input from any key except the STOP key.

    10 GET A$

GO - GO is used as part of GO TO and GO SUB statements. GO usually has meaning only when combined with another U/PL keyword.

GOSUB - GOSUB is used to branch out of a program's "mainstream" to a Subroutine. The GOSUB statement must be followed by a line number to indicate the first line of the subroutine to be executed. A RETURN statement must be used at the end of a subroutine's execution to return control from the subroutine to the main program.

    10 GOSUB 100

GOTO - The GOTO statement causes program execution to "jump" to a specified line number. Many implementations also accept this statement as two words; GOTO.

    100 GOTO 10

HOME - HOME is a command used to clear the screen and position the cursor in the upper left corner. It is similar to CLS found on other systems. HOME can also be included as a program statement to clear the screen before the program creates a graphics display.

    10 HOME

IF - The IF statement is part of the conditional branching statements IF-THEN, IF-GOTO, IF-GOSUB, IF-SET, etc., and is used to indicate the variable to be tested by one of the relational operators (see =,<,>,< = ,> = , <>). For example: IF X = 3 THEN 100 the system branches or "jumps" to line 100 IF X equals 3. If the condition is not met (i.e. X !=3), the test "falls through" and program execution continues on the next line. These conditional IF-THEN tests must be placed last on multiple statement lines because the system either branches to the indicated line number (if the test is true) or falls through to the next numbered line (if the test is false).

```
10 IF X=10 THEN 60
```

IF-GOTO - IF-GOTO is a conditional branching statement using one of the relational operators (see =, <, >,< = , > = , <>) When the condition of the IF-GOTO statement is met, the system executes the branching statement GOTO.

```
10 IF X=20 GOTO 60
```

IF-SET - The IF-SET statement is a conditional SET statement using one of the relational operators (see = ,<,>,< = ,> = , <>). When the condition of the IF-SET statement is met, the system assigns a value to the variable following SET.

```
10 IF X>20 SET X=10
```

IF-THEN - The IF-THEN statement is a conditional branching statement using one of the relational operators (see = ,<,>,< = ,> = , <>). When the condition of the IF-THEN statement is met, the system executes the branching statement number following THEN. For example, IF X = 3 THEN 100 tells the system to branch or "jump" to line 100 if X equals 3. If the condition is not met (i.e. X^3), the test "falls through" and program execution continues on the next line.

```
10 IF X=30 THEN 60
```

INKEY$ - The INKEY$ function is used to read a character from the keyboard each time INKEY$ is executed. Unlike the INPUT statement, INKEY$ does not halt execution waiting for the ENTER key to be pressed. The system just keeps "circling" until it receives a message from the keyboard. Until a key on the keyboard is pressed, INKEY$ simply reads an "empty" string (ASCII code of 0). Since INKEY$ doesn't wait for you to enter a character from the keyboard and "ENTER", it usually is placed in a program loop to repeatedly scan the keyboard looking for a pressed key.

```
10 IF INKEY$="X" GOTO 100
```

INPUT - The INPUT statement allows the user to assign data to variables from the keyboard. When the system executes an INPUT statement, it displays a question mark indicating it is waiting for you to assign a value to a variable. It will continue to wait until the ENTER (or RETURN) key is pressed.

```
10 INPUT X
```

INT - The INTeger function is used to round numbers off to their integer (whole number) value.

```
10 X=INT(X)
```

LEFT$ - The LEFT$(string,n) function is used to extract a specific number (n) of string characters starting from the left-most character in the string. The string must be enclosed in quotes or listed as a string variable. The number of characters (n) can be expressed as a variable, number or arithmetic operation. A comma must separate the string from the number.

LINEINPUT - LINEINPUT is similar to INPUT. It accepts an entire LINE of input up to a maximum of 254 characters and assigns it to a single string variable.

```
10 LINEINPUT N$
```

LINK - LINK is used to load a new program into the system's memory from an external device (such as disk or SD card) and execute that program without additional RUN commands. A program may LINK to any other program, including back to the starting one which may serve as a "menu". The main advantage of LINK-ing is that it permits consecutive execution of related programs automatically without needing to keep more than one of them actually in RAM at a given time. This is especially useful where there is a common file of DATA stored externally which can be accessed and manipulated by programs in the LINK.

If the values of variables are to be carried from one program to another, a separate file must be created for them. Before such a program is allowed to LINK to another, it must save the values of its variables in this file so the NEW program can read them back in prior to its execution.

LIST - The LIST command is used to display each program line in the numerical order in which it appears in the program. Some systems (or terminals) will scroll through the entire program list unless stopped by a specified key function. (Control C, Control S, SHIFT (a, etc.) Others will stop after displaying the first 12, 16, 24 or more lines, then advance one or more additional lines each time the up-arrow, down-arrow or other appropriate key is pressed. The LIST command can also be used in conjunction with a line number to specify a starting point other than at the beginning. Many systems will also accept a start and finish line number. For example, LIST 10-40 or LIST 10-40 will list only those program lines with numbers from 10 to 40.

LOAD - The LOAD command is used to load a program into the system from a disk or SD card.

LOG - The LOG(n) function computes the natural logarithm of any number (n) whose value is greater than 0.

```
10 L=LOG(N)
```

LOG10 - The LOG10(n) function computes the value of the common (base 10) logarithm of any number (n) whose value is greater than 0.

```
10 L=LOG10(N)
```

MAT INPUT - MAT INPUT is used to assign values to each element in an array via the keyboard. A DIM statement establishes the number of array elements that may be assigned values.

```
10 MAT INPUT A
```

MAX - The MAX function is used to determine which of two values is larger.

```
10 Y=A MAX 5
```

MEM - MEM is usually used at the command level with a DISPLAY command to display the amount of unused bytes of MEMory remaining in the system. MEM can also be used in a program statement.

```
10 MEM
```

MID$ - The MID$(string,n1,n2) function is used to isolate a specific number (n2) of string characters that are (n1) characters from the left-most character in the string.

MIN - The MIN function is used to determine which of two values is smaller.

    10 Y=A MIN 5

MOD — MOD is used to compute the arithmetic remainder after the value X is divided by the value Y.

    10 A=13 MOD 5

NEW - The NEW command erases the U/PL program(s) stored in memory. However, it does not erase the interpreter itself, NEW is normally used when a new program is to be entered into the system and the existing program is to be deleted.

NEXT - The NEXT statement is used to return program execution to the preceding FOR statement which uses the same variable. When the range of the FOR statement is exceeded, the system continues program execution at the line following the NEXT statement.

    10 NEXT X

NOT - NOT is used in IF-THEN statements as a logical operator to reverse the condition.

    10 IF NOT(A>5) THEN 60

NOTONE — The NOTONE command deactivates the system piezo-buzzer or speaker. This mutes all sounds, even if they are generated by the TONE command in a program.

NOTRACE - The NOTRACE command is used to disable the trace function (see TRACE). NOTRACE may be used as a program statement to turn the trace off at specified areas in a program.

NUM - NUM is a function that converts a numeric string into its numeric value. That is, a string of digits (including decimal point) is converted to the number it represents.

    10 X=NUM("5.2")

NUM$ - NUM$ is a function similar to STR$. It creates a string of numbers from a numeric expression.

        10 A$=NUM$(A)

ON ERROR GOTO - The ON ERROR GOTO statement is used to branch to an error subroutine when a program error is encountered, without stopping program execution. The ON ERROR GOTO statement must appear in the program before an execution error is anticipated. Any error encountered after the ON ERROR GOTO statement causes the system to execute the line number listed in the ON ERROR GOTO statement.

        10 ON ERROR GOTO 100

ON-GOSUB - ON-GOSUB is a multiple subroutine branching scheme which incorporates a number of IF-GOSUB tests into a single statement.

        10 ON X GOSUB 100, 200, 300

ON-GOTO - ON-GOTO is a multiple branching scheme which incorporates a number of IF-THEN tests into a single statement. For example, ON X GOTO 100, 200, 300 instructs the system to branch to lines 100, 200, or 300 if the value of X is 1, 2, or 3 respectively. If X is less than 1 or more than 3.999 the tests in this ON-GOTO example all fail and execution defaults to the next program line. The integer value of X cannot exceed the number of possible branches in the statement. If the value of X is a decimal, the system automatically finds its integer value and selects the appropriate branching line number.

        10 ON X GOSUB 100, 200, 300

OR - OR is used with IF-THEN statements to create a "logical math" operator to test for multiple conditions. For example, IF A = 2 OR B = E THEN 70 reads, "if the value of variable A equals 2 OR the value of variable B equals 6, OR both, the IF-THEN condition is met, and execution jumps to line 70."

        10 IF A=2 OR B=6 THEN 70

The Utility Programming Language Standard

** The following commands are intended for use with a two-servo Pan/Tilt mount:

> PANCTR - The PANCTR command sends digital control signals through pins defined in the U/PL implementation to position the mount platform horizontally to the fully center position relative to the mounting location.
>
> PANLFT – The PANLFT command sends digital control signals through pins defined in the U/PL implementation to position the mount platform horizontally to the fully left position relative to the mounting location.
>
> PANPOS - The PANPOS command sends digital control signals through pins defined in the U/PL implementation to position the mount platform horizontally to the position defined in the command relative to the mounting location.
>
> PANRGT - The PANRGT command sends digital control signals through pins defined in the U/PL implementation to position the mount platform horizontally to the fully right position relative to the mounting location.

****

PEEK - PEEK is used to examine the contents of a specific address in the system's memory.

```
10 Y= PEEK(X)
```

PING – The PING command is used in conjunction with an ultrasonic distance sensor to return the distance to an object. The distance may be in millimeters, centimeters or inches depending on the U/PL implementation.

POKE - POKE is used to store integer values from 0 to 255 (decimal) in specified memory locations.

```
10 POKE X,Y
```

PRECISION - The PRECISION statement is used to specify the maximum number of digits to be DISPLAYED to the right of the decimal point by a

DISPLAY statement. For example, 20 PRECISION 2 might be used in a program where the DISPLAYED values are to represent dollars and cents. If the actual value is longer than the number of digits specified, the number is rounded to the desired number of places and the right most digits are not displayed.

RAD - RAD is used to make them perform trigonometric calculations in RADians instead of degrees. Most systems are in radian mode when powered up, but some also have the capability of calculating trig functions in degrees. If a DEG statement has been used in a program, RAD is needed to restore the system to "normal" mode. One radian is approximately 57 degrees.

RSEED - RSEED is used to "shuffle" or "reseed" a set of numbers (held in the system) in a random order. These numbers are created as needed for selection by the RND function. Placing RSEED in a program before the RND function causes the generation of a new set of random numbers for the RND function each time the program is run.

READ - The READ statement is used to read data from a DATA line and assign that data to a variable. Each time the READ statement is executed, data is read from a DATA line. The pointer then moves to the next item of data in the DATA line(s) and waits for another READ statement. When the last piece of data has been read from all DATA statements, the data pointer must be reset to the beginning of the DATA list before additional READ statements can be executed. (See RESTORE)

```
10 READ A
```

REM - The REMark statement is used at the beginning of some program lines to make them serve as a "notebook" or "scratchpad" to hold comments about the program. The REM statement is not executed. Everything on a line beginning with REM is ignored by the system. If used in multiple statement lines, those statements preceding the REM statement will be executed, but everything following is ignored. If the REMarks require more than one program line, each such line must begin with REM.

RENUMBER - RENUMBER is used to change the program line numbers. The line numbers used in GOTO, GOSUB, IF-THEN, ON-GOTO and ON-GOSUB statements are changed accordingly to maintain the same branching scheme. If a number is not included in the RENUMBER statement, the system automatically renumbers each program line starting at line 10, and spacing the lines 10 numbers apart.

RESET – The RESET command provides in software the same function as power cycling the system. It is important to differentiate between using the software reset command and an external physical interrupt button. RESET will remove the resident program from RAM, void all variable assignments and restart the system processor. The external interrupt leaves the resident program and variables in the state that they were in when the button was pressed.

RESTORE - Execution of a RESTORE statement causes the DATA pointer to be "reset" back to the first piece of data in the first DATA line. This enables the system to use data stored in DATA statements more than once.

RESUME - The RESUME statement is used as the last statement in ON-ERROR-GOTO routines, telling the system to RESUME program execution at a specified line number. The system does not allow execution of the RESUME statement if it is not preceded by an ON-ERROR-GOTO statement.

RETURN - The RETURN statement is used in conjunction with the GOSUB statement. It is used as the last statement in a subroutine; it tells the system to return to the line containing the GOSUB statement and continue program execution from that point. The system will not allow execution of the RETURN statement if it was not preceded by a GOSUB statement.

RIGHT$ - The RIGHT$(string,n) function is used to isolate a specific number (n) of string characters, counting from the right-most character in the string.

```
10 DISPLAY "THE ";RIGHT$("ALRIGHT",5);"$ FUNCTION
   PASSED THE " ;B$"
```

RND - RND is a function to produce RaNDom numbers. Actual variation in usage between implementations is as wide as any keyword in the U/PL language. Most implementations use RND(n) to tell it to create a random decimal number between 0 and 1.

RUN - The RUN command instructs the system to execute the program or programs held in memory, starting with the lowest line number. With many systems, a line number may be included after the RUN command to specify a starting line other than the first one (e.g. RUN 40).

SDERASE — The SDERASE(File Name) command removes the named file from a SD card reader.

SDFILES — The SDFILES command lists the files present on the SD card attached to the system.

SDLOAD — The SDLOAD(File Name) command is used to load a program into RAM from a SD card reader.

SDSAVE — The SDSAVE(File Name) command is used to save the program resident in RAM to a SD card reader.

SEG$ - SEG$ extracts a segment of a string from a string variable. SEG$ has three arguments: the string variable, the starting position in the string, and the number of characters in the substring.

    10 B$=SEG$(A$,4,4)

SERVOCTR -The SERVOCTR(Pin#) command sends digital control signals through pins defined in the U/PL implementation to cause the servo attached to the defined pin to move to the center position relative to the mounting location.

SERVOLFT - The SERVOLFT(Pin#) command sends digital control signals through pins defined in the U/PL implementation to cause the servo attached to the defined pin to move to the left position relative to the mounting location.

SERVOPOS - The SERVOPOS(Pin#, position) command sends digital control signals through pins defined in the U/PL implementation to cause the servo attached to the defined pin to move to the position defined in the command relative to the mounting location.

SERVORGT - The SERVORGT(Pin#) command sends digital control signals through pins defined in the U/PL implementation to cause the servo attached to the defined pin to move to the right position relative to the mounting location.

SET - The SET statement is used to assign values to variables (e.g. SET A = 20).

SGN - SGN tells us the sign of a number. If its sign is negative we get a -1. If it is zero, a 0, and a 1 if it is positive.

        10 X=SGN(Y)

SIN - The SIN(A) function computes the Sine of the angle A, when that angle is expressed in Radians, (not in degrees). One radian = approximately 57 degrees.

        10 Y=SIN(X)

SINH - SINH(N) is a function that calculates the hyperbolic sine of a number. Hyperbolic functions express relationships based on a hyperbola, similar to the way trigonometric functions are identified on a circle.

        10 Y=SIN(X)

SPACE$ - The SPACE$(n) function is used to insert a specified number (n) of spaces.

        10 A$=SPACE$(10)

SQR - The SQR(n) function computes the square root of any positive number (n).

        10 DISPLAY SQR(225)

STEP - The STEP function is used to specify the size between steps in a FOR-NEXT statement. The STEP value can be positive, negative or sometimes even a non-integer decimal value. When a STEP value is not specified, the value of + 1 is automatically assumed.

        10 FOR X=10 TO 1 STEP -2

STOP - The STOP statement is used to STOP execution of the program and place the system in the command or immediate mode. It can be placed at any point within a program but should not used in place of the END statement. Some implementations will stop the program at the line which contains the STOP statement, while others jump to the line containing the END statement. As an aid to debugging, an interpreted U/PL implementation should DISPLAY the line number where the program stopped, and allow continuation of program execution via the CONTINUE command (see CONT).

STRING$ - The STRING$(n, ASCII code) function is used with the DISPLAY statement to display an ASCII character (n) number of times.

    10 DISPLAY STRING$(9,42);

STR$ - The STR$(n) function is used to convert a numeric value (n) into a string. The value (n) may be expressed as a number or a numeric variable.

SWAP - is a statement that switches the values of two variables or array elements. For example, SWAP A >B results in the original value of A being stored in B and the former value of B being stored in A. SWAP is very useful for arranging values of an array in ascending or descending order. Equivalent to EXCHANGE.

    10 SWAP (A,B)

TAB - The TAB function is used with DISPLAY statements to insert a number of spaces (enclosed in parentheses) before the statement to be displayed. The TAB value must always be positive and should be less than the number of spaces allowed per line.

    10 DISPLAY TAB(5); "TAB 5"

TAN - The TAN(A) function computes the Tangent of the angle A when that angle is expressed in radians (not in degrees). One radian = approximately 57 degrees.

    10 X=TAN(Y)

TANH - TANH(N) is a function that calculates the hyperbolic tangent of a number. Hyperbolic functions express relationships based on a hyperbola similar to the way trigonometric functions are identified on a circle.

TEXT - TEXT is used as both a command and a program statement to change the system's operation from the graphics mode to the normal TEXT (narrative) mode.

THEN - THEN is used with the IF statement to indicate the next operation the system is to perform when the condition of the IF statement is met.

    10 IF X=10 THEN 60

** The following commands are intended for use with a two-servo Pan/Tilt mount:

> TILTCTR — The TILTCTR command sends digital control signals through pins defined in the U/PL implementation to position the mount platform vertically to the center position relative to the mounting location.
>
> TILTDWN - The TILTDWN command sends digital control signals through pins defined in the U/PL implementation to position the mount platform vertically to the fully down position relative to the mounting location.
>
> TILTPOS - The TILTPOS command sends digital control signals through pins defined in the U/PL implementation to position the mount platform vertically to the position defined in the command relative to the mounting location.
>
> TILTUP - The TILTUP command sends digital control signals through pins defined in the U/PL implementation to position the mount platform vertically to the fully up position relative to the mounting location.

****

TONE — The TONE(frequency,duration) command generates a square wave of the specified frequency (and 50% duty cycle). A duration can be specified, otherwise the wave continues until a call to NOTONE. Only one TONE can be generated at a time. If a TONE is playing and another call to

TONE is made, the call will set its frequency. On many systems It is not possible to generate tones lower than 31Hz.

TONEW – The TONEW(frequency,duration) command performs identically to the TONE command with the exception that if an updated call is made TONE it will not play until the current TONE call completes.

TRACE - The TRACE command is used to activate a feature which displays program line numbers as each one is executed by the system. It is used as a trouble-shooting aid. This feature is disabled by the NOTRACE command. Depending on the implementation, TRACE may also be used as a program statement to allow tracing only specific sections of programs.

TRACE OFF - The TRACE OFF command is used to disable the trace function. TRACE OFF may be used as a program statement to turn the trace off at specified areas in the program.

TRACE ON - The TRACE ON command is used to activate a feature which displays program line numbers as each one is executed by the system. It is used as a trouble-shooting aid. This tracing feature is disabled by the TRACE OFF command. TRACE ON may be used as a program statement to trace only specified sections of a program.

TRON - The TRON (trace on) command is used to activate an analytical tool which displays program line numbers as each line is executed by the system. This trace feature is disabled by the TROFF or NEW commands. TRON is intended to be used as a program tracing and troubleshooting aid.

UNTIL - UNTIL is used as both a modifier and a statement. As a modifier, some implementations use UNTIL to make statements conditional.

```
50 GOTO 10 UNTIL X=0
```

VAL - The VAL function is used to convert numbers which are written as strings back into numeric notation. VAL has the effect of stripping off the quotes or dollar sign.

```
10 A=VAL(A$)
```

WHILE - WHILE is the beginning statement in a series which are executed repeatedly until a certain condition is false. Care should be taken when configuring a U/PL implementation to provide a method of user interrupt to escape from a possible infinite loop.

    100 WHILE X<>0

XOR - XOR is used in IF-THEN statements as the "Exclusive OR" logical operator. For example, IF A = 3 XOR B = 3 THEN 80 reads, "if A has a value of 3 OR B has a value of 3, but not both of them, the IF-THEN condition is true and execution jumps to line 80". See OR for more details. XOR is the same as OR with one exception; if both conditions are met, XOR says the test fails, usually by sending us a 0.

    50 IF A=3 XOR B=8 THEN 70

" - Pairs of quotation marks (") are used in DISPLAY statements to enclose letters, numbers or characters to be displayed. If the quotes are omitted, the system recognizes the letters as variables and displays whatever values are assigned to them. For example, DISPLAY "A" displays the letter "A"; while DISPLAY A displays the value assigned to variable A.

, - The Comma is an operator with a wide range of uses. One of the more common is with the DISPLAY statement, where it causes individual items to be displayed in pre-established horizontal zones. Each zone usually allows a maximum of sixteen characters. The number of zones allowed on each line varies from 4 to 8, depending on screen (or printer), line width.

. - The period (.) is used as a decimal point by nearly all U/PL implementations.

; - A semicolon is used in DISPLAY statements to allow several displayed sections to be joined together (concatenated) onto one line. For example, DISPLAY "H" ; "I" is displayed as HI.

The Colon : allows placing more than one statement on a single program line. Not all U/PL implementations will allow for this operator.

Parentheses () are used in arithmetic operations to determine the order in which math operations are performed. Math operations enclosed within parentheses are performed before those outside the parentheses. If a math operation is enclosed in parentheses which is in turn enclosed within another set of parentheses (and so on), the system first performs those operations "buried the deepest". When there is a "tie", the operation to the left is executed first.

The # (number sign) is used to specify individual variables as being of "double-precision". Double precision variables are capable of storing numbers containing 17 digits (only 16 digits are displayed). Single-precision variables are accurate to 6 digits. The # sign must be placed after a variable to define it as having double-precision, each time that variable is used in the program. If the # sign is found with a variable that is listed in DEFSNG or DEFINT statements (within the same program), the double precision character (#) temporarily over-rides their action and declares the variable to be of double-precision.

The $ symbol following a letter or letter/number combination is used to declare that variable to be a string variable. Information declared a string variable in a program statement must usually be enclosed in quotation marks. For example, A$ ="THE BASIC HANDBOOK." If an INPUT statement is used to assign the information entered to a string variable, then quotes are not usually required. (See INPUT and READ.)

The ! (exclamation mark) symbol may be used to specify individual variables as being of "single-precision". Single precision variables are capable of storing numbers containing no more than 7 digits (only 6 digits are displayed). Double-precision means having 17 digit precision. Since variables are automatically single precision, the ! operator is used in programs to change a variable back to single precision after it has been declared double-precision by a previous DEFDBL statement or # operator.

The % sign may be used to define variables as integers. When the % sign is placed to the right of a variable, that variable is then only capable of storing integer values. For more information on the use of the INT function see INT.

The ? (question mark) may be used as an abbreviation for DISPLAY. Most implementations that implement this should automatically change the ? sign to the word "DISPLAY" when the program is LISTed. For more information see DISPLAY.

The most common use of the + sign is in arithmetic addition. Example, DISPLAY A + B displays the sum of variables A and B.

The - symbol is used as an arithmetic subtraction sign to find the arithmetic difference between two numbers or numeric variables. For example, DISPLAY A~B displays the value of variable A minus the value of variable B. The - sign is also used for negation in arithmetic operations. Negation simply means "changing the sign from what it is to the opposite". Example, DISPLAY -(3-8) subtracts 8 from 3 which results in a negative 5. The first - (negation) sign reverses the sign within the parentheses and displays 5 (the + sign is implied).

The / sign is used as an arithmetic division sign to find the quotient of two numeric variables.

The * symbol (asterisk) is used as an arithmetic multiplication sign (instead of the letter "X") to find the product of two numbers or numeric variables.

The = symbol can be used as an assignment operator.

The < sign is used as a "less-than" relational operator to compare two numeric values in IF-THEN statements.

The > sign is used as a "greater-than" relational operator to compare two numeric values in IF-THEN statements.

The <> combination is used as a "not-equal" relational operator to compare two numeric values in IF-THEN statements for inequality.

The <= combination is used as a "less than or equal to" relational operator to compare two numeric values in IF-THEN statements.

The >= combination is used as a "greater-than or equal-to" relational operator to compare two numeric (or string, when allowed) values in IF-THEN statements.

The ' (apostrophe) is used by many systems as an abbreviation for the REM statement. For more information see REM.

The & (ampersand) may be used as the "concatenation" operator, allowing two strings to be coupled together and stored as one string.

APPENDIX 4

EXCEPTION CODES

The following table specifies the values of the EXTYPE function corresponding to the exceptions specified in this Standard. Nonfatal exceptions are designated by an exclamation-mark (!). The numbers in parentheses following each exception refer to the sections in which that exception is specified.

Overflow Exceptions (1000)

1001	Evaluating numeric-constant
1002	Evaluating numeric-expression
1003	Evaluating numeric-supplied-function
1004	Evaluating VAL
1005	Evaluating numeric-array-expression
1006	Numeric Datum for (MAT) READ
1007	Numeric Datum for (MAT) INPUT
1008	Numeric Datum for file input
1009	Evaluating of DET or DOT
1010	Fixed Decimal too large
1011	Fixed decimal assignment
1051	Evaluating string-expression
1052	Evaluating string-array-expression
1053	String datum for (MAT) READ
1054	String datum for (MAT) (LINE) INPUT
1105	String datum for file input
1106	String assignment

Underflow Exceptions (1500)

1501	Numeric-constant
1502	Numeric-expression
1503	Function Value
1504	VAL underflow
1505	Array-expression
1506	Numeric DATA
1507	Numeric INPUT
1508	FILE numeric INPUT

Subscript Exceptions (2000)

2001	Subscript out of bounds

Mathematical Exceptions (3000)

3001	Divide by zero
3002	Negative number raised to nonintegral power
3003	Zero raised to negative power
3004	LOG of zero or negative number
3005	Square root of negative number
3006	Zero divisor for MOD or REMAINDER
3007	Argument of ACOS or ASIN not in range -1 <= x <= 1
3008	Attempt to evaluate ANGLE(0,0)
3009	Attempt to invert a singular matrix

Uninitialized Exceptions (3100)

3101	Number-variable
3102	String-variable

Parameter Exceptions (4000)

4001	VAL not a numeric-constant
4002	Argument of CHR$ out of range
4003	Argument of ORD not a valid character or mnemonic
4004	Index of SIZE out of range
4005	Index in TAB less than one
4006	Margin setting less than current zonewidth
4007	Index of ZONEWIDTH out of range
4008	Index of LBOUND out of range
4009	Index of UBOUND out of range
4010	Second argument of REPEAT$
4101	Value of the string-expression in a set-statement
4301	Parameter type or count mismatch between LINK-statement and corresponding program-name-line
4302	Mismatched dimensions between LINK array parameter and corresponding formal-array
4303	Numeric parameters passed in LINK having different ARITHMETIC options

Storage Exceptions (5000)

5001	Size of redimensioned array too large

Matrix Exceptions (6000)

6001	Mismatched sizes in numeric-array-expression
6002	Argument of DET not a square matrix
6003	Argument of INV not a square matrix
6004	Arguments to IDN do not specify square matrix
6005	First index greater than second in redim, or index less than lower bound
6101	Mismatched sizes in string-array-expression

File Exceptions (7000)

7001	Channel number not in range 0 <= c <= max
7002	Channel zero in OPEN, CLOSE, ERASE, or with record-setter
7003	Nonzero channel in OPEN already active
7004	Inactive channel in file statement other than OPEN or ASK
7050	Keyed file OPEN with wrong collate sequence
7051	LENGTH not greater than zero on OPEN
7052	A device is opened as RELATIVE or KEYED
7100	Unrecognizable file attribute in OPEN
71xx	Implementation-defined failures to provide access to in accordance with file attribute
7202	The record-setter RECORD is used on a file opened with a file-organization other than RELATIVE
7203	The record-setter KEY is used on a file opened with a file-organization other than KEYED
7204	Record-setter SAME following DELETE, OPEN, or exception
7205	Record-setter used on device without that capability
7206	The index of a record-setter evaluates to an integer less than one
7207	A record-setter specifies an exact-search for the null string
7301	Attempt to ERASE file not opened as 0UTIN
7302	Output not possible to INPUT file
7303	Input not possible from OUTPUT file
7305	Attempt to input nonexistent record
7308	Attempt to write existing record
7311	Attempt to erase a device without erase capability
7312	Zonewidth or margin set for non-display file
7313	Zonewidth or margin set for INPUT file
7314	A write-statement or array-write-statement attempts to access a KEYED file, but does not specify an exact-search in its record-setter
7315	A template-identifier is used on a file opened as DISPLAY or INTERNAL
7316	A write-statement or array-write-statement does not have a template-identifier when attempting to access a file opened as NATIVE
7317	(MAT) PRINT to INTERNAL file
7318	(MAT) (LINE) INPUT from INTERNAL file
7321	SKIP REST on stream file

7322	A data modification statement attempts to access a file opened as INPUT or as OUTPUT
7401	Attempt to trace to inactive channel
7402	Attempt to trace to non-display-format or INPUT file

I/O Exceptions (8000)

8001	(MAT) READ beyond end of data
8002	Too few data in input-reply
8003	Too many data in input-reply
8011	End-of-file encountered on input
8012	Too few data in record
8013	Too many data in record
8101	Nonnumeric datum for (MAT) READ or INPUT of number from DISPLAY record
8102	Syntactically incorrect input-reply from terminal
8103	Nonnumeric datum for (MAT) INPUT of number
8105	Syntactically incorrect input reply from file
8120	Type mismatch on INTERNAL input
8201	Invalid format-string
8202	No format-item in format-string for output list
8203	Format-item too short for output string
8204	Exrad overflow
8251	The string-expression of a template-identifier is not a syntactically correct template-element-list
8252	An expression or array-element does not agree in type (numeric or string) with its associated TEMPLATE field-specifier
8253	A template-element with a variable-field-count does not coincide with the first element of an array
8254	There are not enough field-specifiers in a template-statement for all the expressions or array-elements
8255	A numeric value has significant digits to the left of the available digit places in the field of a template
8256	A string value is longer than the length of its field in the template
8301	Record length exceeded on output to file
8302	Input from a record longer than RECSIZE
8401	Timeout on (MAT) (LINE) INPUT
8402	Illegal numeric value specified for time-expression

Device Exceptions (9000)

9000	Size of redimensioned array too large

Control Exceptions (10000)

10001	Index out of range, no ELSE in on-goto- or on-gosub
10002	Return without corresponding gosub or on-gosub
10004	No case-block selected and no CASE ELSE
10005	Attempt to LINK to unavailable program
10007	Break statement executed when debugging active

Graphical Exceptions (11000)

11051	Set-statement boundaries with zero width or height
11052	Viewport boundary not in range
11053	A boundary of the device window is not in the range
11054	A boundary of the device viewport is not in the display space
11056	Set-statement point style out of range
11062	Set-statement line style out of range
11085	Set statement color index out of range
11100	Graphic-output with LINES and fewer than two points, or with AREA and fewer than three points

INDEX

' 65, 100, 116, 145, 270
% 133, 269
& 26, 50, 53, 54, 59, 73, 104, 150, 170, 220, 271
* 11, 12, 13, 26, 33, 35, 36, 44, 45, 52, 58, 60, 62, 64, 66, 68, 69, 70, 83, 86, 91, 93, 96, 101, 102, 109, 119, 122, 126, 127, 132, 133, 138, 148, 149, 168, 169, 181, 193, 217, 220, 225, 226, 227, 228, 229, 230, 231, 232, 233, 234, 237, 238, 239, 240, 241, 243, 244, 245, 260, 266, 270
< 18, 38, 39, 41, 42, 52, 56, 84, 85, 90, 94, 116, 128, 130, 133, 205, 254, 255, 270
<= 56, 84, 90, 270
<> 90, 116, 254, 255, 270
= 10, 11, 12, 13, 21, 24, 25, 27, 28, 31, 33, 35, 38, 40, 41, 44, 45, 49, 50, 52, 53, 55, 56, 57, 58, 59, 60, 62, 64, 65, 68, 69, 70, 73, 74, 76, 77, 79, 83, 84, 85, 86, 88, 89, 90, 91, 92, 93, 94, 96, 97, 101, 102, 104, 108, 109, 111, 116, 117, 119, 122, 126, 127, 128, 132, 133, 138, 148, 149, 150, 164, 168, 169, 170, 181, 192, 193, 197, 198, 199, 200, 206, 211, 216, 220, 223, 225, 226, 227, 228, 229, 230, 231, 232, 233, 234, 235
> 12, 18, 24, 25, 28, 31, 33, 35, 36, 37, 41, 44, 45, 49, 50, 51, 52, 54, 56, 58, 60, 65, 68, 69, 73, 76, 79, 84, 91, 94, 101, 102, 109, 116, 127, 133, 149, 150, 164, 168, 169, 181, 192, 193, 198, 199, 205, 210, 211, 216, 219, 220, 254, 255, 270
>= 270
ABS 16, 37, 38, 40, 238, 246
ACS 246
AND 10, 16, 21, 83, 84, 85, 90, 119, 197, 227, 246
ANSI 2, 3, 8, 9, 12
APPEND 16, 246
ASC 16, 246
ASET 247
ASN 247
AT 16, 220, 234, 247
ATN 37, 38, 39, 47, 238, 247
AUTO 16, 247
Autorun 13, 14, 123, 126
BASE . 16, 62, 64, 65, 66, 178, 185, 238, 248
BEEP 248
BLINKING 248
BREAK 16, 206, 226, 247, 248, 249
CDBL 248
CHR$. 23, 54, 55, 58, 60, 107, 248
CINT 249
CLEAR 16, 216, 219, 227, 249
CLG 249
CLS 249, 254
Command 13, 20
COMMON 246, 249
construct 10, 11, 12, 144, 169
CONT 249, 265
Control Exceptions 277
COS 37, 39, 42, 47, 238, 250
COSH 37, 39, 238, 250
DATA .. 16, 17, 100, 119, 120, 228, 250, 256, 261, 262

DEF...16, 101, 102, 104, 228, 237, 243, 250, 253
DEG 37, 39, 238, 250, 261
DELAY............................... 16, 250
Device Exceptions.................. 277
DIM 16, 62, 64, 66, 185, 229, 250, 257
DISPLAY 13, 16, 20, 30, 54, 86, 90, 94, 116, 126, 127, 132, 133, 138, 139, 145, 146, 147, 149, 154, 155, 157, 158, 161, 162, 163, 166, 168, 170, 172, 173, 174, 175, 179, 183, 184, 187, 188, 190, 191, 192, 195, 199, 200, 205, 215, 225, 228, 247, 251, 252, 257, 261, 265, 268, 269, 270
DRAW............................. 16, 251
DSET.............................. 247, 251
ECMA 2, 3, 8, 9, 12, 58
ECMA-6 3
EDUMP...................................... 251
EEPROM....................13, 251, 252
ELIST... 251
ELOAD 251
ELSE 16, 30, 56, 86, 87, 88, 92, 93, 94, 95, 104, 199, 200, 227, 229, 233, 238, 251
END 16, 17, 19, 25, 26, 56, 92, 93, 94, 95, 101, 104, 109, 111, 116, 155, 156, 161, 164, 165, 170, 197, 198, 199, 200, 205, 228, 229, 230, 251, 265
End-of-line 13
EQ 252
ERASE.......16, 145, 147, 149, 150, 158, 160, 230, 252
Error................................. 14, 16
ERROR....................252, 259, 262
errors 2, 6, 7, 14, 26, 88, 137, 199
ERUN..................................... 252
ESAVE.................................... 252

exception... 5, 7, 8, 14, 15, 26, 27, 33, 34, 37, 43, 52, 56, 57, 58, 61, 68, 72, 82, 85, 88, 99, 100, 105, 107, 112, 114, 118, 120, 121, 123, 126, 130, 137, 139, 140, 143, 151, 152, 153, 157, 158, 160, 166, 167, 171, 172, 174, 175, 176, 180, 182, 183, 184, 185, 186, 187, 188, 189, 192, 194, 197, 198, 200, 201, 202, 203, 204, 205, 206, 207, 224, 227, 228, 230, 245, 267, 268
Exception.5, 14, 53, 96, 184, 197, 224
EXCHANGE......................252, 265
EXIT......16, 89, 90, 102, 109, 164, 170, 182, 197, 200, 230, 252
EXP................37, 40, 99, 238, 253
Expanded U/PL..5, 144, 148, 164, 168, 170, 181, 187, 206
External.............................14, 100
File Exceptions........................275
FILES................................144, 253
FN 250, 253
FNEND 253
FOR 16, 89, 90, 91, 170, 230, 232, 252, 253, 258, 264
Function...................15, 104, 105
GET 16, 253
GO...............16, 86, 232, 238, 254
GOSUB 16, 17, 86, 87, 94, 202, 232, 238, 254, 259, 261, 262
GOTO ...16, 17, 86, 232, 238, 254, 255, 259, 261, 262
Graphical Exceptions 277
HOME 254
I/O Exceptions 276
Identifier......................15, 16, 17
IF 16, 56, 90, 92, 94, 116, 119, 120, 164, 170, 182, 193, 199, 200, 205, 229, 233, 236, 246,

251, 254, 255, 258, 259, 261, 266, 268, 270
IF-GOTO 255
IF-SET 254, 255
IF-THEN . 246, 251, 254, 255, 258, 259, 261, 268, 270
Imperative 15, 18
INKEY$ 253, 255
INPUT ...15, 16, 90, 119, 122, 123, 138, 139, 145, 146, 147, 148, 149, 154, 155, 157, 158, 160, 166, 179, 181, 182, 183, 184, 185, 186, 188, 189, 195, 199, 205, 225, 234, 235, 255, 256, 257, 269
INT 34, 37, 40, 41, 90, 94, 204, 238, 256, 269
Interactive mode 15
Internal ... 15, 100, 117, 119, 145, 146, 175, 188
Keyword 15, 16
LEFT$ 256
Line 17, 25, 27, 186, 247
LINEINPUT 256
LINK 16, 17, 117, 235, 249, 256
LIST 13, 16, 225, 256
LOAD 257
LOG .37, 40, 43, 99, 238, 253, 257
LOG10 257
MAT..16, 66, 68, 69, 73, 138, 139, 145, 147, 154, 168, 169, 170, 178, 181, 182, 183, 185, 186, 193, 225, 236, 242, 257
Matrix Exceptions 274
MAX 38, 40, 51, 56, 216, 217, 218, 219, 226, 238, 257
MEM 257
MID$ 257
MIN 38, 40, 51, 56, 238, 258
MOD 38, 41, 42, 43, 238, 258
Native 17, 146, 175, 188
Nesting 18, 96

NEW 256, 258, 267
NEXT 16, 89, 90, 91, 165, 182, 196, 228, 236, 252, 253, 258, 264
NOT 16, 30, 83, 84, 85, 94, 241, 258
NOTONE 258, 266
NOTRACE 258, 267
NUM 258, 259
ON 16, 86, 206, 207, 212, 214, 228, 238, 244, 259, 261, 262, 267
ON ERROR 259
ON ERROR GOTO 259
ON-GOSUB 259, 261
Operator 15, 18
OR ..16, 83, 84, 94, 116, 229, 259, 268
Overflow 18
Overflow Exceptions 272
PANCTR 260
PANLFT 260
PANPOS 260
PANRGT 260
Parameter Exceptions 274
PEEK 260
PING 260
POKE 260
PRECISION 260
Procedural 18, 19
Program Unit 19
RAD 38, 41, 238, 261
READ ..16, 17, 119, 120, 138, 139, 145, 146, 147, 154, 157, 158, 166, 181, 182, 183, 184, 187, 188, 190, 200, 225, 240, 250, 261, 269
REM 16, 27, 30, 241, 261, 270
RENUMBER 16, 261
RESET 262
RESTORE 16, 17, 119, 120, 241, 261, 262

RESUME 262
RETURN 16, 17, 86, 202, 241, 253, 254, 256, 262
RIGHT$ 262
RND. 28, 38, 41, 80, 238, 261, 262
Rounding 19
RSEED 16, 38, 240, 261
RUN 13, 15, 20, 249, 256, 263
SDERASE 263
SDFILES 263
SDLOAD 263
SDSAVE 263
SEG$ 263
SERVOCTR 16, 263
SERVOLFT 16, 263
SERVOPOS 16, 263
SERVORGT 16, 263
SET . 16, 44, 45, 50, 56, 58, 59, 86, 90, 91, 94, 102, 104, 111, 116, 127, 133, 145, 146, 147, 154, 158, 164, 165, 166, 199, 200, 210, 215, 218, 219, 223, 237, 243, 255, 264
SGN 38, 40, 41, 91, 238, 264
Significant digits 19
SIN 38, 42, 44, 47, 238, 264
SINH 38, 42, 238, 264
SPACE$ 264
SQR ... 36, 38, 42, 43, 97, 238, 264
State 19, 20
Statement 17, 20, 44
STEP 16, 89, 90, 91, 232, 264
STOP 16, 17, 24, 94, 200, 242, 248, 249, 254, 265
Storage Exceptions 274
STR$ 57, 259, 265
STRING$ 265
Subscript Exceptions 273
SWAP 265
syntax. 2, 3, 10, 11, 12, 13, 14, 22, 23, 26, 30, 82, 84, 88, 146, 180, 184, 223, 224

TAB 16, 29, 81, 126, 127, 244, 265
TAN 38, 42, 47, 238, 265
TANH 38, 42, 238, 265
TEXT . 16, 216, 217, 218, 219, 220, 222, 232, 239, 266
THEN .. 16, 56, 90, 92, 94, 95, 116, 119, 120, 164, 170, 182, 193, 199, 200, 205, 229, 233, 236, 254, 255, 259, 266, 268
TILTCTR 266
TILTDWN 266
TILTPOS 266
TILTUP 266
TONE 258, 266, 267
TONEW 267
TRACE 16, 206, 208, 244, 258, 267
TRACE OFF 206, 267
TRACE ON 267
TRON 267
Truncation 20
U/PL i, 2, 5, 7, 8, 9, 12, 13, 14, 15, 16, 19, 20, 21, 22, 23, 26, 27, 30, 31, 33, 37, 43, 46, 49, 58, 68, 72, 79, 80, 100, 101, 118, 119, 121, 126, 143, 144, 145, 146, 147, 148, 149, 151, 152, 153, 154, 155, 156, 157, 158, 160, 162, 163, 164, 165, 167, 168, 169, 170, 174, 175, 178, 179, 180, 181, 182, 184, 187, 188, 189, 190, 191, 192, 197, 206, 246, 248, 250, 252, 253, 254, 258, 260, 262, 263, 265, 266, 268
Underflow 20
Underflow Exceptions 273
Uninitialized Exceptions 273
UNTIL 16, 89, 90, 91, 199, 230, 267
VAL 54, 57, 58, 186, 238, 267
WHILE ... 16, 89, 90, 205, 230, 268
XOR 268

www.ingramcontent.com/pod-product-compliance
Lightning Source LLC
Chambersburg PA
CBHW060825220526
45466CB00003B/973